STUDYING THE PAST
TO SURVIVE THE FUTURE

ABOUT THE AUTHOR

Shirley Andrews lives on the Concord River in Concord, Massachusetts, with her husband, Bill, a professor at Harvard Law School. She is a graduate of Middlebury College and has studied, performed, and taught flute for over twenty years. Her intense interest in Atlantis has always been a part of her and she believes it stems from one or more past life experiences there. After raising six children, Shirley was able to devote time and energy to the study of Atlantis and related subjects, which led her to research in the libraries of the British Museum, Harvard, the University of Chicago, and the Association for Research and Enlightenment (A.R.E.) in Virginia Beach, as well as personal travels to the Azores, the Andes, Central America, monastaries high in the Himalayas, the Dordogne Valley in France, and the Tito Bustillo cave in Spain. She and her husband have traveled extensively, hiking and mountain climbing throughout the world, often focusing on the customs and beliefs of inhabitants in remote areas as they reflect on the spirituality of the distant past. Her foremost desire is to share what she has learned with others and incite their curiosity to discover more about these fascinating subjects.

LEMURIA
AND
ATLANTIS

STUDYING THE PAST
TO SURVIVE THE FUTURE

SHIRLEY ANDREWS

Llewellyn Publications
Woodbury, Minnesota

FIRST EDITION
Fourth Printing, 2006

Cover design by Lisa Novak
Cover images © Digital Stock and Corel
Editing and book design by Rebecca Zins
Maps by Lisa Novak
Photos by Bob Brush and Richard Wingate courtesy of Dick Lowdermilk

Library of Congress Cataloging-in-Publication Data
Andrews, Shirley, 1930–
   Lemuria and Atlantis: studying the past to survive the future /
Shirley Andrews.—1st ed.
           p. c.m.
      Includes bibliographical references and index.
      ISBN 13: 978-0-7387-0397-8
      ISBN 10: 0-7387-0397-4 (trade paper)
      1. Atlantis. 2. Lemuria I. Title.
GN751.A63 2004
398.23'4—dc22   2003061788

Llewellyn Publications
A Division of Llewellyn Worldwide, Ltd.
2143 Wooddale Drive, Dept. J397
Woodbury, MN 55125-2989
Llewellyn is a registered trademark of Llewellyn Worldwide, Ltd.

www.llewellyn.com

CONTENTS

ACKNOWLEDGMENTS

It is impossible to thank the many considerate and knowledgeable people who contributed to my efforts to produce *Lemuria and Atlantis*. First of all, I wish to express my gratitude to my husband, Bill, for his loving support, his patient assistance with the intricacies of computer technology, and his editorial suggestions. Roy Andrews and Susan Andrews provided thoughtful editing, and Gregory Berg's astute research of prehistory revealed many interesting and important facts that are not well-known. My sincere thanks to Dick Lowdermilk for his valuable input, including Bob Brush's photographs. The advice and contributions of Carrie Blakley, Michael Fess, Judie Gerber, Joan Griffith, Joan Hanley, Rich Hansen, Anne Harris, Sarah Hindle, Kathleen Keith, Angus mac Lir, Heather Robb, Mark Roberts, Tristram, Wim Roskam, Lew Ross, and Barbara Wolf all made it possible for this book to come to life. And finally, I offer my warmest appreciation to the many persons who generously shared their memories of Lemuria and Atlantis to enormously enrich this book.

PHOTOS AND MAPS

Time present and time past
Are both perhaps present in time future,
And time future contained in time past.
—T. S. ELIOT, "FOUR QUARTETS"

PREFACE

Following the publication of *Atlantis: Insights from a Lost Civilization*, my readers continued to have questions—What was Mu? Where was Lemuria? When was it there? What were the people like? Was Atlantis in the Caribbean? Why did my obstetrician say that since I have O negative blood my ancestors might have come from Atlantis? Who or what were the "things"? How did Atlanteans use crystals for healing? Were all Atlanteans selfish and corrupt? Were there other civilizations at the time of Lemuria and Atlantis? What really happened to Lemuria and Atlantis? Is there any way to prevent our civilization from going the way of advanced civilizations in the past? Is anyone finding evidence of Lemuria and Atlantis now?

Readers from all around the world sent me their strange dreams and vivid memories of what they believed were past experiences in Lemuria and Atlantis. Some, whose minds were pressing for logical confirmation of their intuitions, were afraid they were crazy, and they pleaded for verification. As I assembled answers to their questions, I realized that to describe the ancient island empire of the Atlantic Ocean without weaving in information about the civilization of Lemuria, which

PREFACE

thrived in the Pacific Ocean at the same time, would be similar to a composer offering only half the notes of a musical composition. The similarities in the customs and beliefs of the two civilizations, plus their joint influence on the earliest cultures of Central America and Egypt, confirmed their connections with each other. Additional insights were needed, and from that journey this book emerged.

Lemuria and Atlantis are deeply imprinted in the consciousness of many who are here today, and the ancient cultures are quietly influencing our lives. In the mid-twentieth century, Edgar Cayce (see his biography in appendix II) said that most of the world's leaders at that time were once Atlanteans. In the twenty-first century, numerous Atlantean healers are here to assist us in ascertaining the source and cause of disease so that we may heal in a natural manner. Spiritually advanced Lemurians have returned to assist us by pointing the way in these times of change. Knowledgeable persons suggest that, in addition to those who are present on this planet today, Lemurians and Atlanteans in another realm are using energy from their minds to guide our actions and help us avoid the catastrophes that destroyed their beloved countries.

Little recorded information from prehistory has survived the ravages of time to assist in painting a picture of the distant past, but there are ancient written words on wood, bamboo, bark, palm leaves, bones, ivory, leather, copper, precious metals, waxed tablets, ostraca (pieces of broken pottery), cloth, silk, and papyrus. Most of these are fragile, however, and marks on stone offer the only relatively permanent method of preserving information. Translation of strange writings we have discovered is a further problem. Some of the numerous undeciphered texts include the Malta tablets, Easter Island Rongorongo; the Linear-A script of the Minoans; Dravidian, which is the undeciphered writing of the Rama in India; and hieroglyphs and strange carvings on monoliths in Venezuelan jungles. Stone tablets the natives of the Canary Islands gave to the

Spaniards in the fifteenth century are carved with unusual hiero-glyphs that are similar to those in caves in Cuba and on Andros Island in the Bahamas.

Understanding that written records would not endure, intelligent people in the past devised reliable ways to preserve information for those who followed them on the path of life, and scholars are slowly acquiring respect for oral histories which have miraculously survived in many parts of the world. Celtic bards were required to study nine years and perfectly memorize 20,000 verses before they were entrusted to tell the tales of their country's legendary leaders. Native Americans also relied on their minds to save their precious histories. For this task they selected young girls, who spent their lives learning and transmitting information. Women were chosen because they were less apt to be killed in conflicts. These memorizers didn't change what they were told; everything was always word-for-word the same. There were also storytellers, and some of their tales related to past experiences of their nations or were symbolic of their beliefs, but they did not repeat exactly what they learned, as did the memorizers.

On the other side of the world, in India, for hundreds of generations, fathers recited extensive historical accounts to their sons. The dedicated boys precisely memorized the long poems, just as their fathers had done before them, and then passed them down to their sons. The exciting stories, which are referred to as "Vedas," never changed. If you listen to a Veda in eastern India today and then travel to western India, you will be able to hear the identical one in exactly the same words. Eventually these histories were recorded in Sanskrit on bark, leather, and palm leaves, and monks thoughtfully hid the precious books in dark caves or in secret libraries beneath age-old temples in Tibet and India, where they have carefully guarded them for thousands of years. Material from Lemurian priests who anticipated the disappearance of their land also hides in isolated monasteries in the Far East.

Numerous people contacted me who are sure that in the past —
in Lemuria and Atlantis—they acquired the skills that enable them
to lead satisfying lives today, and told me they wish to share this
knowledge. For additional enrichment and speculation, I have included some of their dreams and recollections. "Anonymous" indicates those who prefer not to reveal their identity.

No one really understands the origin of these images and concepts that surge to light from the deep unconscious, or perhaps descend from a higher awareness, but they should not be completely
ignored. Readers who consider them implausible should overlook
them, but I hope the ideas they offer will enable others to reach into
themselves and recall their own past experiences, which may further
their knowledge of themselves.

There's an old saying that "what goes around, comes around."
Humanity advances in cycles, not on a straight linear path. In
material and technological development we have arrived at a
place in the cycle that is very similar to the final days of Lemuria
and Atlantis. Our world is facing challenges comparable to the
problems that confronted those renowned civilizations in the
past, and we are on the brink of either annihilating ourselves or
entering a new way of living and thinking. Studying the past will
help us to survive in the future.

So come, travel with me back to prehistory. My previous book,
Atlantis: Insights from a Lost Civilization, is a helpful guidebook to
that country, but it is not essential, for this is new territory. The trail
is not straight and easy. To acquire a thorough understanding of
Lemuria and Atlantis, one must follow dangerous footpaths with
steep drop-offs where there are no railings of proof. With imagination and confidence in your intuition, most of you will not be
forced back or pushed off the side. I have attempted to provide
bridges over the deepest streams of ignorance created by Western
academicians who are unwilling to progress past where their profes-
sors led them, but intelligent travelers must use common sense and

find their own way. Feel free to dismiss as improbable routes I suggest; this is my version. If you are aware and thoughtful, you will be able to travel around obstacles and follow your own path. The broad, open views along the way will offer perceptions and insights into the past, present, and future of ourselves, our world, the universe of which we are such a small segment, and the visible and invisible worlds that comprise the entire cosmos.

1

THE MOTHERLAND OF MU

WIDESPREAD MYTHS AND LEGENDS, the most ancient texts in the Far East, writings on stone in Central America, and esoteric sources (inner secret knowledge of the initiated) all describe a land of considerable size that was once above the surface in the Pacific Ocean. During its long history, this missing country has acquired a variety of names: sacred Tibetan texts remember it as "Ra-Mu"; inscriptions on the American continents refer to it as the "lost Motherland of Mu"; and Edgar Cayce, who had access to the Akashic Records,[1] names it "Muri" or "Lemuria." "Lemuria" may have originated from the word *lemures*, which the Romans used to describe the spirits of their dead ancestors who walked by night.

"Lemuria" also stems from the nineteenth century, when scientists unexpectedly found small nocturnal animals called lemurs living on Madagascar and New

Key:

1 HAWAIIAN ISLANDS	8 SAMOA	15 CAROLINE ISLANDS
2 MARQUESAS ISLANDS	9 TONGA ISLANDS	16 PONAPE
3 EASTER ISLAND	10 FIJI ISLANDS	17 PHILIPPINE ISLANDS
4 AUSTRAL ISLANDS	11 GUADALCANAL	18 BORNEO
5 SOCIETY ISLANDS	12 SOLOMON ISLANDS	19 SUMATRA
6 TAHITI	13 NEW GUINEA	20 SRI LANKA
7 COOK ISLANDS	14 MARSHALL ISLANDS	21 MALDIVE ISLANDS

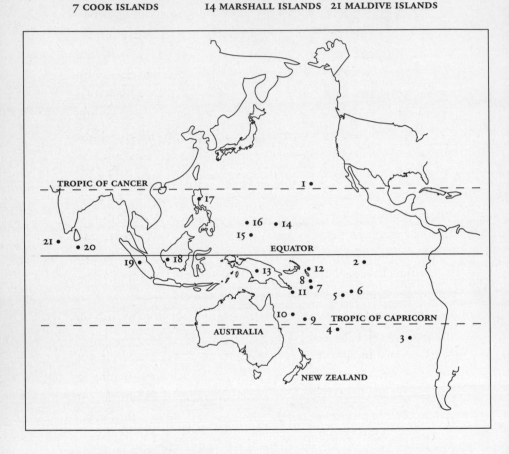

THE PACIFIC OCEAN TODAY

Guinea. They believed the original home of these monkey-like mammals was 250 miles away in Africa, and there was no obvious explanation of how they had traveled so far. The missing land was named "Lemuria" in honor of the lemurs. Today the ancient sunken country in the Pacific Ocean is a place with two names; "Lemuria" and "Mu" are used interchangeably.

During the hundreds of centuries of its existence, the Motherland of Mu, like everywhere else on the fragile surface of our planet, changed in size and shape. Between 50,000 B.C. and 10,000 B.C.,[2] when an immense amount of water from the oceans was incorporated in the snow and ice of the glaciers, sea levels were hundreds of feet lower. Islands everywhere were much bigger and ocean waters ceased to cover the fertile continental shelves. Scholar Egerton Sykes (see appendix II) believes that during this time various separate cultures lived on the large masses of land in the Pacific. They formed a kingdom that was linked by the sea, and communicated freely with each other in their sophisticated ships that held as many as 500 people. Reading the ocean currents and studying the constellations, these earliest navigators of the vast oceans skillfully took advantage of prevailing winds to travel wherever they wished to go.

Col. James Churchward first learned about Mu from records on sacred Naacal tablets in India. (The biography of Col. James Churchward in appendix II will help to confirm that Mu is not just a legend—it was a real place.) After many years of searching in Asia and Central America for further information about the lost country, Churchward believed that, until 10,000 B.C., the largest remaining island of the Motherland of Mu lay in the southeastern Pacific on a broad area of uplifted sea-floor. It extended southeast from Hawaii to Easter Island, with its center somewhat south of the equator. Narrow channels of ocean divided the land into three sections.

To the west, Lemuria's several thousand square miles included the Society, Cook, Austral, Tuamotu, and Marqueses islands, all of which are relatively close together, south of Hawaii and south of the equator. Discoveries of coal and a long history of floral growth on the island of Rapa, one of the Austral Islands, suggest that this portion of the Pacific Ocean was once above the surface.[3] The western section of the large island of Lemuria gradually sank and, as ocean waters threatened their homes and temples, people moved to the higher, safer ground of Sumatra, Java, Borneo, New Guinea, and Australia.

Churchward determined that four major cataclysms, in 800,000 B.C., 200,000 B.C., 80,000 B.C., and 10,000 B.C., were the culprits responsible for nature's tearing the beautiful land in the Pacific Ocean to pieces. Numerous volcanic islands and coral atolls, which endure where Lemuria once stood, confirm the instability of the region. The tiny animals that produce coral only survive in 150 feet or less of water. Since remains of coral are found at depths of 1,800 feet in the Pacific, it indicates that the land that is now 1,800 feet deep was once shallow water, close to the surface.

The instability of the ocean floor in the southeast Pacific constantly subjected the Lemurians to the problems of unexpected earthquakes and volcanic eruptions. As an illustration of the instability, sailors traveling in that vicinity sometimes report islands that are not on maps but, before long, the greedy ocean devours them and they are never seen again. In 1836 the island of Tuanaki, south of the Cook Islands, suddenly disappeared with all but one of its inhabitants, who was luckily visiting a nearby island at the time of the surprising disaster.[4]

Gently rolling hills and tumbling rivers that circled through the land characterized the countryside of early Lemuria. The vaporous steam rising from the abundant, bubbling hot springs gave a surreal, misty impression to the landscape.[5] Gradually, the environment changed as sections of our planet's crust shifted and pushed against each other and forced mountains up from the depths of the Earth. Lemuria became a more hilly country. Some of the islands in the Pacific today are the rocky summits of its mountains.

The Ring of Fire, a chain of active volcanoes that surrounds a large section of the Pacific Ocean, demonstrates the presence of the frightening hot molten lava that was never far beneath the surface in Lemuria. A theory proposes that El Niño and La Niña, weather patterns that occur every four to twelve years, originate in this troubled area. When portions of the Earth's crust expand and contract, it increases or decreases the amount of volcanic activity in the Ring of Fire. As hot lava from deep inside the planet shoots out, it changes the temperature of the ocean water. When the water grows warmer, it produces El Niño. A decrease in ocean temperature induces La Niña.

The lush tropical vegetation of giant ferns and evergreens that covered most of Mu made it a country of unsurpassed beauty. Sacred lotus flowers, one of the first flowers to appear on our planet, glistened like jewels along the shores of its shallow lakes. Coconut palms lined the rivers and fringed the ocean beaches.[6] Just as plant life flourished in the warm climate, so insects grew to an enormous size. Fossilized specimens from islands in the Pacific reveal that in the tropical climate of Mu, roaches were four to five inches long, and two-inch ants with large wings were capable of flying long distances.[7]

Archaeologist Stacy-Judd reports that the natives of Easter Island (Rapa Nui) have said that they are living on the peak of a holy mountain of Mu.[8] They believe Easter Island, which is formed from three extinct volcanoes, is the only portion of their motherland that the sea has not covered. Located 2,300 miles from the coast of Chile, the mysterious island has some of the most impressive structures in the Pacific. Enormous monuments to the dead in the form of huge burial platforms line its thirty-six miles of coastline. The carefully shaped stones of the four- or five-hundred-feet-long platforms weigh two to twenty tons apiece and were put to-gether without mortar in polygonal fashion.[9]

Gigantic statues of human figures without legs that once topped some of these platforms, and others that now lie on the ground, are a tribute to the skills of these long-ago sculptors. At one time, 624 of these huge statues faced the sea, and unfinished ones lay in the quarry of volcanic rock from which they were carved. It is im-possible to explain how some of the stone sculptures, which are ten to forty feet tall and range from fifteen to thirty-five tons,[10] were moved to their current locations on steep hillsides, high above the ocean. The local people say these statues walked up, gaining their strength from mental powers. Many of the figures are unfinished, which indicates that a severe cataclysm interrupted the builders of this tremendous undertaking.

Colossal platforms and statues of legless men are not the only mystery of Easter Island. In 1868, newly converted Easter Is-landers sent to the bishop of Tahiti, as a token of respect, an an-cient piece of wood with long strands of human hair wrapped around it. After removing the hair, the bishop discovered that the small board was covered with writing. An investigation revealed that at one time there were over 500 of these boards or tablets on Easter Island, but only twenty-one have survived, scattered world-wide in museums and private collections. No one has successfully translated Rongorongo, the tiny, strange writing on the tablets, al-though it so closely resembles script from the Indus Valley in India that it must have had a common origin.[11] Evidence of a similar written script has survived in remote Oleai Island, many thousands of miles away from Ponape.[12] There is a theory that to read Ron-gorongo, the writing on the tablets from Easter Island, one starts from the left-hand bottom corner, and proceeds from left to right. At the end of the line, you turn the tablet around before reading the next line. It's like reading a book in which you begin at the bottom of the page and every other line is printed back-to-front and upside-down.

Photo by Bob Brush

**WOODEN TABLET FROM EASTER ISLAND
WITH RONGORONGO WRITING**

Since tiny Easter Island is only seven by thirteen miles, it has never had the means of supporting a population of sufficient size to build the immense statues and their platforms. It is assumed that it was once a large religious center for the surrounding area and temporary residents participated in creating its remarkable stone constructions. When a Dutch navigator discovered Easter Island in 1722, it had a population of about five thousand people. Within 150 years, deadly smallpox and greedy, unscrupulous slavers reduced the number of its inhabitants to 111 destitute individuals.[13]

Cyclopean ruins that survive on numerous other Pacific Islands suggest the skills of Lemurians and their descendants so long ago. On Ponape, in the Caroline archipelago 3,400 miles from Easter Island, remnants of the partially sunken city of Nan Madol cover eleven square miles. The megalithic remains of Nan Madol bear a striking resemblance to Plato's description of the capital city of Atlantis. Two or three walls encircled the city proper, which was interlaced with canals.[14] Constructed from over 250 tons of basalt rock, some of the buildings of this vanished ceremonial center still rise thirty feet above the canals. The huge rocks in the structures, which weigh as much as fifty tons, are from a quarry thirty miles away. These enormous blocks are precisely placed, without mortar to hold them in place. Local legends, similar to those about Tiahuanaco in Bolivia, say that when the buildings were built, the stones were made to fly through the air.

The oldest ruins in the Pacific, such as those near Feefen on the small island of Truk, are underwater. Unlike remains of the buildings of Atlantis in the Atlantic Ocean, which are far below the surface, those in the Pacific are accessible, even to underwater photographers. Fish and scuba divers glide in the shallow water over a submerged megalithic complex off the coast of Okinawa. The entrance to the site's huge submerged temple is near the entrance to Shuri Castle on the western side of the island. On the top of the huge temple sits an immense carved stone turtle who is so massive that his head is many times larger than a person's body. The unusual underwater road that travels around the temple's immense base leads nowhere. Stalactites and stalagmites, which only form above the surface, enhance nearby submerged caves to testify to the long period of time this area was once part of the Motherland of Mu.

NOTES

1 The Akashic Records are pictorial memories of all events, actions, thoughts, and feelings that have occurred since the beginning of time. *Akasha* is a Sanskrit word for the basic substance upon which this information is imprinted, and which surrounds us but exists beyond the range of our senses. The Akashic Records are available to sensitive individuals while in an altered state of consciousness.

2 All dates of 10,000 B.C. and before are approximate.

3 Heinberg, *Memories and Visions of Paradise*, p. 177.

4 Spence, *Atlantis in America*, p. 181.

5 Cerve, *Lemuria*.

6 Churchward, *The Lost Continent of Mu*, p. 47.

7 Cerve, *Lemuria*, p. 99.

8 Tompkins, *Mysteries of the Mexican Pyramids*, p. 366.

9 From private correspondence. Gregory Berg is an amateur archaeologist whose discerning interpretation and astute research into prehistory reveals many interesting and important facts that are not well-known.

10 Ibid.

11 Berlitz, *Mysteries from Forgotten Worlds*, pp. 128–129.

12 Sykes, *Atlantis #4*, 1952, p. 75.

13 Childress, *Lost Cities of Ancient Lemuria and the Pacific*, pp. 286–288.

14 Spence, *Atlantis in America*, p. 183.

2
LIFE IN LEMURIA

*When I lived on Lemuria I understood
very clearly how man had evolved from
spiritual beings, as in early Lemuria we
were in a sense above the earth and not
truly a part of it—sort of moving around
. . . as etheric beings of light. I remember
moving through the great forests as I
floated to Earth, where we gradually
learned to be human. During that time
of the Golden Era at the very beginning,
we were in harmony with the land and
ourselves. Those memories of then are
strong in me.*

—HEATHER ROBB

JUST AS A ROBIN'S EGG CAN
never be reassembled perfectly from the
pieces lying on a sidewalk, although the
lovely blue color of the fragments offers an
indication of the shell's former quality, so

we will never be able to construct a complete picture of the people of the Motherland of Mu, their dreams, and all their accomplishments. However, enough segments of information are available to appreciate and learn about their varied customs and beliefs.

Mu is often referred to as Earth's cradle of the human race.[1] Initially, as in Heather's memories, spirits without physical bodies traveled to Mu, a concept which will be explored more carefully in chapter 11. When they assumed a solid form, humans thrived in Lemuria and, just as the size of insects increased in the favorable climate, so Lemurians prospered physically. Skeletons of men who were nine feet tall were buried on the Pacific Islands, and similar ones have been unearthed in California and in Arizona.[2] On the banks of the Mississippi, in 1885, while quarrying rock for a dam, two feet below the level of the river, workers found the petrified remains of a gigantic human being. The ten-foot, nine-and-a-half-inch long skeleton, with a chest that measures fifty-nine inches around and a massive head that measures thirty-one inches around and was very flat on top, was in a grave that had been dug out of solid granite.[3] Vague legends in Central America report that giants built the highest pyramids in the New World. Numerous references in mythology describe these very tall people, who are often called Titans.

Numerous myths and legends describe the people of the Motherland of Mu as intuitive and nurturing, but it is impossible to accurately picture the hair and skin color of those who lived so long ago. In the thousands of years that have passed since their homeland sank, the descendants of the Lemurians who survived its destruction have mingled with persons on other islands. In addition, these beautiful Pacific Islands have always attracted travelers who stayed, intermarried with the inhabitants, and produced offspring with varied physical characteristics.

Like Col. Churchward, W. S. Cerve also derived knowledge from ancient manuscripts, although he gained access to his information in a very different way. (The biography of W. S. Cerve in appendix II lends credibility to the information that follows about the Motherland of Mu.) Cerve describes an unusual physical feature of many of Mu's people. He reports that at one period in their history, they had a protrusion in the center of their foreheads. Although it wasn't exactly a third eye per se, it was a perceptive sensory organ that, when the person stood still and concentrated on it, offered long-distance impressions that escaped the individual's other senses.[4] It was especially valuable for sensing dangerous animals, who sometimes grew bored with wallowing in wet, marshy areas and went searching for a human being to toy with.

This "sixth sense" also enabled the people of Mu to communicate with the more agreeable animals and to transmit messages to each other when they were far apart. As long as they used the valuable organ, it was available to enrich their lives, but when they gradually failed to take advantage of it, its powers slowly declined and eventually almost disappeared. Many believe that this "sixth sense" or "third eye" was once connected with the pineal gland, which was considerably larger in people in some remote cultures. Scientists have recently begun to correlate the link between the pineal gland and the effect of seasonal variations, such as light on our bodies, as well as other mood changes. In addition to being light sensitive, the gland has many features in common with the retina of our eyes.[5]

When they concentrated on using all their six senses, the people of Mu sensed something more. If they focused on a tree, for instance, they saw its size and color, but they also perceived it as a living being with an intangible relationship to its environment, to nature, to the cosmos. As a result of their extensive knowledge, they believed in a four-dimensional world, and this spiritual aspect of life was of primary importance to them. Through meditation and their concentration on the spiritual, they believed in reincarnation—that they were are all beams of light that would inevitably leave their physical bodies and return to the source from whence they came. The knowledge that there was life after life was enhanced by their close contact with their ancestors who inhabited the other world.[6] Some say the ancestor worship that prevailed until recently in China is a long-lasting remnant of the sensory skills of the Lemurians who long ago emigrated to the Asian continent.

When the people of Mu had accomplished what they believed was expected of them in this life, they were capable of leaving their bodies and making the transition to the spirit world.[7] The symbol of a skeleton with upraised arms and crossed legs is an emblem from Mu that they used in their religious ceremonies to further the impression that there is nothing to fear when the soul leaves the mortal body, for another life awaits. This symbol from the Motherland of Mu, which is part of the Freemasons' liturgy,[8] is found in Egypt, and is repeated many times on the cornices of the west temple at Uxmal in the Yucatan.[9]

> *I had an Akashic reading and I received information about my soul's experience in Lemuria, a place I had never heard of. I was told that when my soul was in Lemuria, I worked with Light. I assume this is Divine Light. Learning this has helped me to understand myself. I have always been very spiritual, but now it has really increased.*
> —ANONYMOUS

Fertile soil, readily available bananas, mangoes, cassava, plantain, taro, coconuts, cashews, and breadfruit assured that the people of Lemuria did not have to work hard to meet their daily needs. Spiritually evolved, they realized the importance of forgiveness, love, and patience in their relations with everyone. During most of their history, they were not interested in material possessions, since they knew their friends would consider only what kind of a person they really were inside—in other words, the level of their soul's advancement. Considerate and kind, they lived together in groups where each individual spent their time contributing whatever he or she was best qualified to offer.[10] Cerve tells us that in early Lemuria there was no money or other form of renumeration for one's work. Members of a community shared everything. Those who enjoyed agricultural pursuits spent their time farming, and surplus was placed in storehouses or traded with distant places to obtain variety. Mining was available to those who wished. Arts and sciences progressed to a high level because talented individuals were free to devote themselves to these areas without concern for daily essentials. To heighten their states of consciousness, Lemurians created lovely gardens full of waterfalls and exotic plants that were available for contemplation and meditation.[11]

Irish folklore offers the following saying: "Knowledge, under the rule of the Golden Serpent, was mostly to be found in the West, while Wisdom, an entirely different thing, was to be found under the rule of the Golden Dragon in the East."[12] Esoteric sources, as reported by David Childress in *Lost Cities of Ancient Lemuria & the Pacific*, agree that the Lemurians applied their admirable wisdom to ruling their widespread kingdoms with excellent results. Their ability to govern was one of their finest achievements. Only one language was spoken, and compulsory education was the primary focus for everyone.[13] As a result of the Lemurians' thoughtful, uncorrupted government, their civilization progressed for thousands of years, steadily advancing in science and technology. As they developed their ability to travel on the ocean's waters to other lands, Lemurians became world leaders in religion and philosophy.[14] Many of them journeyed to Atlantis, where their kindly, loving natures merged with the more mental Atlanteans.

Austrian mystic Dr. Rudolph Steiner wrote that many Lemurians lived in underground dwellings.[15] These homes, safely beneath the surface, offered them protection from unfriendly wild animals whose assaults were a constant threat. Their underground homes also protected them from the midday sun, which forced them to live indoors during much of the day. Due to the sun's burning heat, the early morning or late afternoon hours were the only comfortable times they could work in their fields and orchards.[16]

Stories of ancient, underground dwellings and tunnels prevail worldwide. It is said that hundreds of thousands of years ago, when people chose to live under the surface, they acquired the ability to easily build their large living spaces and the tunnels that connected them. The huge network of caverns in the Yucatan as described in chapter 5 offer one example of extensive underground living spaces that people enlarged and occupied for hundreds of years until volcanic action and earthquakes subsided.

Cerve describes one of Mu's interesting marriage customs, which he believes was practiced in some Pacific islands until very recently. On the day of the big event, everyone assembled in a circle in front of the village temple. The young couple was instructed to remove all their clothing and any other objects from their bodies. They were not even permitted to carry anything in their hands. Accompanied by flutists and drummers, the townspeople escorted the naked woman and man to the edge of the city and instructed them to walk together for at least fifty miles into the wilderness. They were told to stay there for two moon cycles. When the couple returned, they were required to be in good health, without wounds from wild animals, and dressed in protective clothing made from animal skins, feathers, or fibers. If this was the case, and each of them testified that the other had provided for and protected him or her during the ordeal, the wedding took place. If they returned separately, or were unwilling to praise their companion's efforts, there was no wedding service, and they were never allowed a second chance.[17]

Aware of where they had come from, the priests of Mu perceived the laws of the universe and were in tune with all that is.

They guided the people spiritually and taught them in simple, easily understood language. As in Atlantis, the sun was a focus of worship, for it was a physical manifestation of their primary god, the one incomprehensible creator.[18] A picture of the sun, or a circle, which characterized this one god, became a symbol throughout the world. The Japanese flag still carries this ancient Lemurian emblem. A circle also represented their belief in reincarnation for, just as we live eternally, a circle has no beginning and no end.

Lemurian missionaries traveled everywhere to spread their beliefs. Edgar Cayce mentions their presence in the Gobi Desert, Peru, Egypt, the Yucatan, and the western United States.[19] (Please see Cayce's biography in appendix II.) The good people built temples, educated others and, realizing the ultimate fate of their country, constantly worked at imparting and preserving knowledge. When they realized that there was no hope for their beloved continent, to ensure that the Motherland of Mu would always be remembered, the missionaries made a point of carrying information with them and carefully concealing it for future generations like ourselves. The information Churchward discovered, which the Naacals had copied, is an example of the records Lemurians transferred to a safer place.[20]

Stone tablets which Scottish geologist William Niven uncovered in Mexico under several layers of civilizations may also represent Lemurian missionaries' attempts to preserve information about the past when they reached other lands. In 1921, while he was excavating at a depth of twelve feet about five miles northwest of Mexico City, Niven discovered a number of tablets carved from volcanic rock with peculiar pictographs outlined in red.[21] In the years that followed, while exploring in the nearby vicinity, often down to greater depths, Niven found more than 2,000 additional strange stones. From the height of the debris above them, he estimated they were over 12,000 years old and probably closer to 50,000.[22]

The ancient stones are in a variety of shapes and often have figures carved on them as well as strange writing. When Niven was unable to find an archaeologist who could decipher the pictographs, he sent tracings to his friend, James Churchward. Churchward said the writing on the stones was the same language as the Naacal tablets he had seen in India and, after deciphering them, he reported they confirmed his evidence from Far Eastern records. When Churchward said they contained the history of man for the last 200,000 years, the scientific community was disgusted and lost all interest in Niven's find. The areas where the stones had hidden for thousands of years were destroyed by bulldozers as they prepared the ground for the new suburbs of Mexico City. Niven sold many of the tablets when he needed money, and he died in 1930 before scientists recognized the value of his historic discovery. Some of the unusual tablets are available in a private museum in Mexico City.[23] It is reported that many of them were donated to the Museum of Natural History in New York where, in 1976, officials reported they had misplaced them.[24]

Another collection of prehistoric carved stones offers further evidence of the ancient civilizations in South America. Sometimes referred to as a "living library," it is preserved in the Cabrera Museum in Ica, just north of the famous Nazca Lines in Peru. During the past thirty years, Dr. Cabrera has collected over 11,000 carved stones from nearby fields. Their images of medical transplants, people with dinosaurs, blood tranfusions, telescopes, and other advanced technology are truly amazing. Unable to explain the mysterious Ica stones, the Peruvian government once accused Dr. Cabrera of carving them, but that is physically impossible.

When people in the eastern regions of Lemuria realized a major natural disaster was imminent, many of them left their homes and joined their predecessors in Peru or moved to the thriving colony of Mayas in Central America. Widespread sources, including an ancient Hindu text, Chinese and Japanese manuscripts, the

Central American Troano Codex, and carvings on a tomb at Chichén Itzá in the Yucatan refer to the dynasties of twelve kings who ruled over Mayas for many thousands of years. Knowledge from ancient Lemuria, which survived in Peru and has recently surfaced, will be described in chapter 5.

There is a belief that learned Lemurians also traveled into Mount Shasta, which rises to 14,162 feet in northern California. Here they used sound and vibrations to expand an already existing cavern and build the underground city of Telos in preparation for the time when the Motherland would sink into the sea. When the dreadful moment arrived, thousands of Lemurian refugees were able to seek shelter in Mount Shasta,[25] where they were so isolated from their homeland that for several generations they believed they were the only residents of Lemuria who survived the terrible catastrophe that destroyed it. Tales of strange lights on the mountain, unusual visitors to the nearby town, tunnels into the mountain, and nearby UFO activity continue to reinforce the belief that descendants of Lemurians still live deep inside Mount Shasta.

NOTES

1   Scott-Elliot, *The Story of Atlantis and the Lost Lemuria*, p. 85.

2   Countryman, *Atlantis and the Seven Stars*, p. 84.

3   Butler, *Ancient American*, p. 17.

4   Cerve, *Lemuria*, pp.123–127.

5   Hope, *Time: The Ultimate Energy*, p. 94.

6   Ibid., p. 130.

7   Ibid., p. 133. The procedure for permanently leaving one's body is available to those who have learned to enter a deep state of meditation. The person must not "ground" him- or herself at the beginning of the procedure, and must sincerely plan and desire to allow his or her spirit to depart.

8   Churchward, *The Lost Continent of Mu*, p. 150.

9   From private correspondence. Gregory Berg is an e-mail friend who has extensively studied prehistory for many years. Currently he is learning to decipher Mayan glyphs.

10 Cerve, *Lemuria*, p. 152.

11 Ibid.

12 Wilkins, *Secret Cities of Ancient South America*, p. 72.

13 Childress, *Lost Cities of Ancient Lemuria & the Pacific*, p. 28, from *The Ultimate Frontier* (Childress says in the text that this is a work taken largely from the lessons of a group called the Lemurian Fellowship).

14 Scott-Elliot, *The Story of Atlantis and the Lost Lemuria*, p. 19.

15 Walton, *Mount Shasta*, p. 8.

16 Cerve, *Lemuria*, p. 112.

17 Ibid., pp. 157–160.

18 Churchward, *The Lost Continent of Mu*, p. 136.

19 Cayce, *Readings* 691–1, 962–1.

20 Churchward's biography in the appendix contains additional information about the Naacals and their tablets.

21 Churchward, *The Lost Continent of Mu*, p. 223.

22 Tompkins, *Mysteries of the Mexican Pyramids*, p. 358–363.

23 Ibid.

24 Ibid. and Zapp and Erikson, *Atlantis in America*, p. 249.

25 *The Light Messenger*, February 2001, p. 5 (a newsletter from Beverly Dombrowski: pegasusiam@snowcrest.net).

3

ATLANTIS IN THE SUNRISE SEA

In 1954 I was traveling from New York to Europe on a ship called Mauritania. *Midway across the ocean, despite my unpleasant problems from the very rough seas, I began to have an awful feeling of things far below me. I knew nothing about Atlantis. Yes, my sister [author Shirley Andrews] spoke of this place, but I had nothing to do with that. As I grew up, I had no interest in the mysterious land which she said was at the bottom of the Atlantic Ocean. But now I felt Atlantis lying crushed beneath me. Broken land. Smashed cities. I had a sense of dread, doom. This horrible feeling stayed with me as we moved slowly toward our destination. Atlantis was big, very big. A wondrous, civilized, complex society with all its good and all its bad, and as the ship took me toward Europe, I knew it lay shattered and ruined under the water.*

—BARBARA WOLF

When I went to Barbados, I was led to an older gentleman who took me to the top of the island to a little town called "Atlantis"! He further told me folk tales that described the ancient mountaintops of Atlantis as the present islands of the Caribbean.

—ANONYMOUS

The inhabitants of the Motherland of Mu in the Pacific Ocean were the first to develop a high civilization, but in prehistory people thrived throughout the world, just as they do today. In 350 B.C., Greek scholar Plato wrote a detailed description of a country on fertile land he called Atlantis. Plato's Atlantis was an extensive island that, before it sank in about 10,000 B.C., was in the Atlantic Ocean in front of the mouth of the Pillars of Heracles. Long ago, the Straits of Gibraltar were called the Pillars of Heracles because Heracles, an emperor of the African Tuaregs, controlled shipping through that narrow passageway.[1] Before 10,000 B.C., Lemurians traveled to Atlantis and Atlanteans traveled to Lemuria. As we shall see, in spite of some basic differences, the people of the two countries influenced each other and sometimes intermarried.

Three times Plato asserts that his Atlantean information is true. He carefully outlines his sources, and researchers who checked on them confirm that his authorities lived when Plato says they did. The subject of Atlantis fascinated Plato and, to learn more, it is said that he consulted students of Pythagoras (582–500 B.C.) and others who were acquainted with the ancient mythological, historical, and geological lore. Proclus (A.D. 410–485) reports that before Plato wrote about Atlantis he made a trip to Egypt, presumably to confirm his data. In Egypt Plato sold edible oils, probably olive oil, to the Egyptians to pay for the journey. While he was there, he talked with priests at Sais, Heliopolis, and Sebennytus.[2]

For his Atlantean account, Plato also had access to ancient records, such as those in the remarkable library at Alexandria, which Edgar Cayce says Atlanteans established in 10,300 B.C. to include information about cultures and religions from all over the world. For hundreds of years learned people assembled in that attractive North African city to exchange information and contribute to the growing collection of valuable manuscripts. Eventually almost a million scrolls and books from all parts of the western world were available to scholars who traveled to Alexandria.

In A.D. 391, and again in A.D. 642, ignorant invaders completely burned the Alexandrian library's irreplaceable contents, including the collections of information about Atlantis and Lemuria that scholars had so carefully preserved. The fate of Hypatia, a gifted female mathematician and philosopher, demonstrates the zeal of those who compulsively destroyed the precious writings. This very beautiful woman, who was curator of the library at Alexandria in the fourth century A.D. when it was torched and burned, attempted to save some scrolls from the flames. The story is that "Christians" dragged Hypatia into a church, stripped her naked, and cut her into pieces with abalone shells.

Plato refrained from writing about Atlantis until just before he died. It appears that, as he neared the end of his life, he finally wrote about Atlantis in an effort to ensure that the history of the lost civilization would be preserved. He undoubtedly received some of his information from priests who were members of secret brotherhoods who swore him to secrecy. In the past, these mystery schools kept wisdom from those who were not initiated into their society, for it helped to ensure the safety of their intellectual treasures during perilous times when marauders were pillaging the land. It also offered them esteem and a means of controlling the general public. In some situations, the punishment for disclosing sacred hidden knowledge was death. Since the time of Plato, secret societies have continued to appeal to the human race. Their ceremonies are usually not open to the public, but knowledge about the organizations is generally available.

Edgar Cayce depicts Atlantis as a large island that originally lay between the Gulf of Mexico and the Mediterranean. Over a period of thousands of years, the huge country gradually disintegrated into smaller islands. In the *Timaeus*, Plato describes the final days of the main island, when what remained was located on the Atlantic Ridge, a mountainous section of the sea floor that runs north-south in the Atlantic Ocean between the European and American continents. This land is not granite, like continents, but volcanic material that comes through rifts in the ocean floor where sections of the Earth's crust are separating. Proof that portions of the mountainous Atlantic Ridge were above the surface until 9500 B.C. is available in innumerable other books, which offer the results of intensive studies from analysis of core samples, the geography of the terrain, glacial residue, lava rock, coral, sand deposits, and plant growth. The evidence is convincing and readily available. Sources are more fully indicated in my book *Atlantis: Insights from a Lost Civilization*. The proposition that Plato's Atlantis was a Bronze Age society that thrived until 1200 B.C. is impossible to validate, for there is no evidence that substantial portions of the Atlantic Ridge were above the surface after 9500 B.C.

The hills, valleys, and broad central plain of Atlantis are clearly visible on an ocean floor map of the Atlantic Ridge today. The Azores Islands, Madeira, and the Cape Verde Islands, which were the mountaintops of Atlantis, are all that remain of the once-flourishing land. These islands' steep coastal hillsides extend almost perpendicularly down to the sea floor without underwater platforms. The sand beaches along parts of the western and southern coasts of the country, and the coral reefs that offered protection from ocean storms, are also visible far below the surface.

The volcanic soil of Atlantis was rich and nourishing, and the temperate Gulf Stream that circled the island ensured a pleasant climate even during the Ice Age. In this desirable location, with the protection from invaders that the surrounding ocean provided, the

Atlantean civilization thrived. Plato's report of Atlantis includes the geography of the country, an extensive description of its massive capital city, information about the government, the army, the people's extensive use of gold and silver, and much more. (Further details may be found in *Atlantis: Insights from a Lost Civilization*.)

The inhabitants of Atlantis had a major geographical problem. The Atlantic Ridge lies at the intersection of two sections or plates of the Earth's crust, and three sections intersect in the region of the Azores Plateau. Although it is below the surface, it is one of the most active volcanic areas in the world, for these sections of the Earth's surface frequently change positions. The movement is very slow but, when it happens, it stimulates damaging earthquakes and volcanoes. As in Iceland today, which is the only major portion of the Atlantic Ridge above the surface, life-threatening earthquakes and volcanic eruptions were frequent events in Atlantis.

Small islands that occasionally appear and disappear in the Atlantic Ocean demonstrate the instability of the Atlantis Ridge. In March 1882, 200 miles south of the Azores, a British captain and his crew aboard the S.S. *Jesmond* noticed smoke in the distance and quantities of dead fish and mud on the surface of the ocean. The ship continued on and came to an island with smoking mountains that was not on their maps.

When the captain and some sailors went ashore to explore the desolate place, they were surprised to discover that no plants or trees grew on the island. The apprehensive men came to ruins of massive stone walls and, while digging near one of them, they unearthed bronze swords, jewelry, pottery, and a lava-covered stone case that apparently contained a mummy. They took the sarcophagus to the British Museum for safekeeping, but the museum says it is currently lost. The British and American press reported the event at the time, but the ship's log, which was in the offices of the S.S. *Jesmond's* owners, was destroyed in the London Blitz in 1940. The mysterious island soon disappeared and has never appeared again.[3]

In 1808, after a substantial underwater volcanic eruption, a large island appeared among the Azores. It was given the name Sambrina, but before long it, too, sank beneath the waves. During the twentieth century, several additional acres of the Azores island of Terciera rose from the sea, and more land, which is only seven feet under the surface, is currently moving upward.

When the Earth shook too often, the ground beneath their feet flooded and sank, and volcanoes ejected rocks, lava, and hot ashes, many Atlanteans left their island home and moved to more stable lands around the Atlantic Ocean. They thrived in their new locations, and soon the Atlantean civilization was widespread. The Caribbean area, where life was easier, was a favorite destination. Here Atlanteans built extensive cities similar to their old capital that Plato portrays so well. Ruins of Atlantean buildings in these regions are more accessible, and are slowly revealing themselves to the many diligent searchers who hope to find Atlantis. The civilization of Poseidia, the largest island in the Caribbean Sea, and a popular destination of Atlanteans, will be described in the following chapters.

NOTES

1   Hansen, *The Ancient Atlantic.*

2   Temple, *The Sirius Mystery.*

3   Berlitz, *Atlantis: The Eighth Continent,* pp. 76–79.

4

POSEIDIA: THE LAND OF PROMISE

I grew up on a small island off the south-ern coast of Puerto Rico. All my friends and I believe it was once a much larger island and part of Atlantis. We remem-ber that we worked in a temple on that island where people with physical and mental problems came to be healed.

The soil on the island was clay and when we were children, when it was rain-ing hard, we would pick up a clump of the clay and hold it out in the rain in the palm of our hands. The water washed away the dirt, and when it was gone we'd have a handful of little quartz crystals.

—ANONYMOUS

FROM 30,000 B.C. UNTIL 10,000 B.C., when ocean waters were 350 feet lower than today, the continental shelves around the Atlantic Ocean extended out as far as two hundred miles from the present

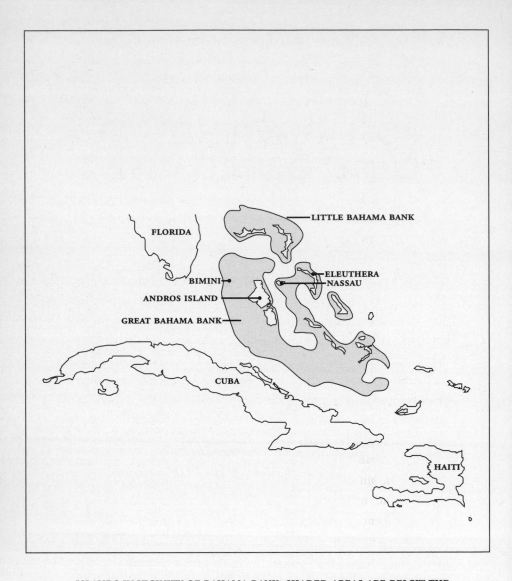

Labels on map: LITTLE BAHAMA BANK, FLORIDA, ELEUTHERA, BIMINI, NASSAU, ANDROS ISLAND, GREAT BAHAMA BANK, CUBA, HAITI

ISLANDS IN VICINITY OF BAHAMA BANK; SHADED AREAS ARE BELOW THE
SURFACE TODAY, AND CLEAR AREAS ARE ABOVE THE SURFACE TODAY

shorelines of America and Europe. Extensive portions of the sea floor of the Gulf of Mexico and the Caribbean Sea were also above the surface. Poseidia was a large, pleasant island in 28,000 B.C. located on the Bahama Bank, which at that time was completely above the surface. The Bahama Bank is clearly visible on any map that depicts the ocean floor. Today Poseidia is about seven hundred small islands and cays that extend from fifty miles east of Palm Beach, Florida, for approximately 760 miles southeast in the direction of Haiti. The exposed continental shelves, plus the larger islands that resulted from less water in the ocean, made Poseidia easily accessible to Atlanteans.

Jacques Cousteau offers some interesting proof that Poseidia was above the surface so long ago. While in his submarine *Calypso*, Cousteau explored around Andros, the largest island in the Bahamas. At a depth of 165 feet, he found a huge grotto or cave with large stalactites and stalagmites. Tests of sediments on the walls of the cave confirmed that it was above water in and before 10,000 B.C.[1] Andros Island, in the center of the Bahama Bank, has many caves with writing on their walls that is similar to ancient written symbols in the Canary Islands. No one has successfully deciphered these far-flung hieroglyphics.

The Lucayan Caverns near Grand Bahama Island are also now submerged, but were once above the surface. Their winding passages extend underwater for eight miles, and include a huge domed hall and rooms with circular sky lights. Human bones in a group of caverns on Grand Bahama Island, which can only be accessed by diving through a lake, provide additional evidence that many thousands of years ago, when this land was above the surface, people lived in Poseidia.[2]

Atlanteans who moved westward looking for a new place to live also settled in Cuba and the Yucatan peninsula of Mexico. When they arrived in the Yucatan peninsula, they were surprised to find people from Mu and Og (Peru) already living in the most desirable locations. The Lemurians and South Americans were helpful and friendly, however, and shared their knowledge with the newcomers. No serious problems arose between the various groups,[3] since they were all compassionate and spiritually advanced. The followers of the virtuous Atlantean leader Iltar and the people from Mu and Og gradually intermarried, and an advanced civilization, the predecessor of the Mayas, developed.

Memories of the people of Mu with whom the Atlanteans met and intermarried in Central America are still evident. Inscriptions on Yucatan monuments indicate they were constructed as memorials to the thousands of unfortunate people in the Motherland of Mu who died when ocean water covered it.[4] Carved figures in the yoga position adorn lintels and walls of ancient, disintegrating buildings in Central America. At Palenque a carved figure sits in the cross-legged attitude of meditation and a beautiful bas-relief portrays a person in a yoga position. These features, which were common in the Far East, demonstrate that travel from the Pacific was possible long ago. Immigrants from Lemuria carried their customs with them as they moved to both Asia and Central America.[5] The name of Guatemala reflects the presence of people from Mu, for "Guatama" is a name given to the Buddha in the Far East, and was probably a sacred word long before the days of the Buddha. In both the Codex Troanus and the Codex Cortesianus, the Maya recorded the sinking of the land of Mu.

Cuba was a larger island during the last Ice Age and included the Puenta del Este caves on the Isle of Youth, which is now about one hundred miles southwest of the Cuban mainland. The circular openings in the ceilings of these interesting caverns offered opportunities for the inhabitants to view the stars, and the numerous astronomical symbols in these Puenta del Este caves indicate the significance of heavenly bodies to those who spent time in them so long ago. The walls and ceilings of the caverns also contain unusual red and black petroglyphs, as well as pictures of bulls.[6] The bull figures are reminders of the importance of bulls in Atlantis, as are the bulls painted 20,000 years ago on walls of the Spanish caves in southwestern Europe.

When sea levels were lower, Atlanteans lived on a long mass of land that included the small island off the coast of Puerto Rico with quartz crystals in the soil. The land extended from Jamaica, across what are now the Lesser Antilles Islands, and continued all the way south to Venezuela. Except for two or three breaks for rivers, this lengthy stretch of firm ground offered a connection between South America and the Caribbean. Along the road, traders led animals loaded with gold, silver, and precious gems from South America, which they used for trade with the people of the Caribbean.

Evidence of humans living in South America long ago offers proof that the oceans were carriers, not barriers, in the distant past. Archaeologists have learned that Monte Verde in southern Chile was home to immigrants possibly as long ago as 33,000 years,[7] and many other areas in South America were occupied between 13,000 B.C. and 18,000 B.C.[8] In a Brazilian rock shelter, 32,000 years ago, artists created permanent paintings in the same style as those which artists made in the caves of southwestern Europe at that time.[9]

Since the time of Lemuria and Atlantis, adventurers have proved it is quite possible to bridge the oceans and reach the American continent from both the east and the west. Thor Heyerdahl's trip in 1947 on a primitive balsa raft across the Pacific Ocean from Peru to Polynesia, and the many brave travelers who have duplicated his exploit, demonstrates that the Pacific Ocean was quite accessible to ancient people. Heyerdahl built his flimsy raft *Kon Tiki* from nine giant balsa logs, just as ancient Peruvians might have done, without using any metal. With five friends, he travelled 3,600 miles across the Pacific, proving that ancient people could cross vast stretches of ocean. Heyerdahl traveled from east to west, but a current north of Hawaii to the southwestern United States, plus the prevailing westerly winds, made the trip in the opposite direction available to Lemurians. Rafts in Micronesia, which go back to at least 60,000 B.C., show that people were not afraid to venture forth. Using the stars, reassuring support from dolphins, the winds, and the ocean's currents, Lemurians went wherever they wished.

After years of intensive research, Egerton Sykes unearthed reports from a variety of hardy Irishmen who traveled as early as 2000 B.C. westward across the Atlantic Ocean to the magical place they described as the Land of Youth, the Land of Heroes, the Land of Promise, the Great Coast, and the Plain of Desire. (Information about Atlanteans who once lived in the Caribbean, which Sykes gleaned from the journals of these early travelers, will be included in the next chapter.) Ignoring the dire warnings of others, and following shorelines or the ocean's currents in the direction of the setting sun, the fearless Irish adventurers crossed the Atlantic long before Columbus. Stone markers, or *inukshuks*, stand where they placed them as they sailed along the coastlines of the North Atlantic. Using simple geometric calculations, they followed these signposts from one point to the next.[10]

The Gulf Stream, a huge circular moving current in the Atlantic Ocean, contains more water than all the rivers of the world. The enormous current is fifty to one hundred miles wide at the surface and often extends over a mile down. It moves in a clockwise direction from the southern United States, up the coast and across to Europe, and down along the coast of Spain and northwest Africa. From there it proceeds across the Atlantic to the Bahamas, and back up to the southern United States. Columbus spent a long month crossing from Europe to the American continent, but recently, sailors in a ship similar to his, with the help of the more southerly section of the Gulf Stream, made the trip in nineteen days.[11] Early Irish sailors were free to travel in the ocean because they were outside the Straits of Gibraltar, which were often controlled by others. Once they learned to correctly follow the clockwise circuit of the current of the Gulf Stream, travel back and forth across the Atlantic was relatively quick and easy.

Ancient Irish stories about the Firbolgs, "the people of the hide boats," who arrived in Ireland from Atlantis when their homeland on the Atlantic Ridge was sinking, may be what inspired the Irish to build their seaworthy crafts of leather. The *currahs*, as the monks called their boats, consisted of wooden frames covered with sewn animal skins. They were small and lightweight and proved more stable in heavy seas than larger vessels, for they rode with and on top of the waves. Close to the ocean's surface, the sailors could more easily "read" its currents. If the small leather currahs did capsize, they were not apt to sink.[12]

Legends and a few ancient Central American books have survived to remind us of the people from Mu and Atlantis and their descendants who once lived there. Abbe Brasseur de Bourbourg, a respected scholar of the nineteenth century, devoted his life to the study of Central American history, philosophy, and religion. In 1845 Brasseur moved to Mexico and learned the local dialects. After he gained the confidence of the natives, they helped him find obscure manuscripts from seventeenth-century Spanish friars, and to translate and understand inscriptions on the stellae that escaped his destructive predecessors. Stellae are stone columns on which the Maya and their ancestors, realizing that records written on softer material would not survive for long, wisely recorded information.

In 1864, Brasseur discovered the Troano Codex in Madrid. It is one of the four Mayan books that escaped the Spaniard's ruinous fires. Apparently a seventeenth-century priest carried the valuable document to Spain, where it lay neglected for almost two hundred years. A second half of the Troana Codex, the Cortesianus, appeared in another part of Spain a few years later. The Troano Codex, which the Maya wrote at least 3,500 years ago from knowledge accumulated over many centuries, consists of fifty-six pages inscribed on both sides. To form each page, the writers folded and doubled an immense strip they ingeniously made from the bark of a fig tree. If the book is laid flat, it fills the floor of a large room. The pages, which are folded like a fan, are completely covered with a whitish varnish on which the hieroglyphic characters are written in black, red, blue, and brown.

Brasseur learned from the Cortesianus that a fearful cataclysm caused a large island in the Atlantic Ocean to sink into the waters with millions of inhabitants. Brasseur's concentrated years of study led him to believe that passing comets, falling meteors, and similar terrible, natural objects from the skies destroyed at least one advanced civilization in the past. These revelations were too much for the nineteenth-century academic community and, in spite of his careful scholarship, Brasseur's colleagues rudely scorned and avoided him for the rest of his life.

Dr. Augustus Le Plongeon and his wife, Alice Dixon, lived in the Yucatan from 1873 until 1885. They learned the language of the Maya, studied their culture, listened to their stories, and participated in their shamanic rituals. He came to realize that beneath the natives' everyday life there existed a strong current of occult wisdom and practice that stemmed from the very distant past.[13] For example, he learned that the ordeals in the rites of initiation to the mysteries that the priests practiced in Xibalba, in the heart of the Guatemalan mountains, were similar to the trials of initiations to the greater mysteries in ancient Egypt.[14] Le Plongeon was a Mason and was amazed to discover evidence of Masonic rites in ancient Mayan sculpture.

Le Plongeon and his wife were the original excavators of Chichén Itzá, which they documented with 500 photographs. From their contacts with the people and a variety of other sources, the Le Plongeons ascertained that some ancestors of the Maya were from the Motherland of Mu. His excellent translation of the Troana about the terrible sinking of Mu reads as follows:

In the year six Kan, on the eleventh Mulue, in the month Zac, there occurred terrible earthquakes, which continued without intermission until the thirteenth Chuen. The country of the hills of mud, the 'Land of Mu,' was sacrificed. Being twice up-heaved, it suddenly disappeared during the night, the basin being continually shaken by volcanic forces. Being confined, these caused the land to sink and rise several times and in various places. At last the surface gave way, and the ten countries were torn asunder and scattered in fragments; unable to withstand the force of the seismic convulsions, they sank with sixty-four millions of inhabitants, eight thousand and sixty years before the writing of this book.[15]

Writings the Le Plongeons translated on a temple at Uxmal, which stated the building was constructed in memory of Mu, the land to the west from whence came sacred mysteries, helped to confirm the startling information.[16] Since assertations of this type were unacceptable to the scientific community, like Brasseur, Le Plongeon lost all credibility and his fellow scholars permanently ignored him. In addition, the Mexican government confiscated many valuable relics the natives had shared with Le Plongeon. Near the end of his life he no longer trusted the Mexicans and lost all interest in sharing his discoveries with the outside world. After he died, his wife revealed that her husband had hidden a precious map to the site of underground rooms where there were perfect records of the Maya. Hopefully, one day someone will rediscover these significant memories of the past.

The Lacandon Indians in southern Mexico are Maya who lived completely removed from civilization for hundreds of centuries until fifty years ago when a startled surveyor stumbled upon one of their villages. The Lacandons believe their language is the oldest in the world.[17] One night in a dark hut, deep in the rainforest of Chiapas in southern Mexico, I listened to an elderly Lacandon chant the songs of his ancestors. As he sang, he changed the notes in pitch, intensity, and amount of vibrato, depending on the meaning of the words. Even before the singsong words were translated from his language to Spanish to English, I understood the main character and his frantic action and terrified feeling as a fierce jaguar attacked and killed him.

The fact that Lacandons continued to use this ancient language, their skills at making cloth from tree bark just as their ancestors had done for thousands of years, and my observations in the village convinced me of the validity of their memories of their origin. Lacandon Kin Garcia asserts the Maya originally came from the land of Atlantis, but they have very strong hereditary connections with the Tibetans and the Indians of North America. Kin reports that these distant ancestors gave his people sacred geometry, knowledge of the universe, and books inscribed on rocks and monuments.[18]

The Aztecs also remember the homeland of their ancestors. When Cortez and his Spanish soldiers invaded Mexico in 1519, these highly civilized people lived north of the Maya in and around what is now Mexico City. As the Spaniards stared at the gleaming beauty of the Aztec capital, with its magnificent pyramids painted pink with volcanic ash and palaces higher than the tallest churches in Spain, it seemed as if they were dreaming. The canals, lakes, freshwater aqueducts, and perfectly paved streets of the city—which was larger than Paris, the biggest metropolis in Europe—added to the scene. Montezuma, the handsome emperor, with his carefully trimmed beard and gracious manners, resembled a European nobleman.

What was the origin of all this civilization? Montezuma told the Spaniards his distant ancestors came from a land to the east called Aztlan, which was now in the sea. In their language *atl* means "water" and *tlan* is "a place" or "land," so Aztlan means "water land" or perhaps "island."[19] The Aztecs remembered that Aztlan had a high mountain, a garden where the gods lived,[20] and many flamingos. Thousands of beautiful pink and orange flamingos still congregate and breed in Andros Island, in the center of what was once Poseidia.

The Aztecs attempted to preserve memories of their past in stone carvings. Many years ago a German archaeologist found a frieze on a temple deep in the jungle of northern Guatemala that apparently depicts a destruction of Atlantis. The relief depicts a scene in which a pyramid or temple is falling apart and slipping into the water (ocean). Next to the blocks of the crumbling building a large volcano is erupting. A man rowing a boat has adornments in his ears, indicating he is a priest. Before him, a drowning person wears a headdress, which suggests he or she represents the lower classes.

For thousands of years, the Caribs of Central America have preserved memories of their ancestors who were members of a large group of seven families who left their homes on a now-submerged land far to the east in the sunrise sea. The seven families traveled to the west in seven fleets of ships, and finally came to an island they called Caraiba, where they settled.[21] The Caribs refer to their original homeland as the old, red land. In a similar way, the Toltecs, predecessors of the Aztecs in Mexico, remember that their ancestors came from the old, old, red land. (Please see the biography of Lucille Taylor Hansen in appendix II, for her interesting research with Native Americans was the source of this information.) A high incidence of red clay in parts of the Atlantic Ridge offers an explanation for the Native American references to Atlantis as the old, red land.[22]

The Caribs told Hansen that descendants of the seven families from the old, red land lived happily in Caraiba for a very long time. Visiting priests from Atlantis taught the people the religion of Tupan and referred to them as the Tupi, meaning "the sons of Pan." "Pan" was another name for the old, red land. Many generations later, a particularly devastating natural catastrophe on

Caraiba compelled the Tupi to leave their sinking island home. They traveled a little further to the west in seven even larger fleets and came to a sea they named Caribbean, after Caraiba.

When they reached the Caribbean, the Tupi ancestors of the Caribs separated. Some settled on nearby mountainous land where they farmed by terracing, a technique their distant forebears employed on the steep mountainsides of Atlantis. Other Tupi moved to the south and journeyed up the Amazon River. The Guarahis of Paraguay continue to worship the god Tupan. At least one of the seven groups of these Atlanteans from Caraiba went north to the Mississippi River Valley. For a long time representatives of the seven extended families met every 104 years to coordinate calendars and compare adventures, but communication became an increasing problem, and they gradually lost touch with one another.[23] In the same way, after many generations, descendants of Lemurians and Atlanteans who settled in Central America gradually forgot the past history of their ancestors.

NOTES

1   Fix, *Pyramid Odyssey*, p. 215.

2   Collins, *Gateway to Atlantis*, p. 330.

3   Cayce, *Readings* 5750–1.

4   Churchward, *The Lost Continent of Mu*, pp. 80–84.

5   Ibid.

6   Ibid., p. 251, 265.

7   *N.Y. Times*, July 22, 1986, from Tom D. Dillehay.

8   *The Economist*, "The First Americans," Feb. 21, 1998, p. 79, 80.

9   Katz, "The Way We Were," *Newsweek*, November 10, 1986, p. 72.

10   *Nova, WGBH Transcripts*, December 15, 1987, *Secrets of the Red Paint People*, pp. 6–7.

11   *Nova, The Gulf Stream*, February 28, 1989.

12   Zapp & Erikson, *Atlantis in America*, p. 285.

13   Tompkins, *Mysteries of the Mexican Pyramids*, p. 166.

14   Le Plongeon, *Sacred Mysteries*, pp. 41–43. For example, the ancient Maya wisemen practiced clairvoyance and with magic mirrors they predicted the future. Surrounding themselves with clouds, they could appear to make themselves invisible and materialize amazing objects. Although there is no proof Lemurians or Atlanteans carried the techniques for these occult skills to Central America, it is impossible to prove they didn't.

15   Le Plongeon, Alice and Augustus, *Queen Moo and the Eastern Sphinx*, p. 147.

16   Hatt, *The Maya*, p. 9.

17   Muck, *The Secret of Atlantis*, p. 129.

18   Red Star, *Star Ancestors*, p. 74.

19   Berlitz, *Atlantis, The Eighth Continent*, p. 56.

20   Tompkins, *Mysteries of the Mexican Pyramids*, pp. 4, 9.

21   Hansen, *The Ancient Atlantic*.

22   Donato, *A Re-examination of the Atlantis Theory*.

23   Hansen, *The Ancient Atlantic*.

5

POSEIDIA AND THE YUCATAN

SHE DREAMED SHE WAS IN A strange land, far from her homeland of Atlantis that was gone forever. It was hot in this foreign country, and she and her friends were surrounded by a forest which seemed to stretch on and on. The nearby sea was also unfamiliar. Noisy, small monkeys filled the air with loud shrieking. Brightly colored birds fluttered from tree to tree, and strange insects buzzed around her. The woman and her companions wore simple, primitive clothing and lived in huts constructed from gray bark. Her hands were rough and calloused from chopping trees for fires and digging to plant grains and vegetables. She was kneeling, pounding some nameless grain in a wooden bowl. Despite the hardships, she was happy.[1]

This dream came to renowned author Taylor Caldwell late in her life, after she wrote *The Romance of Atlantis*. When she was only twelve years old, Caldwell (1900–1985) wrote that detailed novel about the experiences of a princess of Atlantis during the final days of her country on an island in the Atlantic Ocean. Caldwell's father sent the manuscript to her grandfather, a book publisher, who promptly returned it, saying he was horrified and was convinced it was a fraud. He believed the philosophical and intellectual maturity it reflected indicated that someone much older had written it. Taylor Caldwell set aside *The Romance of Atlantis* until she was seventy years old, when she sent it to her friend Jess Stern, who was interested in having it published. At that time Caldwell had this dream about her life after she hurriedly left sinking Atlantis.

Many Atlanteans, like those in Taylor Caldwell's dream who managed to escape from their sinking country during its last moments, found themselves in a difficult, often fearsome situation somewhere on the American continent. Since small groups of refugees did not have the knowledge or the equipment to reproduce the high standard of living they had enjoyed in their homeland, their lives soon disintegrated to primitive living conditions. The more fortunate last-minute refugees from the Atlantic Ridge reached the island of Poseidia on the Bahama Bank in the Caribbean. Here they joined the thousands who had moved there since 28,000 B.C.

The first to arrive in Poseidia were people whom Cayce identifies as Children of the Law of One. Throughout most of its long life, the majority of the inhabitants of Atlantis were spiritual individuals who loved and respected each other. Gradually, with the passage of time, the leaders divided into two groups, the Children of the Law of One and the Sons of Belial. The Children of the Law of One are also referred to as the "Sons of Light," and the Sons of Belial are called the "Sons of Darkness." Similar terms are found in the Dead Sea Scrolls.[2]

The Sons of Belial were selfish, materially oriented individuals who focused on the pleasures of satisfying their own physical appetites and desires, with no respect for others. As their lives filled with thoughts of material objects, they came to believe, like many of us today, that the acquisition of more and more would bring them happiness. When disaster threatened Atlantis, they were so involved in the material world they did not heed the advice of wiser individuals, who urged everyone to leave if they wished to continue their lifetime on this planet.

The main principle of the Law of One is that we all are related; we all are one. The Children of the Law of One focused on love and practiced prayer and meditation, hoping to promote everyone's spiritual knowledge. They followed the Golden Rule, and also believed that whatever they did to others would happen to them. They honored the Creator from whence they came, who gave them their soul.[3] Many individuals on the Earth today are Lemurians and Atlanteans who have returned to participate in another struggle between the forces of good and evil for control of this planet. Some believe that if the creases of the lines that are visible in the palm of your hand when you close it slightly form the letter "M" you were probably one of the Children of Light. A curved "S" or "C" indicates the Sons of Darkness.[4] However, one's actions or thoughts in Atlantis or Lemuria are not really important. What is significant is that today we are all here to help make our world a better place. The Children of the Law of One will continue their good work, and the Sons of Darkness will have an opportunity to redeem themselves.

I dreamed that my ex-husband and I lived in a big house that had large arched porticoes and very filmy, sheer, light drapery hangings of some type. The house was on a hillside, open to fresh air and ocean breezes on all sides. I could feel the breeze and the curtains were flowing softly from the windows. Life was wonderful and I was very happy; I knew that we were living in Atlantis.

—ALLISON

In a city on a beautiful hillside overlooking the sea, the devout Poseidians erected lovely temples, some with large pillars of onyx and topaz inlaid with precious stones that reflected the sun's light.[5] Two of the temples, the Temple Beautiful and the Temple of Sacrifice, became the center of the lives of numerous Atlanteans who wished to raise their level of consciousness ever higher. It is said that "Beauty in mind, body, and soul" was inscribed over the door of the Temple Beautiful, where men and women were equal and they worked together in harmony.

Edgar Cayce says that active participants in the Temple Beautiful and the Temple of Sacrifice wore special headgear and garments, but he does not describe them.[6] Like doctors, nurses, train conductors, and royalty today, their clothing was similar to a uniform and indicated one's field of service. From psychic Betty Bethards we learn that those who participated in the temple's activities wore a wraparound garment with large sleeves that hung down, resembling one of our hospital gowns. It was tied at the waist with a shiny lightweight metallic band, unlike any metal we know.[7]

British author Murry Hope (please see her biography in appendix II) adds that the basic color of their garments and their sash, earring, pendant, ring, bracelet, or headband indicated whether they were a healer or student or teacher, and also showed what level of enlightenment they had attained.[8] When Atlanteans started the journey toward priesthood, the novices wore pale green robes. As they advanced, light blue clothing distinguished them, and finally they were permitted to don the white garments reserved for the highest-ranking orders. Unique deep-blue gowns were passed down from one generation of sages to the next and worn only on special occasions. A healer with a silver headband specialized in mental healing, and an orichalcum headband indicated proficiency in physical medicine or surgery.[9]

The orichalcum in the headband was a popular metal in Atlantis, but its composition is somewhat of a mystery. In ancient Greek, the word simply meant "gold metal." Plato says that orichalcum was something that in his time was only known by name, but was once a precious metal that "sparkled like fire."[10] It was probably an alloy of gold and copper or meteorite iron. Memories of the orichalcum of Atlantis appeared 600 years before Plato's time in the works of the Greek poet Homer, who mentions it in the *Hymn of Aphrodite* as a golden metal. Hesiod, another pre-Plato Greek poet (eighth– –seventh century B.C.) also refers to orichalcum.

The Temple Beautiful and the Temple of Sacrifice offered students opportunities to participate in a variety of activities intended to purify their bodies and minds. In the Temple Beautiful, the primary goal of the participants was to acquire a thorough understanding of themselves so they would be better equipped to serve others. As they progressed in the seven stations of the Temple Beautiful, a variety of techniques, such as musical experiences and expressive dance forms, furthered the participant's ability to interpret their emotions and to purge, heal, and unify themselves.[11]

Young women went to a Temple Beautiful to prepare for the self-sacrifice of motherhood, and to learn how their actions affected the lives of their offspring.[12] When they were ready, music assisted them in preparing their bodies and minds for procreation.[13] At one station, teachers offered advice to unselfish individuals who wished to become missionaries.[14] After completing their training, a group of teachers and caregivers from Poseidia went to Egypt and built a Temple Beautiful in a pyramid shape,[15] and a Temple of Sacrifice modeled after the one in their homeland.[16] The Temple of Sacrifice was similar to our hospitals and will be described in chapter 11.

Murias was the largest city in Poseidia. From Celtic myths and records and diaries of adventurers who crossed the Atlantic searching for treasures and legends, we know that Murias was the seat of government for the area. Its extensive facilities included a hospital, a home for travelers in distress, and a shipyard with repair facilities. On a hill above the city, the Atlanteans built an exquisite healing temple which offered such remarkable cures that memories of it have never completely disappeared.

> *Today, for the first time, I read about the "mythical" Atlantis on your website. I was in tears when I read the section about a temple with crystal windows because in the not-so-distant past I had the most vivid dream about a similar place, and the memory of this dream haunts me still.*
> —ANONYMOUS

The architecture of the exquisite healing temple above Murias is thought to have incorporated the vibrational and numerical aspects of sacred geometry, which intensify and focus various subtle cosmic energies for the sensitive person. It also displayed sophisticated knowledge of the structure of the universe, the solar system, and planet Earth in a manner similar to the Great Pyramid in Egypt.[17] The temple's most unusual feature was its translucent rock crystal windows, which local people still remember in contemporary times. The building was dedicated to the Bennu bird and the god Min, both symbolic of rejuvenation, and one of the sources of the island of Bimini's name.

In 10,000 B.C., rising ocean waters completely covered the thriving city of Murias, but the swelling waves stopped climbing before they reached the healing temple with the crystal windows. The unusual structure was safe, but at the water's edge. The medical opportunities available in Murias were well-known throughout the Western world and enticed Irish, Egyptian, Greek, Phoenician, and Carthagenian travelers to the area for thousands of years.[18] Inevitably, earthquakes disrupted the land, broke the temple's retaining walls, and toppled sections of the beautiful building as if it were a glass toy.

Unusual temples were not the only accomplishment of the Atlanteans in Poseidia. Employing engineering techniques from their earthquake-torn homeland, they erected sturdy pyramids to represent the spiritual life of the soul as it rises to its highest point from a strong base. Although the ocean finally covered the buildings, sonar scans and aerial surveys taken when the water is calm reveal their outlines. Scuba divers also refer to the ruins of ancient buildings under the surface, but the information receives almost no publicity, for authorities rightly fear that treasure hunters will strip them of valuable objects or employ damaging dynamite to explore beneath them.

From the ocean floor on the Bahama Bank, divers brought up limestone discs or "sea biscuits," as they are called, which many believe were possessions of the Atlanteans who once lived here. In 1949 the Geological Society of America dredged a ton of similar sea biscuits from the sea floor south of the Azores.[19] In the shape of a plate, with a depression in the center of one side, the plates are all approximately six inches in diameter and one and one-half inches thick. Their surface is relatively smooth, except rough in the depression. Tests determined that sea biscuits are about 12,000 years old and that they are manmade from limestone, which formed above the surface.[20] In the past, Atlantean descendants in Scandinavia placed fresh fruits and vegetables on plates similar to these and left them in rock crevices or carried them to hilltops as a way of paying tribute to the forces of nature.

Just as religious groups left England in the seventeenth and eighteenth centuries to establish colonies in the New World, where they hoped to be free to worship as they pleased, so, as conditions changed in Poseidia, devout people moved away from their pleasant island home to Central America. In 10,600 B.C., a virtuous and moral leader named Iltar led a small group from Poseidia to the Yucatan. The followers of Iltar lived their lives as symbols of the Spirit of the One God and understood the importance of manifesting compassion for others. Focusing on their religious services rather than on acquiring unnecessary material possessions, they constructed energized circles of stones as sites for their worship.[21] Circles and pyramids offer opportunities for increased healing and enlightenment, for they enhance the energy fields created by the emotions of those who spend time in them.

A ceremonial circle similar to those the Native Americans have used for hundreds of centuries, or just a circle of crystals on the ground with a lit candle in the center, provides a positive link to the power of the universe and the Creator. If appropriate rituals are performed in a circle and each person intensely focuses on the same desired outcome, it is possible to improve their intuitional facilities or to assist an individual in healing his or her mind and body. In their strong sacred circles, Iltar and his Poseidian followers conducted ceremonies that were designed to cleanse their bodies and minds of anger, hatred, impatience, greed, and other selfish traits.[22] Atlanteans regarded Earth as a living creature that responds to the same stimuli and harmonies that are pleasing to humans, and to that end they spent time in stone circles giving strength to the planet. They realized that the health and condition of the Earth was bound up with their own actions and attitudes. In their ceremonies they used the stone pillars of the circles like acupuncture needles to transfer energy from the heavens above to the earth below and provide the living planet with a harmonious source of strength and vitality.

The large, flat-sided stones these prehistoric builders erected in circles are usually positioned so as to reflect sound toward the center. They appear to have been designed to act as giant loudspeakers. The amplification of the strong vibrations of drums played during rituals would have had a moving and powerful effect on the emotions of everyone within the circle.

On the coasts of Spain, Portugal, and Morocco, and throughout southern England, western France, and Scotland, prehistoric builders arranged immense boulders in circles resembling those

Cayce describes Poseidians erecting in the Yucatan. Remains of similar circles are also found on Pacific Islands. These constructions, in lands where Lemurians and Atlanteans and their descendants settled, help to demonstrate the remarkable knowledge of our distant ancestors and their concern for Mother Earth.

The spiritual people of the past preferred to build their homes in a circular or octagonal shape.[23] They considered a round home to be more harmonious to the spirit, and believed the geometric shape would better channel the energy of the universe. Cayce says a circular home contributes to a person's ability to be productive. Many Native Americans lived in circular tents. Numerous ruins of round houses built from stone are found in several parts of Easter Island.[24] Almost all ancient cities in Central America were circular,[25] and of course Plato tells us Poseidon constructed the Atlantean City of the Golden Gates in the same pattern.

Since the early residents of the Yucatan were almost totally attuned to the spiritual, the priests and priestesses were the government. Unselfish leaders like Iltar were convinced that the welfare and happiness of the people was their most important responsibility. The Golden Rule was really the law of the land. To ascertain how to improve their governing of the people, in a manner similar to shamans in indigenous cultures, the priests and priestesses used their psychic abilities to talk and listen to the one great Creator. Unlike many of us today, they communicated and prayed regularly, not just when they were in trouble.

The diet of these early inhabitants of Central America is slowly coming to light. Using slash-and-burn agriculture, 10,000 years ago people grew corn, squash, and pumpkins. Fruits and nuts were readily available in their natural state, and coconuts from the Pacific reached the American continent at least 12,000 years ago.[26] Since the distant past, spiritual individuals have realized that meat consumption is not conducive to developing the psychic aspect of one's mind, so meat was probably not included in their meals.

Natural destructions are unusually severe in the unstable lands of Central America, and the catastrophes that bruised the Earth's fragile surface severely threatened the survival of those who lived there. Time and time again, tidal waves covered cities in low areas along the coast and earthquakes toppled buildings and stimulated fiery volcanoes to fling out deadly rocks and boiling lava. During these difficult periods, the massive underground caves in the Yucatan, Guatemala, Belize, and the northern regions of El Salvador and Honduras offered safe shelter to hundreds of fortunate families.

Prehistoric people made use of these caverns for innumerable centuries before the Mayan culture is commonly thought to have existed. The immense cave system, with its innumerable interconnected caverns of spacious rooms and high ceilings, is a natural formation, but residents also carved out additional areas, which are referred to as the Loltun Caverns. Often priests used captives to carve the stepwork and chambers and, when the work was completed, the priests sacrificed the workers to keep the location secret and unknown to outsiders.[27]

Abundant artworks in the caves reflect the Lemurian and Atlantean ancestry of these early inhabitants. Painted symbols and bas-relief carvings on the walls, such as circles, spirals, swastikas, and equidistant crosses, are similar to those people left in the Canary Islands, South America, and southwestern Europe. Many inscriptions that embellish the Loltun Caverns were fashioned over 15,000 years ago. They demonstrate the interminable hours that artists spent in the dark, damp caverns, waiting for the day when floods, earthquakes, and volcanic eruptions would cease, and they would be free to return to a more normal life.

Certain symbols can be powerful, for each one contains vibrations that are related to the original thought that created it. If a person intensely concentrates on a symbol, it can lead to an altered state of consciousness and comprehension of that initial concept. Remote indigenous people, isolated from our current civilization, retain a belief in the power of symbols as they tattoo spirals and other signs onto their bodies. They believe these characters help them to gain added strength from the energy of the Earth and all that is beyond.

Early occupants of the Loltun Caverns carved and reshaped the huge stalactites, stalagmites, and rock pillars of the caverns into strange stone figures. When Manson Valentine explored here in the mid-twentieth century, he found various male faces carved with facial hair, including a nine-foot-tall giant with a full beard. The features of the sculptures are quite different from the current local Mayan population, who have no knowledge of those who created them so long ago.

Some of the most striking drawings in the Loltun Caverns are outlines of hands with mutilated thumbs or cut-off fingers.[28] These gruesome depictions are similar to those left in the caves of southwest France and in the Pyrenees,[29] and they imply that the artists had a common origin. The most prevailing belief is that the hand prints are the artist's signature. There is no logical explanation for the mutilation—perhaps it was incorporated into a magical or initiation ceremony.

In certain areas of the Loltun Caverns, sensitive visitors experience intense, concentrated forces, which they believe radiate more energy than the Great Pyramid of Cheops in Egypt.[30] Artworks offer evidence that these rooms were set aside as sacred places where priests or shamans, during hallucinatory out-of-body experiences, gained access to what they refer to as "the other world." Some priests describe communicating with their ancestors in this invisible place. Others seem to enter another dimension where knowledge is more readily available to them, like Cayce's searching the Akashic Records. To these skillful communicators with the spirits of the past, birds symbolized the flight of the soul. Paintings deep in the Loltun caves of the Yucatan depict a figure wearing a mask and a bird headdress. They are almost identical to pictures of bird-shamans in several European caves, such as the one with claws for hands, wearing a bird mask, which enhances a wall in the depths of the Lascaux cave in France. The French bird-shaman's penis is erect, something that frequently occurs during trance states, and it points toward a speared bison whose head is turned to look at his own intestines falling from his wound.[31] Next to the depiction of the bird-shaman in the Loltun Cavern is a staff similar to those still carried by shamans today, topped with a bird. Phallic monuments stand outside three sites in the Yucatan that contain pictures of these bird-shamans. A similar figure and his staff are depicted in an ancient Arizona rock engraving.[32]

In the seventeenth century, when the Spaniards were so cruelly destroying the Maya's advanced civilization, the Loltun Caverns offered local people excellent hiding places for their irreplaceable books and riches. There is a report of an old Mayan hermit who guards priceless treasure hidden in the Yucatan, deep in these caves.[33] The hermit's precious valuables may refer to something tangible, or perhaps the account alludes to the superior insights and higher spiritual knowledge of the Maya and their ancestors that we have yet to fully comprehend. The caverns in the Yucatan are especially extensive and confusing, with narrow, winding passageways and steep cliffs, so explorers have not completely investigated them. Someday a skillful searcher will discover valuable records of the civilizations of Mu and Atlantis, and perhaps even some of their treasured gold and crystal possessions. Books of the Maya are another possibility, or the map to Mayan records that Le Plongeon secreted away in a cave.

The sea eventually covered countless buildings off the coast of the Yucatan. Like ghosts of the past, ruins of the structures are visible under the water today, as well as roads that travel from the coastline and disappear into the Caribbean Sea. Scientists have recently confirmed that prior to 9000 B.C., people lived in Belize on the southern coast of the Yucatan peninsula. Someday Western archaeologists will acknowledge the Lemurians and Atlanteans and their descendants who settled here.

NOTES

1   Caldwell, *The Romance of Atlantis.*

2   Cayce, Edgar Evans, *On Atlantis*, p. 70.

3   Cayce, *Readings* 877–26.

4   Bethards, *Atlantis*, p.28

5   Cayce, *Readings* 364–12.

6   Ibid., *Readings* 1007–3 and 2690–1.

7   Bethards, *Atlantis*, p. 33, 34.

8   Hope, *Practical Atlantean Magic*, p. 153.

9   Ibid.

10   Plato, *Critias.*

11   Cayce, *Readings* 1207–1.

12   Ibid., *Readings* 2454–3.

13   Ibid., *Readings* 2581–2.

14   Ibid., *Readings* 1678–2.

15   Fix, *Pyramid Odyssey*, p. 100.

16   Cayce, *Readings* 1193–1.

17   Sykes, *Atlantis*, Volume 27, No. 4.

18   Ibid.

19   Donato, *A Re-examination of the Atlantis Theory.*

20   Ibid.

21   Cayce, *Readings* 5750–1.

22   Cayce, *Readings* 5750–1.

23   Hope, *The Ancient Wisdom of Atlantis*, p. 111.

24   Brown, *The Riddle of the Pacific.*

25   Zapp and Erikson, *Atlantis in America.*

26   Ibid.

27   Gregory Berg, private correspondence.

28   http://www.students.tulane.edu.

29   Hadingham, *Secrets of the Ice Age*, p. 145.

30   Umland, *Mystery of the Ancients.*

31   Halifax, *Shamanic Voices*, p. 17.

32   Bahn and Vertut, *Images of the Ice Age*, p. 190.

33   Walton, *Mount Shasta*, p. 11.

6

NORTH
AMERICA

JUST AS SUGAR CONTINUALLY
attracts ants, so, over a long period of time,
portions of the North American continent
that escaped the damaging Ice Age enticed
people from Mu, the Atlantic Ridge, the
Caribbean, and Central America. Evidence
of their presence is slowly emerging. Every
year archaeologists and other scholars push
back their dates for civilization in areas
where descendants of Atlanteans and
Lemurians once lived. Human bones in
the Meadowcroft Rockshelter in Pennsyl-
vania date to 12,500 B.C., and debris indicates that human beings were living there
for thousands of years before that time.
Tools and other residue found at Cactus
Hill and Saltville in Virginia, and at the
Topper site in South Carolina, confirm
that people settled in this country long before 10,500 B.C.

Not only do researchers regularly uncover older sites, but scientists have recently proved that radiocarbon dating, which had been accepted as a rough guide to the age of an object, can be inaccurate by thousands of years. British and American scientists, checking with uranium dating, a newer and more accurate method, found that radiocarbon dating became more out-of-date as they went further back in time.[1]

Dr. Johanna Nichols of the University of California, Berkeley, after analyzing the way languages have changed and diversified in this country, suggests that people have been here for 30,000 to 40,000 years. Theodore Schurr of Emory University in Atlanta, Georgia, reached a similar conclusion after studying the DNA of the hair of wild goats in prehistoric sites where humans made their homes.[2]

Just as the first Atlanteans to move to Poseidia and the Yucatan were those who unselfishly focused on loving and caring for others, so spiritually attuned Lemurian priestesses who taught the Law of One were among the early settlers in the lands of Arizona, New Mexico, Nevada, and Utah.[3] Legends of the Hopi and Zuni Pueblo allege that their distant ancestors came from Mu and traveled to Arizona and New Mexico.[4] These memories are reinforced by the Maya of Central America, who believe that Lemurians came to the land where the Hopi now live and, as they deposited their knowledge, activated it as a new spiritual place.[5]

On a cliff in Grapevine Canyon, Nevada, Lemurians carved the ground plan of a temple they erected as a tribute to the innumerable souls who perished as the Earth shook and their Motherland sank into the sea. Another story on stone in Nevada says that Mu, the Empire of the Sun, which lies across the ocean in the direction of the setting sun, is now in darkness.[6] Throughout the southwestern United States and Central America, Lemurians and their descendants enhanced rocks and temples with carved backwards swastikas; their beautiful, sacred lotus flower; and the plain equal-armed cross that represented the four great creative forces of earth, air, fire and water.

Like bee colonies searching for a new homesite whenever their nests are disturbed, when unstable conditions disrupted their lives, thousands of Atlanteans and their descendants left their homelands between 50,000 B.C. and 10,000 B.C. Some crossed the ocean from the Atlantic Ridge, while others traveled northward from Poseidia and the Yucatan on a land bridge that stretched from Cuba almost to the Key West chain of islands. In small boats, different groups reached and traveled up the Mississippi River. The variety of their tools, teeth and bones, legends, and earthworks reflect this long period of time during which the habits and physical characteristics of the incoming refugees changed.

The Cherokee were among the first to reach North America. In her recent book *Voices of Our Ancestors*, Cherokee Dwyani Ywahoo reveals her decision to share teachings her people have carefully preserved since the beginning of their time. Dwyani received the knowledge from her grandparents and great grandparents, who learned it from their grandparents. The Cherokee history begins with the people from the stars known as the seven dancers (the Pleiades), who settled in Atlantis and lived there happily for many generations. When the islands began to disintegrate, their descendants moved westward to the American continent, where they were known as the Cherokee.

The Cherokee's way of life and their advanced mathematical skills, detailed knowledge of astronomy, and legends of their sources of power reflect the wisdom and accomplishments of their Atlantean ancestors. The Cherokee believe that mindfulness and love and care for others and for their natural environment maintain the balance of the planet, and therefore harmony in the universe. Their medicine people once utilized crystals to capture and manage the Earth's positive energy for their own use. They believed this positive energy came from forceful dragons they called

Ukdena, who represented the wave pattern of the Earth's magnetic energy. With crystals and ancient sacred rituals, the Cherokee controlled that energy and maintained a harmonious balance of power from the sun, the moon, the Earth, and the universe. They grew bountiful crops and lived happily. Immersed in their natural world, they led full, satisfying lives until Western civilization encroached and the number of Cherokee medicine people decreased, the rituals diminished, and the shamans lost the dragon power and their beneficial relationship with the energy currents of the universe.[7]

Edgar Cayce describes another group of early visitors from Atlantis who camped at a site near Talladega, Alabama, to make use of healing techniques they brought with them. The waters of a nearby river were helpful in offering relief to people with fevers, infections, and digestive disturbances. Following the instructions of a tutor from a temple in Poseidia, the Atlanteans built cedar conduits that would carry the beneficial water to people's homes.[8]

The Dakota remember that their forebears once lived in cities on islands to the south, many of which are now beneath the sea.[9] Legends of the Iroquois, Sioux, Mandans, and Delaware refer to the home of their ancestors as an island that sank but was once in the Atlantic Ocean "in the direction of the sunrise."[10] These people all retain the aquiline noses, high cheekbones, and long skulls of their Atlantean ancestors,[11] physical characteristics that are completely different from immigrants from the Far East who settled in the western United States.

Large numbers of big game hunters, known as the Clovis people, first appeared at the mouth of the Mississippi River in about 10,000 B.C., when Lemuria and Atlantis disappeared. Their weapons, called Clovis points, were bifacial, fluted stone points, often ten inches long. Archaeologists used the word "points" because they weren't sure of the size of the Clovis people. If the hunters were tall, the points were arrowheads, if the hunters were short, the weapons were spearheads. From the mouth of the Mississippi, the Clovis people spread to the southeast and eventually over much of North America.

Although they were not the first to migrate to this continent, a variety of sources indicate that the Clovis people came from the direction of Atlantis. The weapons of the Clovis are identical to the older ones of the Solutrean people who lived in southwestern France and Spain on the seacoast and along the banks of rivers that led to the Atlantic Ocean before the final sinking of Atlantis. No Clovis points have ever been found in Siberia or northeast Asia. Experts believe it is highly unlikely that the similarity in the complicated, intellectual process of duplicating the Clovis and Solutrean stone weapons was a coincidence.

The Clovis on the North American continent and the Solutrean people in Europe practiced many similar customs. They both buried their dead with exquisitely fashioned stone tools in caches filled with red ocher and used similar items in their ceremonies. Both groups shaped mammoth ivory in the same way to weight their weapons, and they straightened their spears with shaft wrenches. Genetic research also points to their common place of origin, for these people who entered the Americas in 10,000 B.C. were from a DNA European Caucasian group labeled haplogroup X.[12] The island of Atlantis, in the ocean between their continents, is a likely possibility for their initial homeland.

Evidence of a previous civilization is being discovered beneath original Clovis sites of 10,000 B.C. The tools of these earlier settlers, such as those archaeologists are studying near Allendale, South Carolina, which dated to at least 16,000 years ago by optically stimulated luminescence, were very different from the stone tools of the Clovis.[13] The pre-Clovis people were more dependent on fishing, which indicates they probably came from an island home, where the ocean waters surrounding the land made fishing a natural occupation.

Shamanism, which until recently was the most practiced method of obtaining healing advice on this planet, is widespread in Africa, the South Pacific, and South America, all places where Lemurians and Atlanteans lived. For over 12,000 years, Native American shamans, following in the footsteps of their intuitive ancestors, have used their minds to travel to the shady area where the mundane and spiritual worlds overlap and mingle. Drumming, chanting, dancing, sweat lodges, and specific drugs made from plants and herbs enable them to enter that mysterious place and seek the assistance of spirit helpers. Once they are there, the shamans receive guidance in healing and access to the infinite wisdom of the ancestors.

Edgar Cayce explains that archaeologists find few remains of the bodies of the early settlers on this continent because the first Atlanteans who came here, and their immediate descendants, cremated their relatives when they died.[14] In North America, bones of prehistoric inhabitants occasionally appear but, due to the 1990 Native American Graves Protection and Repatriation Act, study of them is almost impossible. Native Americans who believe their people did not migrate from another continent, and that they have been here "since time began," were instrumental in passing legislation which states that all prehistoric skeletons found in the United States must be reburied. Even though archaeologists demonstrate that the features of these skeletons exhibit no relationship to any modern tribe who lives in the area where the bones were found, the scientists do not receive permission to test them. The intention of those who advocated the law was to protect their ancestors' sacred remains from grave robbers but, in practice, it has enabled tribal activists to prevent the study of the DNA of ancient people, making it difficult to learn their place of origin.

In July 1996, along the bank of the Columbia River in Kennewick, Washington, two men discovered the skeleton of a five-foot, nine-inch man who fished in that river about 9,300 to 9,600 years ago. The skull's long, narrow face is completely different from the nearby American Indians in the northwest United States, and scientists are hopeful thay will receive legal permission to study it fully. Seven complete skeletons similar to "Kennewick man" have been found in North America, as well as fragments of at least twenty others. Two ancient American skulls, which are very different, also remain a mystery.[15]

Edgar Cayce says that second-generation Atlanteans who journeyed northward from the Yucatan were among the mound builders of Kentucky, Indiana, and Ohio.[16] Long before written history, people throughout the south, central, and eastern United States moved tremendous quantities of earth to erect immense artificial hills. Early Europeans referred to these strange constructions as "mounds." Exactly when the mounds were built is difficult to determine and estimates vary, for new ones were often constructed over remains of ancient sacred structures. In the same way, Christians placed the cathedrals of St. Pauls in London and Chartres in France at strong spiritual sites where prehistoric pagan people, who sensed the areas' high energy, once built temples.

Atlantean descendants in North America erected numerous mounds in the shape of a pyramid, whose sides were often oriented to correspond exactly with the cardinal points of the compass.[17] A pyramid as large as the Great Pyramid of Cheops in Egypt once stood at the intersection of the Missouri and Mississippi Rivers in East St. Louis. When this huge mound was decimated in the nineteenth century, it contained embroidered materials, beautiful gold, silver, and copper jewelry, and parchment that appeared to have writing on its surface.[18]

In 1890, on behalf of the Smithsonian Institution, Cyrus Thomas made systematic "explorations" of hundreds of these artificial hills in the southeastern United States. His work consisted of gutting and demolishing the ancient structures. In the same area, well-meaning people also destroyed huge towers, walls over 800 feet in length, and canals as long as fourteen miles.[19]

The innumerable ley lines in the United States may help to explain the Cherokee's Ukdena, the dragons who represented waves of the Earth's magnetic energy. Ley lines, perfectly straight man-made paths that are visible from the air on every continent, were first documented in England by Alfred Watkins in his book *The Old Straight Track.* The lines stretch for hundreds of miles over all sorts of terrain, deep into valleys and directly up high hills in Great Britain, Germany, China, and the United States. In Great Britain, churches, mounds, crossroads, cemeteries, mark-stones, castles, and fords continue to identify the ley lines that are always perfectly straight.[20]

The large mound at Portsmouth, Ohio, from which groups of mounds extend in concentric circles into West Virginia and Kentucky, is located on a ley line which runs from Marietta, Ohio, over 65 miles away, to Lexington, Kentucky, 190 miles in the other direction. The line is 59 degrees from true north, the exact angle of the sunrise at Marietta on June 21, the day of the summer solstice.[21] We do not know the purpose of ley lines, but this angle correlates with the legends in Great Britain that assert when the sun shined directly down one of these courses at sunrise, the Druids rose in the air and moved along them. Scientist John Mitchell suggests that ley lines were built to channel the flow of the Earth's magnetic energy.[22] In 1987, officials of the city of Seattle, Washington, began a comprehensive project of mapping the lines in their vicinity. They plan to place a series of environmental artworks at key power spots to mark and perhaps enhance the invisible energy.[23]

Prehistoric builders often constructed mounds where ley lines crossed, for they believed that enormous vortices of energy were created at these sites. As we learn more about the mysterious lines and the magnetic energy grid which surrounds the Earth, it may be possible to perform rituals at powerful places that would send energy along the ley lines to promote peace and compassion.

NOTES

1   BBC News, Sci/Tech, June 29, 2001.

2   *The Economist*, February 21, 1998, "The First Americans."

3   Cayce, *Readings* 851–2.

4   Red Star, *Star Ancestors*, p. 213.

5   Mayan elder Hunbatz Men to Nancy Red Star, *Star Ancestors*, p. 91.

6   Churchward, *The Lost Continent of Mu*, p. 206, p. 203.

7   Ywahoo, *Voices of Our Ancestors*, p. 16.

8   Cayce, *Readings* 707–2.

9   Hansen, *He Walked the Americas*, p. 76.

10 Goodman, *American Genesis*, p. 37.

11 Hansen, *The Ancient Atlantic*.

12 Little and Van Auken, *The Lost Hall of Records*, p. 269.

13 *Neara Transit*, Spring 2000, p. 6.

14 Cayce, *Readings* 914–1.

15 *The Economist*, "The First Americans," February 21, 1998, pp. 79, 80.

16 Cayce, *Reading* 3528–1.

17 Hansen, *He Walked the Americas*, p. 181.

18 Hansen, *The Ancient Atlantic*, p. 39.

19 Mertz, *Atlantis: Dwelling Place of the Gods*, p. 103.

20 Watkins, *Ley Hunter's Manual*, chapter 2.

21 Ted Bauer in *The Marietta Times*.

22 Michell, *The New View Over Atlantis*.

23 Plantier, Ann, "Finding Places of Power In Your Own Backyard," *Fate Magazine*, May 2001, p. 25.

7

SOUTH
AMERICA

WHEN LEMURIANS REALIZED
their land would disappear, in their desperate attempts to preserve knowledge, they
carried records and artifacts to the east to
South America, and to the west to India
and Tibet. Those who went to Peru were
especially successful at saving the valuable
information, for they moved far inland to
secluded areas in the mountains where
their descendants avoided contact with
contemporary civilization.

In addition to precious knowledge,
priests carried their valuable and unusual
Golden Disc of the Sun to South America.
Since the dim past, the disc had rested on
an altar in the Temple of Divine Light in
the Motherland of Mu. Symbolizing the
Great Cosmic Sun or Creator, in addition
to serving as a focal point of concentration
during meditation, the disc had other, more
remarkable functions. When combined

with certain gold mirrors, lenses, and reflectors, it was capable of producing a light that healed, and when it was struck by a priest-scientist who understood its operation, it gave off extremely powerful vibrations.[1]

When they reached South America, the Lemurians took their precious Golden Disc to the Monastery of the Brotherhood of the Seven Rays at Lake Titicaca, where the native Quechua guarded it. After a long period of time the Inca arrived in South America, and when they were advanced enough to use the Lemurian disc for the benefit of others, the Quechua took it to them. The Inca hung the valuable object in the Temple of the Sun in Cuzco using ropes of gold. The holes for the ropes are still visible at the Convent of Santo Domingo, which is built on top of the ancient Inca Sun Temple. When Pizzaro and his soldiers arrived in Peru, the Quechua quickly removed the Golden Disc and carried it from Cuzco to a secret hiding place, either in the Andes or at Lake Titicaca. A group has recently organized to search for the Golden Disc of the Sun.[2]

I believe a branch of an ancient brotherhood from the Andes is reenacting spiritual practices once used in Lemuria.
—LEW ROSS

A Peruvian wise man, Anton Ponce de Leon Paiva, has emerged from deep in the Andes to bring secret teachings and the true history of the past to the outside world. In *In Search of the Wise One*, Anton tells us that as a young man he was blindfolded and taken to a hidden village where the Quechua, predecessors of the Inca, have secretly guarded information from their ancestors for hundreds of years. While he was in the village, Anton was initiated into the Brotherhood of the Sun, a South American branch of the White Brotherhood, which has existed since the time of Lemuria. Near Cuzco, Peru, Anton established a center that gives a spiritual ceremony venerating sacred geometry and offers additional spiritual information from Lemuria.

*We came from the old, red land when the fire god crawled out
of the caverns, and thrust his long tongue through the sea, for in
this land the earth walked, and the sea came up in mountainous waves and covered the smoking, burning temples. We came
in ships, sailing to the high mountains of the southern snows.*
—APACHE CHIEF ASA DELUGIO[3]

After leaving Atlantis, Asa Delugio says his ancestors found temporary shelter in immense, ancient tunnels in the high South American mountains. Eventually savage warriors forced Asa Delugio's predecessors to move northward through underground passages to Central America, where the families wandered with their seeds and fruit plants for many years before finally settling in Arizona. The Sioux apparently followed a similar route to reach North America. Years later when Sioux Chief Shooting-Star made a trip to the high Andes, the Peruvians welcomed him with their ancient private sign, which was identical to the greeting sign of the Sioux. Shooting-Star suddenly realized that his ancestors also journeyed to their present homeland by way of South America.[4]

Asa Delugio's description of underground tunnels in South America correlates with numerous reports from early Spaniards, native people, and adventuresome explorers. Some accounts describe a network that at one time made it possible to travel underground for 400 miles from Cuzco in Peru to Tiahuanaco in Bolivia. Radar images have recently confirmed the presence of what appear to be ancient rooms and tunnels 100 meters below the city of Cuzco. One tunnel links the Temple of the Sun with five other Inca buildings in Cuzco that are in perfect astronomical alignment. A seven-foot doorway to the underground areas offers access to a passageway that leads to the archaeological site of Sacsayhuaman, a former

Inca fortress on a hilltop above Cuzco. It is said that Incas in Cuzco fled from the Spanish through a tunnel that took them to the forests and mountains east of Cuzco, possibly to their lost city of Gran Paititi that lies in that direction.

In 1923 the Peruvian government sent a group from Lima University to explore the mysterious network. They used an entrance at Cuzco as their starting point. After a few days the members of the expedition who were on the outside lost touch with those who had gone in, and all was quiet. Twelve long days later, one starving man emerged. He reported confusing labyrinths and trapezoid-shaped, dark passagways.[5] Stories say that one of the tunnels from Cuzco leads to a royal tomb where carved stone slabs pivot and turn so suddenly that potential robbers are trapped.[6] This may be what happened to some of the numerous curious people who disappeared in the passageways before officials closed the entrances at Sacsayhuaman and Cuzco in 1923.

Ancient South American tunnels are visible in other areas. In 1972 a severe earthquake in Lima, Peru, exposed long underground passages that seem to lead to the mountains in the east. It was impossible to travel in them, for they were in very poor condition after such a long period of time. At the ruins of Samaipata in eastern Bolivia there is an entrance to an unexplored, manmade tunnel. The passageway leads to the northwest, probably to a mountain about fifteen kilometers away, and possibly farther.[7]

Situated on a mountaintop many miles west of Sao Paulo in Brazil, the tourist town of Sao Tome das Letras features an elaborate manmade tunnel that is a real engineering feat. Carved out of dirt, it is at least seven feet high and sufficiently wide for a person to travel easily. Members of the Brazilian army once attempted to explore the passageway. After four days underground they came to a room with openings for three tunnels, plus the one they used to reach the room. After exploring for some time from the room, they gave up and returned to the surface. A man who lives in the town of Sao Tome das Letras says he knows the tunnel and that one section of it goes all the way to Machu Picchu in the Peruvian Andes.[8]

In a reading he gave to a client, who was once a girl named Amammia living on this continent around 10,000 B.C., Edgar Cayce offers an example of an Atlantean who went to South America. Amammia was a follower of the Law of One, but when she traveled to Peru she fell in love with material things, especially the abundant gold. Amammia hoarded her wealth, aspired to power over the minds of others, and focused on beautifying her physical appearance. Cayce told his client that as a result of her experiences in that past life, she was fearful of people who focused on material objects rather than the spiritual.[9]

Explorers encountered the strange white-skinned Paria, with fair hair and blue eyes, who lived in the village of Atlan in the virgin forests between the Apure and Orinoco Rivers in Venezuela. The Paria may be descendants of Atlanteans who went to South America and remained there, for they told the adventurers that their distant ancestors were a noble and prosperous race who lived on a huge island in the ocean, which a catastrophe destroyed. When nearby Venezuelan natives learned about the Paria females with the curious white skin, they captured the women and used them as concubines. In the sixteenth century, the Spaniards found harems of white Paria women, some of whom were blind from being kept in semidarkness.[10] In the future, translations of monoliths in Venezuelan jungles that are covered with hieroglyphs and strange carvings may offer further information about these early settlers.

Intriguing reports of *banderistas*, missionaries, and natives depict elaborate ruins deep in the Amazon jungles of Brazil, near which lived "strange white Indians" with beards.[11] Whispered stories tell of the remains of large cities like El Dorado, whose tumbled stones are overgrown with dense vines and trees. Tales portray white and gold metal and even gold ingots and beautiful jewels

Photo by Bob Brush

FATHER CRESPI AND THE ENGRAVED TUSK (ABOVE)
PLATINUM HEALING WANDS (ABOVE RIGHT)

that the inhabitants left behind in El Dorado as they hurriedly left their homes. Inspired by these accounts, intrepid explorers have coped with and often succumbed to malaria and other deadly diseases, snakes, dangerous swamps, and ferocious unfriendly natives as they search in vain. British Colonel Percy W. Fawcett spent nineteen years attempting to find ruins which he believed were once Atlantean cities. These cities were said to have stones on tall pillars that glowed at night from sun power stored in underground reservoirs. Fawcett reported that he did successfully reach his goal. But he never returned.[12] Ten years later, his wife hired Geraldine Cummins, a medium, who successfully contacted Fawcett. He communiated he was not dead, but in a semiconscious state in the South American jungle—a prisoner in a small village.

A more tangible account of the riches available in South America concerns Italian Father Carlo Crespi, whom the Vatican sent to

Photo by Richard Wingate

Photo by Bob Brush

FATHER CRESPI AND THE COPPER CROWN (TOP)
UNDECIPHERED WRITING ON METAL PLATE (BOTTOM)

Photo by Richard Wingate

Photo by Bob Brush

A RELIC MADE FROM METAL THAT DOES NOT CORRODE (TOP)
WHAT FATHER CRESPI SAVED FROM THE FIRE (BOTTOM)

Photo by Bob Brush

FATHER CRESPI AND A SOLID GOLD CROWN

a remote area of Ecuador in the mid-twentieth century. After he became friends with the natives, they brought Father Crespi objects of gold, silver, and precious stones which they said were hidden in a mountain cave at the time of Pizarro. These included several crowns of gold and one very unusual copper crown that was much too large for a normal-size person. Crespi gradually accumulated silver plates with hieroglyphic-type writing on them; an elephant tusk carved with figures and designs in the Chinese style; unusual metal and stone sculptures; long platinum wands, one of which was surrounded by entwined serpents (caduceus); and many additional treasures. Father Crespi, perhaps from conversations with the natives, came to believe that Atlanteans and Lemurians brought the treasures from their countries when it was sinking. This was the only explanation for the sophisticated techniques involved in their production.

With the permission of the Vatican, Crespi built a museum to house his valuables. In 1960, it was one of the largest collections of artifacts in Ecuador and he was recognized as an archaeological authority. In 1962, someone set fire to his extraordinary museum and it burned to the ground. Father Crespi managed to save a few articles, which he stored in two long, narrow rooms, but they remained in total disarray, for he was too elderly to care for them. The photographs Bob Brush and a friend took when they visited Father Crespi in the early 1970s are the only evidence of these priceless artifacts from the past. David Childress searched for them in vain in 1991, but Father Crespi had died and nothing remained. Childress could find no one at the site who would even admit that they ever existed.

In 1532, Pizarro, the Spanish conqueror of the Incas, captured Inca King Atahualpa and held him hostage. Pizarro told the natives that he would not release Atahualpa until they filled the room in which he was holding the captive with gold as high as King Atahualpa could reach. To meet his demands the Incas loaded sturdy donkeys with precious objects and began to carry them to

Pizarro. Pizarro rejected anything that wasn't gold, and when the room was only half full, he killed his hostage. When this terrible news reached the pack trains that were on their way to Pizarro to save Atahualpa, they quickly turned around. Eventually the natives hid their cherished cargoes in secret caves. Crespi believed the priceless gifts the natives brought him were part of the treasures that were once on the way to Pizarro.

In numerous readings, Edgar Cayce refers to people bringing culture and civilization from Lemuria and Atlantis to the American continent. In their new locations the immigrants served as priestesses and healers, developed agriculture, built temples and lengthy walls for protection from the sea, preserved information, worked with young people, improved the relationship of individuals to each other, and promoted profound respect for the natural environment. For thousands of years, Native Americans preserved this knowledge. As they become confident that their information will be treated with respect, they will continue to share it with others. To understand their distant past is to understand our own.

NOTES

1   Brother Philip, *Secret of the Andes*, p. 18.

2   Additional information about the Golden Disc of the Sun is available in *Secret of the Andes* by Brother Philip.

3   As quoted in *The Ancient Atlantic*, by Lucille Taylor Hansen, pp. 274–275.

4   Hansen, *The Ancient Atlantic*.

5   Childress, *World Explorer*, Vol. 2, No. 3.

6   Wilkins, *Mysteries of Ancient South America*.

7   Childress, *World Explorer*, Vol. 2, No. 3.

8   Ibid.

9   Cayce, *Readings* 1183–1.

10   Braghine, *The Shadow of Atlantis*, p. 39, 40.

11   Wilkins, *Secret Cities of Old South America*, p. 254.

12   See *Atlantis: Insights from a Lost Civilization*.

8

ATLANTEAN PRIESTESSES AND THEIR TEMPLES

During the session I was back in Atlantis. The whole sky is in flames. There are earthquakes and volcanoes and everything is falling. It's chaos!

I am a tall woman, with long blond hair, and I am wearing a white robe. I am about forty-five years old. My name is Aiija. I am sitting with other priestesses around a table in a beautiful room, but it is strange, there is a lot of ozone in the air, a lot of lightning-type of energy and . . . fear. We are talking about it, but there is nothing we can do.

This is a lovely room and it's part of the temple, but pieces have been falling down from the ceiling and the walls have cracked, it's not really safe here anymore.

We are talking because we know that this was possible or coming, but we hoped that it would not happen. I feel regret about everything that is disappearing; this wipes Atlantis completely out

. . . you see the flames against the sky . . . all that light and fire and
stuff coming out, and that noise . . . it's so much noise . . . and the
people don't know what to do . . . they are just running back and
forth.

I die, getting buried under buildings and rubble and mud.
It happened in that time of the year we call December.

That is why I am always filled with sadness during that time
of the year. A deep, deep memory of something I will never be
able to forget.

—HERMA

This tragic account from my friend Herma is a familiar description of the last hours of Atlantis. Similar experiences, or other memories that relate to drowning in very deep water, are buried in the subconscious minds of many of us who perished with our beloved country.

Herma is an attractive woman with dark hair, but she describes herself as a priestess with blond hair. Many dark-haired people lived in Atlantis, but her reference to being a blond Atlantean also correlates with recent archaeological discoveries. Mummies in caves in the Canary Islands, and elsewhere around the Atlantic Ocean where Atlanteans settled, often have red or blond hair. They exhibit the physical characteristics of Cro-Magnons, a race of people who were *Homo sapiens*, as we are. Cro-Magnons were first known as the "Atlantic People" because evidence of them stretched along the Atlantic shore from North Africa to the British Isles. They were physically strong, with a brain cavity somewhat larger than ours, long narrow skulls, high cheekbones, and prominent chins.

Cro-Magnons created the sophisticated artwork in the caves along rivers that lead to the Atlantic Ocean from southern France and northern Spain. Their beautiful paintings and sculptures date to the era of Atlantis, from 30,000 B.C. to 10,000 B.C. The artists may have come from the island of Atlantis, where pleasant climate, even during the Ice Age, offered them the opportunity to perfect their outstanding artistic skills. It was a short distance from Atlantis to these rivers along the coast of southwestern Europe. In the next chapter we shall consider other factors which also indicate that many Atlanteans were Cro-Magnons.

The light, fire, and resounding noises of Herma's unpleasant experience were from earthquakes and erupting volcanoes in the last hours of Atlantis. If the building she remembers was on a mountain, which wasn't a volcano, it might have survived when the ocean covered the land. Four temples of Atlantis, built high above the sea, did endure the final destruction. One temple was at Gorias on Gran Curral of the Madeira Islands, 300 miles north of the Canary Islands. Another, the Temple of Finias, stood on the island of Tenerife in the Canary Islands. In the westernmost section of the Canary Islands, the Temple of Falias was above the surface on San Miguel, and far to the west across the Atlantic in the Caribbean, the Temple of Murias, which was described in a previous chapter, remained standing.

When the ocean waters started to rise and earthquakes shook their country, the Atlanteans who realized the final destruction was imminent quickly climbed up to the sacred buildings. When conditions stabilized, the few fortunate survivors were amazed to discover that the ground had dropped and the water had risen so much that they and their temples were safe on land, but close to the water's edge. Before long, the priestesses in the temples in the Madeira and the Canary Islands established regular contact by sea with each other. Using the clockwise circuit of the Gulf Stream's strong current, they also managed occasional communication with the inhabitants of the faraway Temple of Murias in Poseidia.[1] The intensive research of scholar Egerton Sykes offers interesting information about the Atlantean priestesses, lay workers, and soldiers who worked in the four temples. For untold centuries these sites were used for religious services and offered medical and repair facilities to visiting ocean travelers. Each extensive complex had clinics, schools, barracks for soldiers, and houses for those who worked at the temple.[2] Women priestesses usually directed the temples' activities. This was partly due to the strong influence of lunar fertility goddesses at that time, and also because during some of its various civilizations, Atlantis was a matriarchal society.

In North America, the Iroquois, whom Edgar Cayce says were direct descendants of Atlanteans, preserved the matriarchal culture of their ancestors. The earliest European records indicate that Iroquois women controlled the government and owned the land that, when they left this world, passed down to their daughters. The Iroquois men, who were expected to hunt and help plant the crops, had to live with their wife's family. If the husband did not produce up to his spouse's expectations, he was forced to leave the home and find another place to live.

Music was important in the Atlantean temples, for priestesses used it extensively in their healing practices. It was especially helpful with periods of depression and other mental disorders. The Atlanteans realized that every person has a certain vibration, and disease results from conflicting or discordant vibrations.[3] If music is correctly employed, it may eliminate harmful vibrations and offer a channel through which the natural rhythm and balance of the patient can be restored. Before becoming priestesses, women were required to attend special colleges where Muses trained them to be excellent musicians and successful healers.[4] They learned to play flutes and stringed instruments, including harps and lutes, and to sing a variety of chants.

Murias, since it was renowned as a healing center, attracted priestesses who were interested in caring for others. At the temple, which was similar to a combination clinic and health spa, people received advice about their physical problems and also learned how to improve their habits so they might enjoy a healthier and happier life. Early explorers and treasure seekers, when they returned to the European continent, elaborately depicted Bimini as a site for the restoration of health and youth—hence the widespread belief that there was a wonderful Fountain of Youth somewhere in the Caribbean area. Hundreds of years later, these tales inspired the voyages of De Soto and Ponce de Leon, who daringly crossed the Atlantic Ocean hoping for rejuvenation.

Sykes believes the remedies the priestesses brewed in their cauldrons from herbs and plants led to the potions that Calypso, Circe, Medea, Medusa, the Witch of Endor, and Morgan Le Fay prepared. He points out that surviving stories attribute the power of the witches' mysterious concoctions to the cauldron itself, not the ingredients, for apparently most people believed the power was in the "magical" container, not its contents.[5] Edgar Cayce identifies the Bimini area as a place for improving one's health. He suggests the development of a center for regeneration there, which would take advantage of the minerals in the water.[6] In the midst of the salt water mangrove swamps on North Bimini, investigators discovered a hole of fresh water that appears to be spring-fed. This area, which resembles a very large well, is referred to as the "healing hole" or the "fountain." Swimmers report a dip in the water has the happy effect of raising their spirits and making them feel cheerful and lighthearted. Some believe spending time in the "healing hole" improves their arthritis. The water in the Bimini area may stimulate the adrenal and pituitary glands to produce beneficial hormones, which could contribute to an uplifting, rejuvenating effect.

The workers who assisted in maintaining these four surviving temples of Atlantis were chosen partially for their skill in keeping records. Many of them were Tuatha who, when they left the sacred buildings, moved to the British Isles, taking their documents with them. The Celts incorporated the Tuathas' data into myths and legends that provided Egerton Sykes with extensive information about the temples of Atlantis. From these sources and others, Sykes even provides us with the names of priestesses from each ancient location, such as Medusa, Sthenno, Eurayle, and Andromeda, who served in the Temple of Finias in the Canary Islands.

For numerous generations, priestesses remained on the islands to serve others, but eventually many of those from Falias, Gorias, and Finias joined the Amazons, a large tribe in nearby Africa with women rulers. As Amazons, these descendants of Atlantean priestesses maintained their knowledge and skills until Christianity and Islam finally eliminated them. Renowned for their especially vicious, well-trained female soldiers, the Amazons forced their women fighters to remain virgins until they completed military service. Hannibal employed fierce Amazon cavalry-women who fought with lances and carried shields of serpent skins.[7]

Precious treasures stored in the Atlantean temples were very carefully guarded, for stories about the valuables were widespread. For thousands of years, adventurers who were eager to acquire the valuable articles organized elaborate expeditions in hopes of reaching the islands and acquiring a precious Atlantean relic. The brave soldiers, who dedicated themselves to protecting the temples and their unusual treasures, were primarily Aesirs and Vanirs from Scandinavia.

The first recorded group of treasure seekers were from Ireland. They included Fionn, the Tuirenn brothers, and Labraidh, who was chosen to be a ruler of Labrador, and after whom the country is named. Labraidh's daughter Fand became queen of Labrador and married two explorers; first, Mannannan, who deserted her and went to the St. Lawrence estuary, and then Cuchulain, who is a hero in many Irish epics.[8] Sykes tells of a second group of brave adventurers whom Pepi the First of Egypt sent in 2800 B.C. to explore islands in the Atlantic. Their records refer to a visit to the Azores, where they found a temple on Santa Maria that was surrounded by a wide wall. In his diary, one of these Egyptians describes a white cat that jumped among the many white stone pillars of the temple. Perhaps the cat had escaped from a ship where it was expected to help with the problem of mice and rats. Other explorers who traveled to Santa Maria returned with stories of a woman named Calypso who was politically entangled with Neptune, Oceanus, and Ogyges. At a temple on San Miguel, the Egyptians report inspecting an extensive vineyard.

Homer wrote *The Odyssey* many centuries after the adventures of these intrepid voyagers, but stories of their exploits are thought to have provided him with the basic data for this classic masterpiece. Homer never sailed in the Atlantic himself, so he confused the sequence of Odysseus' experiences. However, Sykes' research revealed that an Odysseus was shipwrecked on Santa Maria, where the Calypso of the day lent him an ax to cut trees and an auger to drill holes. These tools, plus some sail cloth she gave him, enabled Odysseus to construct a vessel strong enough to carry him back to Gibraltar.

Some of those who sought Atlantean treasures were successful in their aggressive endeavors. The daring Tuirenn Brothers of the Tuatha, who worked in the Temple of Falias as scribes, stole an ancient seat and carried it to Ireland, where it was known as the Throne of Tara. Royalty used the magnificent chair for many years, even though it apparently had some property that delivered a small shock. There is a story that if an impostor didn't know about its energy, he or she would cry out in surprise when they sat on it.[9] One of the most priceless Atlantean treasures at the Temple of Gorias on Gran Curral in the Madeira Islands was a royal crown that became the property of the Amazon queens when they took over the island. Like other articles of infinite value, it was often the basis for the evil behavior of aggressive attackers. Amazon Queen Hippolyte traveled to a nearby island with the crown, believing it, and she, would be safe there. While she was on the island, wearing it and carrying a flag of truce, a group from North

Africa murdered her. The valuable jewelry last appeared in France at the outbreak of the First World War, but Sykes learned that it vanished during the German occupation. Necklaces and bracelets from the Temple of Gorias were last seen in a North African museum during the 1930s.[10]

The Temple of Gorias is also remembered because it was adjacent to the orange grove that was famous in the ancient world as the location of the Golden Apples of the Sun. In ballads and stories, people in the Western world passed down memories for thousands of years that portrayed Perseus, Hercules, and others eagerly searching for what they believed were balls of solid gold.[11]

The Atlantean Temple of Finias on the island of Tenerife in the Canary Islands was renowned for its twelve towers of gold and emeralds (which Sykes believes were probably lapis lazuli or jadeite). Finias was an important center for metal workers, and when the treasure-seeking Tuirenn brothers returned home to Ireland from Finias, they took many valuables with them. These included the Findrine belt and shoe buckles, the sword of Lugh, the spear of Nuda, and the wine press of Tuis.

The Temple of Finias was also famous for its horse and dog breeding, which produced Pegasus, the steed of Perseus, and several special hunting dogs.[12] A full-size, solid gold replica of the Chariot of Poseidon that Plato describes, complete with horses and driver, was the most priceless possession of the priestesses and soldiers of Finias. On special occasions, everyone cautiously moved the heavy vehicle down the seven steps from the altar in the temple on which it stood and carried it out to the street for the festivities. As a result of these public displays of the valuable carriage, stories of it circulated around the world for centuries. The knowledge was still current in 330 B.C., when the historian Budge wrote in his *Life of Alexander the Great* that Alexander was invited to visit the temple at Finias with its full size, solid gold Chariot of the Gods, which the Chariot of Poseidon was called hundreds of years later in Alexander's time. No information about what happened to the chariot has survived, but Sykes believes it probably lies in the sea between Tenerife and Lanzarotte and will never be found.[13]

Edgar Cayce's readings contain several references to other Atlantean temples and to the priestesses who lived and worked in them. These include the Temple of the Sun or Light and the Temple of Ichakabal, both in the Yucatan. Here, like Mother Teresa and many of those who minister to needy people today, the devoted women focused their lives on service to others rather than their own selfish goals. In his readings, Cayce tells us that priestesses used symbols and signs, numbers, astrology, astronomy, ritual, and plants as well as music to help their patients overcome their physical problems and to advance their spiritual development.

Cayce gave a past life reading to a person who long ago was an Atlantean girl named Quellar. Quellar left Atlantis when the land was breaking up and moved to the Yucatan, where she became a priestess. She spent her life working in the temples and spreading knowledge and teaching others. Cayce suggested his client might find the temples in the Yucatan very interesting, since she was interested in the occult.[14] When meditating and reflecting in these sacred buildings, it is possible to receive an illuminating glimpse into other worlds, including the distant past.

Another priestess from Poseidia, named Alyne, traveled to the Yucatan where she worked to establish a temple. She became so upset with the activities of people from Mu and Og (Peru) who moved into the area that, to avoid all the distressing problems they created, she intentionally went within herself, withdrew from her physical body, and left the Earth. She escaped to Jupiter, where she hoped to repair the damage to her soul.[15] Cayce sometimes refers to souls spending time on other planets in our solar system between material lifetimes on Earth. This is interpreted to mean the soul enters the dimension associated with a particular planet. These visits offer enriching learning experiences.

Highly evolved Atlanteans like Alyne had so much control of their minds and bodies that they could concentrate and focus their thoughts and depart from their body (physically die) if they wished to. Lemurians had the same facility. When they believed they had accomplished all that they could in their present circumstances, they passed through transition, even though they were still young.[16] If we wish to, we will once again learn to leave the material world. Some animals are capable of accomplishing this feat. There is an account of two wolves who were captured in a park, put in a cage in the back of a truck, and driven for several hours to a zoo. When the truck arrived at its destination the two wolves were no longer alive. Mystified scientists could find no physical problems to explain the wolves' departure from this Earth. Obviously, it was the trapped animals' decision to abandon their physical existence on this planet.

NOTES

1   Sykes, *Atlantis*, Volume 27, No. 3, p. 44.

2   Ibid., p. 40.

3   Winston, *Music As the Bridge*, p. 13.

4   Sykes, *Atlantis,* Volume 27, No. 3.

5   Sykes, *Atlantis*, Volume 27, No. 4, p. 67.

6   Cayce, *Readings* 587–4.

7   Spence, *Atlantis in America*, p. 130.

8   Sykes, *Atlantis*, Volume 27, No. 4, p. 76.

9   Sykes, *Atlantis*, Volume 27, No. 3.

10 Ibid.

11 Ibid.

12 Ibid.

13 Ibid.

14 Cayce, *Readings* 3412–2.

15 Cayce, *Readings* 823–1.

16 Cerve, *Lemuria.*

9

BLOOD TYPES AND GENES

When I was pregnant with my first child, after my obstetrician learned I had type O blood that was RH-negative, he said: "You must be of Atlantean descent." I wasn't sure how serious he was, but I like the suggestion.

—ANONYMOUS

A VARIETY OF FACTORS LED this astute OB to make his comment. Between 50,000 B.C. and 10,000 B.C., when the earth shuddered in Atlantis, frightened Atlanteans left their comfortable homes and settled on the fertile continental shelves. Gradually, when it was possible, they moved inland to safer home sites in the mountains. Atlantean descendants who survived in these isolated places have a much higher percentage of type O and RH-negative blood than the rest of the world's population. It predominates among the Basques in the Pyrenees Mountains, amid the Berbers in the Atlas Mountains on the Atlantic coast of North Africa, and mummies of early residents of the Canary Islands. Similarities in the languages of Atlantean descendants offer another indication of their common place of origin.

Genetic mapping shows that the Basques first entered the Pyrenees Mountains between France and Spain about 35,000 years ago. These independent people really believe that, as Edgar Cayce says, their ancestors were from Atlantis. Proud of their Atlantean heritage, and because of their isolation, they have refrained from marrying outside of their lineage. Their blood type is as much as 75 percent type O, whereas the French and Spanish are primarily type A or AB. The Basques also have the highest frequency of Rh-negative blood in the world.[1] The Rh-negative factor is considered a mutation of unknown origin that occurred in Europe about 25,000 to 35,000 years ago when large numbers of people with this type of blood spread into what is now Spain, England, and Ireland. A reasonable assumption is that they came from Atlantis, a nearby island in the direction of the setting sun.

The obstetrician's interest in Rh-negative blood was related to the health of his patients. If the fetus of an Rh-negative woman is Rh-positive because that is her partner's status, her body will react to the baby's blood as if it was a foreign substance. During the first pregnancy this immune response is not as strong as in subsequent ones, although it is an important factor to consider. In the following pregnancies, if the fetus is Rh-positive, antibodies from the mother may cross the placenta and begin to attack the baby's red blood cells. Today injections of Rh-immune globulin control the problem, but in the past it resulted in severe newborn jaundice, miscarriages, and stillbirths. Atlanteans with the Rh-negative factor had difficulty producing more than one child with partners whose blood was not the same as theirs, and therefore they and their descendants retained their Rh-negative status.

In 1878, Basque poet Jacinto Verdaguer published a beautiful poem titled "L'atlantida" about his Atlantean homeland. The poem is available in Catalon, a language that is a combination of French and Spanish and widely used in Barcelona and vicinity today. With intense feeling, Verdaguer portrays a country with gigantic ferns, lemon trees, lovely flower gardens where the singing nightingales lived, and yellow wheat like golden hair slides between trees and sprouts, all very different from his native Pyrenees Mountains. Tales passed down by the Basques through the generations come alive in his poetry. Even the famous grove of golden oranges is included, as Verdaguer depicts Hercules killing the dragon that guarded the Golden Apples of the Sun.

Verdaguer's reference to wheat in Atlantis is interesting because in 13,000 B.C. wheat was cultivated in the Nile Valley, where there was no population pressure and plenty of food. Wheat was not indigenous to Egypt, so people must have carried it there. Refugees from Atlantis are a possibility. Diodorus Siculus, the respected Sicilian geographer and historian, reinforces this concept. In the first century B.C., he wrote in his book *The Historical Library*: "The Egyptians were strangers who in remote times settled on the banks of the Nile, bringing with them the civilization of their mother country, the art of writing, and a polished language. They had come from the direction of the setting sun and were the most ancient of men." The setting sun is toward the west, where Atlantis was the only advanced civilization prior to the first century B.C.

In 1402 Spaniards discovered a tall race of Cro-Magnon people with brown complexions, light hair, and blue or gray eyes living off the coastlines of North Africa in a secluded area of the Canary Islands. The Spaniards referred to these unusual, isolated humans as the Guanches. Like those who settled on the coasts of France, Spain, England, and North Africa about 30,000 years ago, the Guanches had retained their pure Cro-Magnon characteristics. Although the Guanches fought valiantly, disease and the Spaniards completely annihilated them within 150 years. A high percentage of the mummies of their deceased relatives that the Guanche placed in caves on the shady side of their valleys were type O negative. This correlates closely with the Basque's blood type, and that of other Cro-Magnons. The ancient art of mummification was practiced in Egypt, Mexico, and Peru in a strikingly similar manner to the Canary Islands. Atlantis provides a link for this progression.[2] Polynesians from the southwest Pacific also mummified their dead.

The Guanches of the Canary Islands were so terrified of the waters of the ocean that they did not have boats. They believed their Atlantean ancestors saved themselves from the dangerous sea by climbing to the mountain peaks of a now submerged land. Scholar Lewis Spence (please see his biography in appendix II) offers further interesting information from early Spanish records about the Guanches' terrible fear of the ocean waters. While in a trance or hypnotized under the power of a high priest, a sect of virgin priestesses, the Magades, served as oracles and also engaged in symbolic dances. If dreaded earthquakes shook the land, or volcanoes were active, the virgins sacrificed themselves to the ocean, hoping to prevent the omnipotent sea from covering everything as it had in the past.[3]

The Spaniards discovered that the Guanches were still practicing customs that Plato attributed to their Atlantean ancestors, such as sacrificing bulls, and electing ten kings to govern their land. In spite of the abundance of seafood, it was not included in the Guanches' diet of goat meat, cheese, fruit, and toasted wheat. Legend has it that they refrained from eating fish because they reasoned, as did the Tuarags of Africa and some Native Americans, that fish devoured their distant forebears who drowned when Atlantis sank, so eating fish was like eating their ancestors.

As the Spaniards carefully explored the Guanches' region in 1402, they found the remains of an irrigation system, pottery, mummies, and prehistoric cities. The beautiful paintings the

Guanche artists left on cave walls were almost identical to those painted in similar places in southwestern Europe from 30,000–10,000 B.C. Their ceramics, some dating to 20,000 B.C., were decorated with images of the sun and other patterns similar to the designs on early South American pottery. The Guanches showed the Spaniards ancient stone tablets with writing on them, but the invaders destroyed most of them. No one has successfully deciphered the few that remain.

Ruins of six stepped, black stone pyramids on Tenerife, one of the Canary Islands, also suggest the Guanche's distant origins. After a native showed them to Thor Heyerdahl, he persuaded a Norwegian businessman to buy the site and clean up the debris of centuries. Archaeologists reported that the pyramids are many thousands of years old and perfectly astronomically oriented to the sunset at the summer solstice. Recent excavations under one of them yielded artifacts identified with the pre-Spanish inhabitants,[4] who were the Guanches. Early Spanish records report that the Guanches danced, performed games, and participated in sacred ceremonies on the flat tops of these terraced stone pyramids.

The disproportionate amount of the Rh-negative blood factor is characteristic of other indigenous people who live in the vicinity of the Atlantic Ocean. These include isolated tribes of Berbers in the Atlas Mountains of northern Africa and the Maya Lacandones of southern Mexico, who were described in a previous chapter. The Lacandones' aquiline faces with dark complexions closely resemble the Basques. The surveyor who discovered them recorded that the Lacandones constantly played a rough ball game that was very similar to "pelote Basque," the national game of their distant cousins.[5] The unusual game of pelote consists of two teams who attempt to send a hard ball through a small hole in a stone that protrudes from a high wall. As they struggle to pass the ball through the opening, the contestants, without using their hands, bounce it off various parts of their body.

Their languages provide further evidence of the connection between remaining Atlantean descendants. Usher, the speech of the Basques, is thoroughly unique and not traceable to any other tongue. Apparently it has a common origin with the language of a tribe of Maya in northern Guatemala, for when a Basque missionary from the mountains of Spain preached to these Central Americans in the Basque language, the natives clearly understood him.[6] In the sixteenth century, the Spanish and the Portuguese began to study the speech of the Tupi-Guarani, who once lived deep in the Amazon River basin far from civilization. Today it is the most widely researched Native American tongue. Researchers have learned that many of its words are similar to those of the Basques and the Berbers.[7] The Tupi-Guarani appear to be descendants of the Caribs' Tupi ancestors, who were originally from Atlantis and went to South America. (See chapter 4.)

Gene-based anthropology continues to offer additional clues to our origins. Ancient bones and teeth provide helpful information about those who lived long ago and, to test the heritage of contemporary individuals, a small brush rubbed gently against the inside of a person's cheek furnishes plenty of cells. Mitochondrial DNA is found in human cells, outside the nucleus. It is simpler than nuclear DNA and easier to analyze. Since it mutates at a fairly steady rate, scientists use it to estimate when a group of people migrated from their primary group. The amount of difference between the mitochondrial DNA sequences of two individuals indicates approximately how long ago they shared a common ancestor.

The geographical origin of haplogroup X is unknown, although it is found in areas around the Atlantic Ocean where Edgar Cayce reports Atlanteans settled. When researchers from Trinity College tested individuals in Ireland for haplogroup X they discovered that the relatively isolated Irish on the far west coast of that country, closest to where Atlantis was, have the highest concentration of this type. Haplogroup X is present among the Basques, the Finns, and the Spanish.

Northern Native Americans, such as the Ojibwas of the Great Lakes, the Sioux, the Yakima, and 25 percent of the Iroquois tribes display haplogroup X. A small amount is also found among the Na-Dene-speaking Navaho. The North American strain of haplogroup X is somewhat different from the European strain, which indicates that the ancestors of those with it were related so long ago that its presence here is not a result of recent intermarriages. Genetic evidence indicates that the first haplogroup X people arrived in America in 34,000 B.C. Others came in 28,000 B.C. and the great majority entered between 10,000 B.C. and 8,000 B.C., all times when Edgar Cayce depicts large numbers of Atlanteans leaving their stricken land. Haplogroup X is not found in Asia, except for a very small pocket in the Gobi—another site that Cayce says attracted Atlanteans.

Scientists say haplogroup X may be of European origin. They are unwilling to designate Atlantis as a site of origin since it does not exist today. It is very possible that when humans with haplogroup X genes departed from the central point of Atlantis some went to the American continent in the west and others traveled to Europe. This would explain the striking similarities between tools and customs of the Solutrean people of southwestern Europe and the Clovis people on the North America continent. (See chapter 6.)

The numerous diversified physical characteristics of residents of the Pacific Islands, such as straight hair, curly hair, dark hair, light hair, long heads, round heads, tall people, short people, and a variety of skin colors, indicate that in the past people freely journeyed over the ocean and intermarried. As scientists work on identifying the frequencies of variations in diverse populations that are apparent only at the genetic level, they are revealing the initial heritage of this vast area, and evidence is emerging that some of them originated at a central, unidentified point.

Like haplogroup X around the Atlantic Ocean, the origin of the ancient genetic haplogroup B is unknown. It is found in aboriginal groups in coastal Asia and the southwestern United States. Haplogroup B genes were also present in people who moved to the western coast of South America, some of whom reached that continent before 35,000 B.C.[8] The majority with haplogroup B arrived on the Pacific coast of South America around 11,000 B.C., a time when Cayce described earthquakes and volcanoes disturbing the peaceful land of Mu.

The sophisticated research of scientists who continue to study the mitochondrial DNA of people of the islands in the Pacific reveals that some islands appear to be the place of origin of people with haplogroup B. The mountainous area of New Guinea provided shelter to hardy families forty thousand years ago, and there is no trace of an earlier site for their forebears. Thousands of years later their courageous descendants traveled eastward in double-hulled canoes to live in the Solomon Islands.[9] Similarly, in the South Pacific, the haplogroup B ancestors of current residents arrived in that area so long ago that scientists can only say it was their place of origin.

Genetic research is in its infancy and scientists have accessed the genomes of only a small number of ancient bones and living people. However, it is confirming that human beings sailed in the distant past, such as from New Guinea to the Solomon Islands. It is also indicating that waves of individuals emanated from a central point in the Pacific Ocean, perhaps the Motherland of Mu; for Hawaii and Rarotonga in the Cook Islands in the South Pacific are 3,000 miles apart but there is a positive link between their inhabitants.[10] As the scientists who are striving to document the genetic makeup of all the people on the Earth compile evidence from current DNA, their tests will offer many more clues to the ancient heritage of the human race and confirm that maritime civilizations once lived on ancient islands in the Atlantic and Pacific Ocean.

NOTES

1   Cavalli-Sforza, Luigi Luca, "Genes, Peoples and Languages," *Scientific American*, November 1991, p. 108.

2   Spence, *Atlantis in America*.

3   Spence, *The Occult Sciences in Atlantis*, p. 100.

4   *Science Frontiers*, March/April 1999.

5   Muck, *The Secret of Atlantis*, p. 131.

6   Braghine, *The Shadow of Atlantis*, p. 187.

7   Homet, *Sons of the Sun*, p. 231.

8   Little, Van Auken, and Little, *Ancient South America*, pp. 58–60.

9   Sykes, *The Seven Daughters of Eve*, p. 103.

10 Ibid., p. 93.

10

GODS AND GODDESSES FROM THE SKY

The destruction of Atlantis and the subsequent migrations through Mesoamerica lie within the mystery of Indian knowledge of our ancestors from the sky. The Star Beings showed us where we came from. They taught us how to read the stars, how to build pyramidal ceremonial centers, how to keep a cosmic calendar. They taught us how to honor our place of origin from the stars, how to reconnect with it and with those who seeded us here.

—FROM NANCY RED STAR, "STAR ANCESTORS," P. 57.

PLANETS SURROUND MORE than one-half of the 100 billion known stars in the galaxy. Recent observations using powerful telescopes indicate that uncounted numbers of these worlds may have water and Earth-like atmospheres. Life in the cosmos is everywhere, and has been since long before we appeared on this planet.

Carefully preserved legends and scholarly literature show that some of the beings who developed in these distant worlds advanced their scientific skills enough to leave their homelands and travel in space to our desirable small planet. The Earth, with its luxuriant plant growth and pleasant climate, has always attracted guests, some of whom spent a considerable amount of time here in the past.

Edgar Cayce refers to visitors from other worlds who came to this planet during the time of the Maya, and numerous memories of guests from far away are preserved in the records of ancient cultures throughout the world. Often the travelers are described as gods descending from the skies. The Zulu and Dogons of North Africa remember the visits of these gods as the oldest thing in their history. The ancient Order of Egyptian Ammonites and Central America's Popul Vuh tell us that their visitors used the compass, knew the Earth was round, and understood the secrets of the universe.

Plato says that in the beginning, people on Earth were ruled by the gods directly. Greek mythology represents them as real people, complete with emotions and sexual powers. Possessing powerful weapons and traveling at immense speeds, they were involved in human affairs, but inaccessible. Plato also recounts that the god Poseidon went to Atlantis, married an Earth woman, and performed superhuman feats as he constructed a city with gigantic buildings.[1] Poseidon, the god of the sea, helped the Atlanteans build ships and sail to distant ports. Edgar Cayce was aware of Poseidon's influence on Atlantis and referred to it as the Poseidon land, or as Poseidia.

The Far East offers a wealth of information about the gods from the sky. Brahmin books claim friends from the cosmos brought previously unknown fruits and grains to the Earth. The first emperors of China maintained that they were not descended from human beings on this planet; their ancestors came from the heavens above in metal dragons that spit fire. The Japanese claim that they are offspring of seven spiritual gods who were succeeded by five terrestrial spirits.[2] Ancient Indian epics contain numerous references to the presence of the gods and their ships that flew in the air.

Chariots were the primary means of transportation when biblical information was assembled and interpreted. Therefore, in the Bible space vehicles are referred to as "swift clouds" or "cloud chariots," or simply "chariots." Pilots are "charioteers" and liftoffs are "whirlwinds." Ezekiel 1:4–5 offers one of the more graphic descriptions:

> *As I looked, behold, a stormy wind came out of the north, and a great cloud, with brightness round about it, and fire flashing forth continually, and in the midst of the fire as it were, gleaming bronze. And from it came the likeness of four living creatures.*

One of the greatest mysteries in the study of the evolution of the human race is the sudden appearance on the Earth's surface of Cro-Magnon peoples who were described in a previous chapter. For hundreds of thousands of years before the appearance of Cro-Magnons the human race was unchanged, and individuals retained the same physical characteristics, worked with simple stone tools, and searched for food in similar ways. Suddenly, Cro-Magnons emerged in widely separated areas. Zecharia Sitchin offers an explanation for the relatively abrupt appearance of Cro-Magnons. (Please see the biography of Zecharia Sitchin in appendix II.) From information he deciphered from 25,000 clay tablets in the ancient Sumerian library in Nineveh, on the east bank of the Tigris River in Assyria, Sitchen believes the abrupt emergence of the Cro-Magnon people was the result of "when the sons of God came into the daughters of men, and they bore children to them," as stated in the Bible in Genesis VI.[3] Airplanes, spaceships, and rockets were unknown in the early twentieth century when the texts at Nineveh appeared. At that time scholars did not understand the Sumerians' references to all-powerful gods who came to their country in ships from the heavens. From his up-to-date translation of the texts, Sitchin learned that advanced beings from the sky lived in the Sumerian lands between the Tigris and Euphrates Rivers for hundreds of years during and after the third millennium B.C. They resembled humans, wore helmets, and were the source of the rapid appearance of the Sumerian's sophisticated written knowledge of architecture, astronomy, metallurgy, complex mathematics, and advanced medical techniques. Sitchin refers to them as the Annunaki and believes they were from a tenth planet whose long elliptical orbit circles our sun once every 3,600 years.[4]

Atlantis and Lemuria were extremely attractive places to live in prehistory. Lemuria was centered around the equator, and warm winds from the Gulf Stream ensured Atlantis would not suffer from the ice and snow that covered so much of Europe and North America. An abundance of food from the land and the oceans meant Lemurians and Atlanteans did not devote all their energy to working for survival, and they had time to expand their minds as well as their technical progress. The result was an open and inquiring population with whom the highly developed extraterrestrials enjoyed communicating. Quasi-crystals, which will be explained in chapter 13, assisted them as they acquired information from their visitors.[5]

From their contact with these advanced beings, the Lemurians, the Atlanteans, and their descendants learned the power of pyramids and how to cut and move the huge boulders to build them. The texts from Nineveh relate that gods from above supervised the construction of step pyramids with flat tops in Sumeria.[6] Similar prehistoric buildings are prevalent in Mexico, Egypt, and China, all places favored by visitors from the sky. The earliest pyramids in Egypt were originally constructed with flat tops where religious services were held, but because of the heat worshipers were forced indoors, and the sides of the building were extended up to a point.

Throughout the Pacific Islands, the people of Mu constructed massive ceremonial structures from huge, cut stone blocks. Some of their megalithic buildings have survived the rocking and shaking of earthquakes for over 10,000 years. Even tiny, uninhabited Malden Island, which lies near the equator, east of Tonga, is covered with ruins of platforms and temples built long ago from coral blocks. On top of these places of worship, the builders placed large stones arranged as dolmens.[7] Roads, which once connected these pyramids with the rest of the world, currently just disappear into the sea. With one exception, the over-100 pyramids in Shensi and Chinkiang provinces in China also have flat tops. The Chinese pyramids were constructed from blocks of clay, but many of the buildings are very large. One is as tall as the Great Pyramid of Cheops in Egypt. No one knows what secrets of life on our planet in the past are hidden inside these mysterious buildings, for the Chinese maintain a close watch on the pyramids and keep interested people away with the reprimand that the opening of the huge constructions is for the next generation.

They say they get abducted; we get visited.
—JOSE LUCEROQUOT, SANTA CLARA PUEBLO[8]

Native Americans have maintained contact with sky gods since the beginning of their time. The Sioux tell of a beautiful, pale-white, radiant person from the stars who, as is usually the case with extraterrestrials, was a woman. She appeared to two Dakota scouts, who named her White Buffalo Calf Woman. White Buffalo Calf Woman gave the scouts spiritual teachings, ceremonies, and important instructions about the origin of the Sioux people.

When they are in a receptive state, like their Lemurian and Atlantean predecessors, many Native Americans are capable of communicating with their star ancestors without speaking aloud. If we wish to establish contact with extraterrestrials in space, it is suggested that sound and light are too slow for such vast distances. We must employ thought transmission, which is so rapid that it is almost immeasurable.

The Pleiades, the closest star cluster to Earth, are about 300 stars that lie within the constellation of Taurus the Bull. Although they are far from our sun, six of these stars are visible to the average eyes, and keener vision can detect several more. Legends of indigenous cultures everywhere on this planet contain references to the Pleiades, and to their inhabitants' frequent visits to the Earth. Cherokee, Sioux, Maya, and other Native Americans believe their ancestors came from the Pleiades to Atlantis, where they settled and developed an advanced civilization. Initiation of young men into the Hopi spiritual ways takes place only when the Pleiades are directly overhead.

Legends from Great Britain describe the Pleiades as the dwelling place of giant sky gods who once visited the Earth. Prehistoric stone monuments in Scotland, like the one at Callanish, line up with the position of the Pleiades in the sky at the equinox or on other significant astronomical dates. The ancient occasion of Halloween occurs when the Pleiades are directly overhead in Great Britain. Greek Temples, such as the Parthenon, are oriented toward the Pleiades.[9] The distant stars' beams of light, even though they are too weak to be seen by the human eye, shine into their inner sanctums on an equinox or solstice.

When our civilization first discovered the Dogons of North Africa, they had an extraordinary knowledge of astronomy. The Dogons told the first scientists who interviewed them that long ago visitors from the vicinity of Sirius, the brightest star in our sky, taught them their extensive information about heavenly bodies that are not visible to the naked eye. Although the Dogons believe there are three stars in the Sirius system, our scientists did not find evidence of Sirius C until 1995, when two French astronomers discovered a small red dwarf star that seems to exist in the system of the star Sirius.[10] The Dogons say that Sirius C is very light and has a satellite. Although Sirius B is so tiny that our telescopes can barely reveal it, the Dogons assert that Sirius B is extremely heavy, it rotates on an axis once a year, and it revolves around Sirius A once every fifty years.[11] Our astronomers have not yet confirmed the Dogon's complex information about these two stars.

The ancestors of the Dogons came from Egypt, where some of the most ancient Egyptian temples are aligned with the star Sirius. Hieroglyphic writing on the temple at Denderah, which was erected in the first century B.C. on the site of an earlier temple, says the sacred building was constructed according to plans which dated to the time of Horus. This was well before the beginnings of dynastic Egypt.[12] Legends from Denderah maintain that at certain times when Sirius rose in the sky, its light would travel down the main corridor to the altar in the inner sanctum of the temple. When the beam of light from Sirius reached the altar, it was transformed into Sothis, the Star Goddess.[13]

Native Americans believe that representatives of seven galaxies are present on the Earth today. Further information about these various extraterrestrials is available at the extensive International UFO Museum, which opened in Istanbul in December 2001. The museum displays statues of different advanced beings based on information from observation reports. In addition to statues, photographs, illustrations, written documents and models of UFOs are available. A worldwide sighting map, descriptions of archaeological ruins, NASA cover-ups, and traces and inscriptions of ancient cultures and their connection to extraterrestrials may be found in the museum. Mars research, reports from institutions and universities, and other information further enhance this distinctive museum.

The star gods are coming for a variety of reasons. Some may be here to attempt to exploit and control us, but many have helpful motives. Since they are hundreds of years ahead of us technologically and they have survived, they are more knowledgeable and could be of immense assistance as we strive for a united world in which all are equal and Mother Earth is once again healthy.

We're quite aware that our mental and spiritual pollutants are contaminating this planet's environment, but the cosmos beyond is also feeling the effects of our corruption, and the star gods know we are following a dangerous path. As I stood on one of the tallest mountain peaks of France on a clear day, I was shocked to see that for hundreds of miles in all directions, a thick, dark atmosphere covers the Earth. Those who inhabit other solar systems realize that our technological development is advancing more rapidly than the natural evolution of our emotional condition, and Native Americans believe these representatives of the Star Nations are returning to assist us in growing spiritually. Vehicles from the heavens came to Atlantis toward the end of its civilization to warn the people of its impending destruction[14] and, in the same way, they are here today to caution and advise us.

To avoid disaster, it is essential that we do what the people of the past did *not* do. They were a spiritual society overwhelmed by scientific advancements. We must rework our culture in reverse order and change the emphasis from scientific to spiritual. With this new level of awareness, it is possible that love and understanding will solve our mutual problems, and we will live in peace and harmony with nature. Aggressive behavior is not solving our problems. It is time for a change.

Numerous people believe the crop circles, which appear all over the Earth, are the work of heavenly visitors who wish to communicate with us. They are trying to tell us that we are not alone. Strange lights and UFOs are often seen near the crop circles, and no one has offered another satisfactory explanation. For many years "great circles of the Gods," as they are called in South Africa, have mysteriously appeared overnight. The large circular depressions of different geometric designs that occur in fields and along embankments affect all types of plants in a similar way. The stalks of the vegetation are carefully bent in the same direction and, although circles may be as large as football fields, the delicate plants are never harmed or broken. Some patterns are easily recognized, such as a DNA spiral, an illustration of circles, a hexagon with rotated triangles, or a circle within a triangle within a circle. Others are more cryptic. No one knows how the diverse designs are created.

South Africans, who believe star gods communicate by means of the strange circles, set aside special fields for them. When a new circle appears, the people rush to erect a restricting fence of poles around it. For several days they joyously dance and perform sacred rituals honoring the star gods and the Earth Mother.[15] Hundreds of crop circles have appeared in England since 1978, and 99 percent of them are within the Wessex Triangle, a forty-mile triangular area that includes the sacred sites of Glastonbury and Stonehenge. While searching for answers to ancient mysteries, scholar Mark Roberts, after carefully studying the British crop circles, believes he has successfully deciphered some of their messages. Further information is available on his website: http://home.earthlink.net/~pleiadesx, Stargate Manuscript, Chapters V and VI.

Just as priestesses in Lemuria and Atlantis used symbols and signs to advance the spiritual development of others, in a similar way extraterrestrials are trying to reach our unconscious minds with the designs. Those who work with the circles believe an unusual energy emanates from them. When they study the mysterious patterns, investigators report that their sensitivity expands. As they integrate these experiences into their lives, many researchers experience an inner transformation, which includes a profound awareness that human beings and the planet they live on are undergoing a change.

The prophecy talks about people coming out of the sky to help us. That is what the talk has been from my grandmother, my grandfather, their grandparents, and back. But nothing will happen until we make it happen. We have to decide what we want. The Star People won't interfere.

—FRED KENNEDY[16]

UFO investigator Ralph Winters believes star beings will not interfere with our actions—that they have a policy of noninterference as long as the inhabitants of a planet are not technically advanced enough to leave their own solar system. They do have the power to guide us, however. Perhaps every space visitor is not here solely to advise and assist us, but we all came from the same source. Just as we are different, so advanced beings vary but, like humans, they are not entirely evil-minded. Nonhostile gods from space have visited our planet since the time of Lemuria and Atlantis, and they have not destroyed us. We, the citizens of the Earth, should follow the example of our distant ancestors and optimistically welcome those who once again offer advice and help.

NOTES

1   Plato, *Critias.*

2   Le Plongeon, *Sacred Mysteries.*

3   Sitchin, *The Twelfth Planet.*

4   Ibid.

5   Hope, *The Ancient Wisdom of Atlantis*, p. 106.

6   Sitchin, *The Twelfth Planet.*

7   Childress, *Lost Cities of Ancient Lemuria and the Pacific*, p. 196.

8   Red Star, *Star Ancestors.*

9   Pinkham, *Return of the Serpents of Wisdom*, p. 79.

10   Temple, *The Sirius Mystery*, p. 3.

11   Ibid., p. 68.

12   Hope, *Atlantis: Myth or Reality*, p. 140.

13   Further information is available on his website: http://home.earthlink.net/
     ~pleiadesx/. Go to free Stargate Manuscript Chapters V and VI on the right
     side of the front/first page.

14   Cayce, *Readings* 1681–1.

15   *The Circular*, Issue 41, Spring 2001, p. 33.

16   Red Star, *Star Ancestors.*

11

"THINGS"

ONE DAY, AS I WAS TALKING about *Atlantis: Insights from a Lost Civilization* with the owner of a local store, a nearby customer overheard our conversation and excitedly joined us. He obviously wanted to talk with me about something that was upsetting him. The man (I'll refer to him as John because I never learned his name) related the following story.

I heard you mention Atlantis, and I just have to ask you a question. I occasionally dream of a time when I lived in Atlantis, and those dreams are usually pleasant experiences from which I learn something. But this dream, which was so vivid I can't get it out of my mind, was different and I don't understand it—it makes me feel that I behaved in a really inadequate way. Can you please try to explain it to me?

A friend and I were walking down a wide path through a pine forest. I somehow knew we were in Atlantis, because it just seemed like it. The temperature was very comfortable, a light rain had recently fallen, and it was like a green fairyland with tall trees full of branches, different kinds of ferns along the sides of the lane, moss-covered rocks, and just a sense of natural beauty all around me.

Anyhow, as we went around a corner we suddenly saw two creatures tied to a tree next to the trail. I say "creatures" because at first I thought they were large men, but then I noticed that one of them had ears like a donkey and the other had a big wide tail like a horse, and their feet were strange shapes. As soon as they saw my friend and me they started to struggle and they shouted "Help, help, untie us, set us free."

We quickly ran up to them and started to untie the vines which bound them to the pine tree, but a husky man came striding out of the woods and started throwing rocks at us and we rushed away to save ourselves. I feel so sad for the creatures and have been trying to figure out who or what they were and how I could have helped them.

—JOHN

John experienced a very probable event in early Atlantis. His description of the temperature, the light rain, and the lush plants that thrived in the rich volcanic soil are all characteristics of the Azores Islands on the Atlantic Ridge, some of the remaining mountaintops of the main island of Atlantis. When I visited the Azores, I was amazed at the prolific growth and deep colors of the flowers. The hydrangeas were in bloom, and the dense, six-foot high plants that lined the narrow roads were covered with huge white, blue, and pink flowers. Farmers used hydrangeas as fences to define fields, so when you looked out you'd see squares of field outlined by blue or white flowers. People in the Azores say they plough lupins under for fertilizer because they're so prolific.

The strange creatures of John's oppressive dreams, which are often referred to as "things," really did live in Atlantis and elsewhere in prehistory. Edgar Cayce offers an explanation of their origin that is similar to Creation myths and legends of indigenous people around the world who believe that humans arrived first spiritually and then physically. Cayce explains that in the beginning there was the Creator, an infinite expanse of universal consciousness. The Creator, from itself, made shapeless sparks of light Cayce called "thoughtforms." The thoughtforms had good, moral souls, and they lived in a truly spiritual way in accordance with divine laws. When they found our beautiful planet, millions of these original light souls projected themselves onto it. They watched animals having a wonderful time eating and playing together, and they wanted to experience the pleasures of touching, tasting food, and the sexual act. As simple thoughtforms, this was impossible, but gradually some of them succeeded in mixing with the life forms that were already on the Earth.

At first the soul-entities could enter or leave their unique frames at will, but as they focused on the delightful sensual pleasures available when they were in a physical form, their vibrations grew increasingly dense and it became more and more difficult to move in and out. It was like being stranded on an island in the middle of a deep, surging river. Eventually the thoughtforms lost their multidimensional consciousness, and they were trapped inside physical bodies. After thousands of years of pleasure and enjoyment, most of them completely lost contact with their Maker and became immoral and self-centered. They focused on satisfying their own needs, which resulted in a huge amount of strife and discord. The situation on Earth was extremely rotten and unpleasant.

Cayce tells us that a soul named Amilius saw this bad state of affairs and decided to go to the Earth and attempt to raise the consciousness of the souls so they could once again travel freely to and from this planet's sphere. Many other virtuous thoughtforms with similar good intentions joined Amilius in this unselfish venture.

After studying the varied mixtures that were a result of the creatures indiscriminately multiplying for a long time, Amilius assumed a shape like a human body, which he believed would be the most suitable physical form for the Earth.

Cayce goes on to say that Amilius created human bodies similar to his for the thoughtforms who accompanied him to the Earth. The new people appeared simultaneously in five places on our planet. Amilius worked with the thoughtforms who came to Earth with him, trying to keep their hearts and minds pure as they assumed their new physical shapes, but he was not completely successful. Some of them selfishly succumbed to sensual pleasures and mixed with the animals. The results were often grotesque, part-human and part-animal offspring. They came to be called "things,"[1] and are the ones that John, the man who spoke with me in the store, tried to help in his dream. The peculiar creatures were primarily humans, but often had animal parts or appendages such as paws, tails, wings, and cloven hoofs or claws instead of feet. Thick fur or feathers covered the bodies of some, others were dwarfs. Cayce's references to the "things" are confined to the early period of Atlantis when, although they were usually intelligent and could learn to read and write, the "things" were definitely outcasts of society, and treated very harshly. Vague memories of the strange creatures continue, for old books refer to hybrids of men and animals living together in tribes in ancient times. Graphic examples of creatures that are part animal and part human are found in Egyptian and Assyrian inscriptions. In Greek mythology there are references to satyrs and centaurs, which were like people with the ears and tails of a horse, and minotaurs, who were half man and half bull.

I was one of the "things" in Atlantis. Part of my mission in this lifetime is to promote acceptance of all life forms, as well as to remind humans that even the clones who are being cloned today, like the "things"/others in Atlantis, are part of God and therefore have spirits/souls.

    —RUTH SOMMA

In Atlantis, the Children of the Law of One and the Sons of Belial totally disagreed about treatment of the "things." The Sons of Belial, who had completely lost touch with their spiritual souls and believed no divinity existed in nature beyond their own physical selves, employed hypnosis and mental telepathy to thoroughly exploit and dominate the "things." They offered them few comforts, treated them harshly, and even bred them for slave labor. Forced to draw water and pull plows, or sometimes harnessed to machinery, the poor beings led miserable lives.[2]

We lived in a walled compound because of the wild beasts. There were many rooms inside of the compound. It was a sprawling edifice/place to live. The "things" did the housework, but in our compound they were treated kindly.

    —ANONYMOUS

The Children of the Law of One believed that we all are related, we all are one. They constantly tried to befriend and help the unfortunate "things," but their methods were inadequate for combating the Sons of Belial. Despite the strenuous objections of the followers of the Law of One, for innumerable years the "things" were cruelly persecuted in Atlantis.

My husband was a scientist and we eventually parted ways — he to destroy Atlantis and I went into a Temple of Healing full-time. I worked in a Temple of Healing with the "things" to help them to remove their appendages—the sense is it was their coming into physical form willy-nilly that trapped them.

    —ANONYMOUS

Cayce describes one possibility for relief that was available to the unfortunate creatures, although the difficult procedure might require several dedicated lifetimes. If one of the "things" and their descendants entered a Temple of Sacrifice, skilled technicians, using drugs as sedatives, performed operations to remove their animal appendages and worked on perfecting a human body.[3] Advice on how to improve their diet and live a healthy life was also available in a Temple of Sacrifice. Some of the "things" who volunteered for experimental electrical operations to remove their claws, tails, or horns had the additional hope that offering themselves for experimentation might advance the development of their souls.[4] After the "things" acquired a more normal appearance, it was easier for them to cleanse and improve their minds, and they moved on to a Temple Beautiful. Here, generous, compassionate followers of the Law of One spent long hours utilizing art, music, crystals, scents, and dance to help the sufferers regain their original purity and raise themselves to a higher level. Cayce describes healing music, such as the singing of tones, while repeating syllables such as *Ar-r-r-r-r, Ou-u-u-u-u,* and *Ur-r-r-r.* The object was to free the mind and allow the body's vibrations to absorb light from the universe and heal itself. Dance programs in a Temple Beautiful not only encouraged better posture, but also offered a healing opportunity to troubled people, similar to the calming effects of tai chi movements.

As the "things" proceeded through the seven stations at a Temple Beautiful, they learned to forgive their distant ancestors who were responsible for their fate, and to release their anger against those who had treated them so unkindly. Paul Solomon, a twentieth-century ordained minister who offered successful medical diagnosis and treatment as well as accurate predictions of future events, reports that these temples were constructed as pyramids with a geodesic dome. The shape of the interior, plus the dome, was the source of the powerful energy that the workers employed to help others.

In the early eighties, I had the opportunity to be hypnotically regressed to several of my past lives. The first was as an Atlantean priest, surrounded by a number of priestesses dressed in the clothes and robes of that time. The second was merely the words "an Egyptian slave boy, eaten by a lion"—I never gave too much thought to this second life that showed itself only in words, until about a year ago. At that time, I met a woman with whom I shared similar interests. At Christmas she gave me three ankhs as a gift. Although I was wearing an ankh, she did not know that I collected them, and that I understand their truer meaning. She had treasured these ankhs for some time before she gave them to me.

Part of my daily ritual is to go for a walk in the evening. It's a form of meditation. One evening, shortly after she gave the ankhs to me, while holding one that was in my pocket, I had a recall or vision of that Egyptian life. I was what was unkindly called a half-breed—part human, part lion. I was the chattel of an Atlantean who had lived on the last island to sink off the coast of Bimini. I was of a very low mentality, and not fully aware of my plight. But I was fortunate enough to escape from there, to what is now Egypt. That was some twelve thousand years ago, when Ra returned from exile in Nubia, bringing back some followers with him. One of those who returned with him was a Nubian princess who became a neophyte under his teachings. She was involved with the healings and surgeries that allowed me to become more like a man in appearance and mentality. We became fast friends in that life. Even though she passed over before me, I made a promise that I would remember her. She was the one who recently gave me those ankhs that enabled me to remember that lifetime. That memory allowed me to see the pyramids as they were back then, and what a sight they were.

—ANONYMOUS

Ankhs, which are available today as amulets or good luck to-kens, are in the shape of a small two-armed stick figure. The head is a hollow loop. In ancient Egypt ankhs were called "the Cross of Life" and considered to be extremely powerful, like a living soul. When properly used, an ankh was an amplifier of energy and of thought. When it was held by the loop, it was used to transmit, and when held by its arms, it received. In Atlantis and Egypt, priests directed sound with their ankhs, like a tuning fork. The powerful energy from that sound could increase and return like a boomerang and harm the sender, so highest integrity and careful training in their use were essential.[5] Ankhs were said to have power over life and death. They were especially helpful in meditation and enabled the priestesses and priests of Atlantis to be out of time, out of body, out of space, and in other dimensions. Learned and expe-rienced priest-scientists used ankhs to shape life, to heal and to communicate with extraterrestrials.

Once the descendants of the "things" dealt with their grosser physical deformities in a Temple of Sacrifice, and refined and de-veloped their mental aspects in a Temple Beautiful, a final step for their progress was available. A select few were permitted to enter the Great Pyramid and undergo the initiation process to increase their awareness. Even though the abnormal physical manifestations of the past have almost completely disappeared, we are still work-ing to raise the level of our souls to their original higher dimension through the ever-repeating cycle of karma and reincarnation.

NOTES

1   Una Marcott, Lecture at Association for Research and Enlightenment, October 15, 1999.

2   Cayce, Edgar Evans, *On Atlantis*, pp. 69, 72.

3   Cayce, *Readings* 2067–6 and 5118–1.

4   Montgomery, *The World Before*, p. 130.

5   Marciniak, *Bringers of the Dawn*, p. 192.

12

HEALING

IN HEALING CENTERS IN AT-
lantis, skilled practitioners used crystals,
pyramids, sound, colors, and their minds
to stimulate the patient's own healing
process and provide relief from dis-ease.
People still practice these ancient methods
in remote areas because they work for
them.

In a small room during a conference
at the Edgar Cayce Institute in Virginia
Beach, I watched a Native American healer
use a quartz crystal, sound, and healing energy from his hands to calm a young man
who was having a seizure. For sound, he
first blew on a small shell flute from prehistoric Peru, and then he filled the room
with low, vibrating tones from a didgeri-
doo, the long flute-like instruments the
Australian aborigines play to evoke Dream-
time.

I worked in Atlantis as a healer for many lifetimes. I remember that I worked with crystals in conjunction with light and sound, maybe some music as well. In this lifetime I retain some of my healing skills from those past lives, for as a young adult, I became aware that I had healing abilities that I can project out through my eyes.

To heal, I put my left hand on the person's body above an injury nearest to the heart and my right hand below the problem. Then I stare at the injury. My field of vision goes sort of milky white but in the center of it is an absolutely clear space about three inches in diameter that is focused on the injury. As I look at it, my vision goes further into the body and I began to see the circulatory system like a thousand tiny little red rivers running in all directions. Then, as I continue to look at the injury, I go further into the body and I can see a brown shadow where the injury or infection is. Then I step up the energy coming out of my eyes (and the inner corners of my eyes sort of tickle with the energy). As I focus on the infection, I can hear snapping and popping, just like popcorn. The infection is being vaporized by this energy. People usually say they feel heat when I work on them.

For a bone injury, I imagine lots of little molecules of bone and I summon them to the end of the bone to assist in the healing. I worked on a friend from a bank who broke her wrist in six places in a car accident. She had two rods bored into her hand and two into her forearm with long supporting rods in between to stabilize her wrist with its broken bones. I visited her once a week to give her a twenty-minute treatment. When she went back for a checkup her doctor said, "Now we can set you up for physical therapy." "How much would that cost?" she asked. "Oh, about $11,000." "Forget it!" she said, and her doctor was angry with her. However, when she went back for her first x-ray, he was amazed at how fast the wrist had healed. I *laughed with delight. "Did you tell him what the two of us had been doing to heal your wrist?" "No, of course not!" In any case I go to see her in the bank now and then and see her typing away just as well as if she never had an injury. I am truly amazed and grateful that I could help her.*

—KATHLEEN KEITH[1]

Although crystals cannot generate energy, they do have the ability to move and transform it, and perhaps to retain it. Navaho healers realize this and utilize crystals to amplify and focus their beneficial energies toward their patients. Just as crystals are used in radios, televisions, and computers to continue the flow of electric energy, so they are capable of assisting the human body. Each of our cells has a small electrical charge that makes us a moving mass of energy, connected to and interacting with the energy that surrounds us. What we think and feel is transmitted along our vast electrical network of nerve cells. Imbalance in the vibrations from the cells of our bodies can lead to dis-ease or illness. Quartz crystals can be very helpful in healing since they assist in improving communication between the cells.

Quartz crystals are formed as silicon cools after it is ejected from the center of the Earth. They were abundant in Mu and Atlantis, where the first soil was formed from the lava and rocks of erupting volcanoes, or from materials spurted from rifts in the ocean floor where tectonic plates separated.

Three months ago a very powerful clairvoyant told me that I was a healer from Atlantis. I've always been fascinated by crystals and gem stones. I believe this was the source of their (our) power, I am not sure how we used them but I can feel that we did.

—ANONYMOUS

Numerous souls who were healers in Atlantis have returned to the Earth, and many of them are skillful practitioners, successfully utilizing techniques from prior lifetimes involving crystals.

> *I am a spiritual healer, and as such heal all debilitating disorders, from broken bones to ALS. I have been blessed with not having the "veil of forgetfulness"—I remember all that I have done in past lives. The energy of Hermes Trismegistus was in three of those lives. This energy did in fact do many things throughout the period of Lemuria, Taucadia, and Atlantis, or as I know it, the Red Land. . . . The energy that I connect to does the healing and I only direct that love and energy.*
>
> —ANONYMOUS

> *I use tuning forks to balance energy and unblock chakras. I have some new crystals and the results are phenomenal. My trainer says I was a healer in Atlantis.*
>
> —REV. EVELYN URBAN-WERN, M.ED.[2]

Evelyn is an energy healer who believes the basis of all dis-ease and sickness is a result of an imbalance or interference with the life force energy system over a period of time. When she works with a patient, using techniques from Atlantean days, she facilitates the flow of energy through the body from the top of the head to the tips of the toes and fingers. If any blockages occur, she clears and directs the natural flow of the energy using special crystals. The benefits one can realize from the experience include greater love, improved health, soul growth, and heightened awareness, all of which will assist in the fulfillment of one's goals.

> *Using quartz crystals we are very successfully aligning our patients' chakras and helping them with physical and mental problems.*
>
> —TWO HEALERS FROM NEW HAMPSHIRE

Chakra is a Sanskrit word that means "wheel of fire" or "wheel of light." It refers to the seven major energy centers in our bodies. The concept of chakras, which dates back to the healers of Lemuria and Atlantis, survived or was perceived again in Egypt, India, Tibet, and among the Maya in Mexico. In the Taoist philosophy, the chakras are related to the seven ductless glands of the body's endocrine system, and they affect all levels of our being.[3] In the earliest civilization of Atlantis, people wore clothing to protect their chakras, for they believed that covering their body ensured that the power of the energy centers would stay with them.[4]

> *When I heal, I place myself in that energy and thus I see the chakras and other areas of the body. I may see the chakras as a spiral, a flower opening, or as a vibrating color. They are a gateway to the universe of the body, waiting to be explored. How they spin, how close together the lines of vibration are—how balanced or crooked they are, all these are indicators of wholeness or illness.*
> —HEATHER ROBB

Each of the individual chakra centers is associated with certain physical, emotional, and intellectual or spiritual functions, and each has a different color, sound, and vibration. If one of these wheels of energy is unbalanced, the body will be prone to a disorder.[5] One of the most interesting chakras, which is also referred to as the third eye, is in the center of the forehead just above the eyes. Violet or very bright blue are associated with this center of our intuition. The third eye enables us to see another person's energy aura—a colored field of light around the body. Modern technology is capable of photographing auras, but it is possible to learn to see them as colored, moving rays of energy. Early religious artists portrayed these auras or energy fields as bands of light around their subjects. Native Americans refer to auras as "sacred fires." Reiki healers study the colors and the shapes of the aura to diagnose and heal physical and mental problems. When a person is under stress, his or her energy field shifts in color and shape, offering tips to the astute observer of the presence of fear, insecurity, greed, worry, and other deep troubles.[6]

> When a person places a crystal over the third eye, if the stone is fully concentrated on, it seems to emit an energy that more or less will "pop" the third eye wide open. Your sixth sense becomes more active, your thoughts go into a subconscious awareness— more of a dreaming state, and you can feel the pressure on your third eye as it opens. This should not be forced too long, or you will get one splitting headache.
>
> —CARRIE BLAKLEY[7]

The vision of the third eye opens us to the knowledge that one's identity goes beyond the physical form. Some Native Americans wear a headband that holds a crystal or another stone over their third eye to connect the third eye with their crown chakra and increase their intuitive abilities.

> To wear a stone over my third eye, I make a wire wrap of the stone, just as I would do to make a pendant. With the wire, I make two broad loops on the back of the stone, then run a ribbon or a folded bandanna through those loops and tie it around my brow.
>
> —ANONYMOUS

One healer reports that stones placed in the area of certain chakras are effective in relieving problems associated with them. She suggests that once a month, right before or immediately after a menstrual cycle, women place a crystal over the second chakra, in the lower abdominal regions just below the navel. She has found this helps to maintain an emotional balance, and seems to slow the flow of hormonal chemicals that contribute to premenstrual syndrome. This technique is also effective in relieving menopausal symptoms, which normally result from a lack of those hormones. In either case, a balancing seems to take place which includes a positive cleansing feeling.[8]

Indigo is the color associated with the crown chakra on the top of the head. The Chinese call its gland, which is the pituitary, the Gate of Heaven, perhaps because it is connected to the hypothalamus gland, which creates pleasure when stimulated. The crown chakra is the doorway to higher or cosmic forces. It influences all the energy centers and affects the central nervous system. Physicians often refer to the pituitary as the master gland because it coordinates numerous functions of the other endocrine glands.

Recalling valuable skills from their days in Atlantis, healers employ quartz crystals to focus during meditation and facilitate the natural movement of vibrations through the body. As the stones receive energy from the mind of the healer, they enhance and move the rhythm throughout the body of the patient, just as they transmit energy in computers. The blockages which are the result of dis-ease and depression diminish, the natural flow of energy improves, and the immune system grows stronger.

A typical healing ceremony in Atlantis might have followed a similar pattern. Large crystals were positioned so as to absorb and disperse positive forces to the patient. The caregiver placed the crystals at the head, feet, and sides of the person, who lay on a low couch or sat on the floor in a cross-legged, seated position. The person held an additional crystal in each hand while the healer thoughtfully arranged more of the sparkling stones on the top of the recipient's head (the most important site), the navel, on the third eye, and on other receptive areas of the disordered body. Friends who were present concentrated on meditating to send intense love and healing energy through the crystals, which expanded it and conveyed it to the recipient.[9]

A variety of factors influence the potency of crystals. It is important to clean them prior to use. Putting the stone in a bowl of soapy water in direct sunlight for three days is quite effective. A simpler approach, which takes only a few minutes, is to place the crystal in a dish of distilled water or spring water that contains several drops of pennyroyal flower essence.[10] The color of the crystal is also important. Quartz crystal is usually colorless, but if the cooling lava contained metallic dust, the crystal will be colored.

In Atlantis, healers employed the rose quartz in spa treatments, and people used it in their daily lives. They usually went to a medicine priest who helped perform the "ritual" of concentration, so they would use the stone properly.
—CARRIE BLAKLEY

Rose quartz is pink, purple quartz is called amethyst, and yellow quartz is referred to as citrine. Rose quartz works best on the heart, the center of the head near the third eye, and other pulse areas of the body. It is most effective in treatment for emotional instability, rather than for physical problems. For this reason it is referred to as the "love quartz." When it is properly used, the rose quartz brings on feelings of tranquillity, inner peace, and harmonic balance. These are similar to the sensations people experience when they encounter true (not just sexual) love.[11] Rose quartz has inclusions of titanium dioxide, which is white, and iron oxide, which contributes the red color. The iron content is affected by magnetism and may enhance the energy of a person's thoughts and be responsible for the pleasant "love" frequency.

The color of smoky quartz crystals ranges from a light sky gray to a dark charcoal gray. Like the black onyx, smoky crystals help us to recall blocked memories of unpleasant events. They assist in ejecting the negative vibrations of these disagreeable experiences from our minds and bodies and create a space inside so we may heal ourselves. Smoky quartz crystals are also effective in treating postpartum depression and other mild cases of "the blues." Since the energy emitted from smoky quartz crystals may have unanticipated effects on the user or on the patient, a skilled healer is recommended. One should not attempt self-application of the smoky quartz crystal.[11]

Clear quartz crystals are the most powerful crystals in healing and meditation. With clear quartz it is possible to adjust the body's energies in a relatively short period of time and more quickly achieve a high state of mental and spiritual awareness. To encourage the most complete equilibrium, skillful healers enhance the ceremony with chanting or music. Candle light and the odor of burning amber, copal, moldavite, and frankincense are also effective in helping the patient to relax, to be receptive to the healing, and to remember how it feels to be healthy. The experience increases the patient's faith that this event will help him or her to regain health; it is well known that strong belief can heal.

Cayce suggests wearing a crystal; not just as a good luck piece, but because it has a helpful influence on the body's vibrations.[13] Some healers recommend placing a clear quartz crystal on the crown of your head, for they believe the stone will pick up the electromagnetic frequencies of the brain and balance and realign it. A crystal under your pillow is thought to stimulate pleasant dreaming and peaceful sleep. A quartz crystal in the center of a garden may promote stronger plants.

Crystals served Atlanteans as healing tools in a variety of other ways.

Walls and ceilings of Atlantean birthing rooms were inlaid with sparkling green crystals, providing a beautiful sight and feeling to a being as it entered the world.
—HERMA WALDTHAUSEN

Quartz crystals were helpful in diagnosis,[14] a technique trained healers make use of today. As they move the stone slowly over a person's body, its color changes slightly in a problem area. Hopi Blue Wolf says that with crystals his people are able to see the "spin of energy" coming from a person.

Many years ago, I experienced a "visit" to a crystal room in Atlantis. I think the room was circular, or the walls were arranged in a circular fashion. There was much light in the room, and I saw the ceiling was a dome. I am told I worked with crystals, light, color, and sound to heal and balance. This was about 15,700 B.C. In Atlantis, I apparently saved the lives of four women whose current names I have, but I have not crossed their paths as yet.

—ANONYMOUS

Several people remember crystal rooms in Atlantis. The rooms were located over soil that was rich in crystals and contained a variety of the helpful stones for use in healing and expanding the mind.

The ingenious Atlanteans used crystals to burn destructive forces from the body in a way that encouraged it to rejuvenate itself.[15] This procedure was successfully performed in a secret rejuvenation chamber in a temple in the main city of Atlantis. While in the chamber, the patient reclined in a comfortable chair, and technicians precisely focused the sun's rays through a crystal onto the elderly body. Simultaneously, the healers produced and magnified varied frequencies of sound, whose energy regenerated the tiny molecules of each cell, reactivating aging tissues. The operation restored the person's hormone balance, wrinkles disappeared, and energy returned. Skill and caution were important, since if the crystal was tuned too high it destroyed the body.[16] One visit was usually adequate, for Atlanteans learned that, as they grew older, like a vacation that is too long, events they once enjoyed offered less satisfaction when repeated several times. Eventually, the prospect of spending more time in the physical body was not as appealing as the pleasant experience that was to come after departure from the Earth.

Structures in the shape of a pyramid were common sights in Mu and Atlantis, and researchers have learned that a mysterious energy operates within these buildings. When investigators found ancient garbage and dead animals in the Great Pyramid at Giza, the age-old objects were fresh, not rotten. They did not smell and they appeared to be mummified. Researchers propose that, given the proper conditions, the energy of pyramids is capable of sharpening razor blades, improving the taste of tap water, stimulating plant growth and seed germination, recharging batteries, facilitating the healing process, and increasing vitality and virility.[17]

One important thing about the pyramid is its energy that works strongly on people's karma, speeding it up, accelerating it, feeding it with energy. And so, for example, if one person needs to learn certain aspects of life (which karma is about), it might happen faster using pyramid energy. Which means he/she might lose a relationship. But look at this in a positive way—one might get a new relationship because the old one was not good. But it might mean that such a person, if he/she slept in the Queen's Chamber of the Great Pyramid, could die shortly afterward, having completed that life's karma in no time!

—WIM ROSKAM, THE NETHERLANDS

Lemurians and Atlanteans often built their temples in the shape of a pyramid, where energy channeled from the universe was more readily available. For additional power, they placed a powerful quartz crystal near or at the peak of the building. These were places to replenish and rebuild, for when one is in a meditative state in a pyramid it is possible to pick up the structure's enhanced vibrations and restore one's energy.[18] The plans of many ancient Mayan cities reflect the knowledge that descendants of people from Mu and Atlantis who lived and worked here passed down to their offspring. The focal part of these cities consisted of four pyramids that faced a sacred central enclosed plaza. The buildings were placed to correspond with the sunrise and sunset of the summer and winter solstices. The Maya explain that their ancestors arranged their important buildings in this manner because that was how the gods did it when the world began.[19]

Presumably the position of the pyramids enhances the distribution of the energy these unusual shapes produce. An e-mail friend describes a dream of a similar complex. His vision depicted a large central plaza, formed by four pyramids arranged according to the four directions. In the center of the plaza stood a tower with a uniquely shaped crystal that collected energy from the universe and transmitted it to crystals on the tops of the four pyramids. He believed people in the buildings used the power from the crystals for healing.

The sensitive people of long ago understood that subtle forces from all realms exert influence on our minds and bodies, and they realized it was important to place buildings so as to take advantage of helpful energies from the Earth and the universe. To choose the most favorable location they utilized the science of feng shui or geomancy. The contours of the land, the location of underground streams, and the presence of other natural factors, such as crystals in the soil, were carefully considered for their influence on the energies resulting from the surrounding gravitational, electromagnetic, and electrostatic fields.[20] Until recently feng shui was mainly practiced in the Far East, and it is enjoying a resurgence in our society.

Damanhur, a unique spiritual community of 800 people in the Valchiusella Valley in the alpine foothills of northern Italy, is based on Atlantean technology. The residents maintain that their ability to time travel to Atlantis has provided them with the information to construct this replica of life as it was so long ago in the lost land. In Damanhur, everyone lives around a huge circular cathedral and its beautiful grounds. A spectator who was allowed to film a six-hour video of Damanhur offers an accurate portrayal of ceremonies in this temple, in which music plays an important role. The building's huge dome of sparkling quartz is arranged in a mosaic pattern, and when the sun shines through the crystal it spreads colorful rainbows around the interior of the cathedral.

> *A master technician, who claims she brought Reiki to Atlantis, recently taught me to be a healer. I know that five of us who work together here were together doing Reiki in Atlantis. Just as the technician was attuning me to Reiki for the first time, a vision came to me of a Temple of Healing in Atlantis. The five of us were on the east-facing porch looking toward the rising sun. After many thousands of years, it is happening again here.*
> —ANONYMOUS

Utilizing love and focused thought, Reiki healers send out energy from their head, heart, and palms to strengthen and encourage the inner electric frequencies of their patients and stimulate their healing process.

> *In addition I have personal memories of other lifetimes in Atlantis, of being a healer in the great healing temples. I worked primarily with Reiki energy and sound to balance the human body. Wonder of wonders, when I came here to this city I met a lady whom I remember from Atlantis as a fellow healer. She now is my own personal massage therapist. She remembers me from there also.*
> —ANONYMOUS

Musical tones radiate on various frequencies and, when combined with other forms of energy therapy such as Reiki, offer a more complete balancing. Taoism, as well as the martial arts, Druidism, Paganism, Wicca, Romany practice, Egyptian shamanism, and Amerindian shamanism combine musical tones with focused thoughts of love to treat their patients. This basic understanding was passed down to many of them from their ancestors.

> *The beginning of the crystal bowls was in Atlantis. There was one Being, a High Priest, who found that when he put together some crystalline sand material, it gave a very pure sound when he touched it, so he began to experiment with patients. . . . He sat people in the Crystal Temple near a quartz cluster and experimented with the bowl-like crystal.*
> —RENEE BRODIE[21]

Crystal bowls offer healers another source of sound to balance the body's energy patterns. Made from silica sand, which is pure quartz, or from crushed and powdered quartz crystal, the bowls send forth a bell-like tone when they are struck with a rubber mallet. Depending on their construction, each bowl will produce a clear, open tone of the musical scale.

Scientific research has rediscovered that certain sound frequencies, or notes on a scale, relate to specific parts of the body. Dr. William Tiller of Stanford University asserts that "each atom and molecule, cell and gland in our body has a characteristic frequency."[22] The note F will benefit the lungs; G the liver, gallbladder, spleen, and stomach; and C the base of the spine.[23] In healing ceremonies, crystal bowls are struck simultaneously or in a sequence while the therapist focuses on clearing away unwanted energies and restoring balance to the afflicted area.

Sounds lift the vibrational quality of this planet; sound alone has the power to heal as well as to create, to manifest, to bring into being.

—ANONYMOUS

Tuning forks and crystal bowls are not the only way evolved healers have used sound since the time of Atlantis to enhance healing vibrations. Musical tones and group songs, drum beats, and repetitious vowels, such as *Ooommmm, Ahhhhh,* and *Huuuu,* all arouse the emotions and open the chakras and the glands of the endocrine system.

The flow of energy from the cells of our body is referred to as the bioplasmic body. Acupuncture, yoga, polarity therapy, and psychic healing all manipulate the energy flow of the bioplasmic body, and are beneficial in improving physical health. Edgar Cayce suggests two pseudo-electrical healing devices, the Radial-Active Appliance and the Wet Cell Appliance, for working with the electrical energy in the body. Many believe his detailed instructions for the construction and use of these tools originated in Atlantis, where the healers understood that our cells contained an important electrical component. Both instruments balance and rejuvenate the neurological system at a cellular level.

Skilled practitioners successfully use these devices today, enhancing them with massage or osteopathic manipulation and dietary improvement.[24] Cayce also suggests including prayer in the treatments. The Radial-Active Appliance is recommended for insomnia and headaches, and the Wet Cell Appliance, which is stronger and produces a minute voltage, has produced improvement in the treatment of multiple sclerosis, muscular dystrophy, paralysis, and Parkinson's disease.[25]

I had a vision of going back into Atlantis. I visited my home in the hills above the temple, and saw my father at work in the halls of the Senate . . . then walked down to the dock at our own bay, watched and laughed as my grandfather played with his pet dolphins and swam with me in the warm waters. My grandfather and I walked hand in hand along the sand till supper time at our house . . . sat by the fire and watched and sang as the sunset came. He stayed with me for a while under the many-starred heavens.

—ANONYMOUS

Dolphins, so plentiful in Mu and Atlantis, are a potential source of healing energy. Plato tells us that gold statues of dolphins, with graceful sea nymphs riding on their backs, surrounded the gigantic statue of the god Poseidon standing on a chariot in the Temple of Poseidon in the main city of Atlantis. Innumerable dolphins lived in the waters around the island, and the people regarded them as special pets.[26]

Researchers using EEGs learned that people who spend time with dolphins experience an increase in theta waves, which indicates that they have entered a deeply peaceful state, similar to one achieved in meditation. Intimacy with dolphins also expands the body's ability to produce and utilize neurotransmitters such as dopamine, which may affect the entire endocrine system.[27]

Atlanteans probably knew and enjoyed the additional therapeutic effects of the compassionate nature of dolphins. Healing comes from within ourselves and when people are with dolphins they cannot help but react with the same feelings of acceptance and unconditional love the animals project. Spending time with dolphins also boosts levels of immunoglobulins and T-killer cells, thus strengthening the ability of our bodies to resist dis-ease. Dolphin contact has helped people with severe depression to improve their self-esteem and outlook on life.[28] Most of us do not have the opportunity to swim and communicate with dolphins as the Atlanteans did, but we do have the privilege of seeking out the healers who have returned to share their unique skills with us.

NOTES

1 In addition to being a successful healer, Kathleen is a retired army officer. Under the pen name of Jane Egan, she has recently completed a book titled *The Mothership Chronicles, A Wider World of Hope and Joy*. In it she tells of some remarkable personal experiences. Using astral travel, she went up to a Mothership high above the gravitational field of the Earth. There she worked in a healing center alongside Pleiadean extraterrestrials. They were intent upon healing soldiers with severe injuries who had been beamed up from wars on the Earth. Her book is available from Amazon.com or from www.1stBooks. com.

2 Evelyn Urban-Wern is a spiritual energy healer. E-mail: evurwn08@aol.com; www.prayevelana.com.

3 Hunt, *Elephants and Chakras*, p. 39.

4 Bethards, *Atlantis*, p. 11.

5 Brodie, *The Healing Tones of Crystal Bowls*, p. 19.

6 Cayce, Edgar, *Auras*.

7 From private correspondence. Carrie Blakley is a freelance scientist who specializes in the areas of holistic and alternative medical therapies. Her website is http://www.geocities.com/carrienjerry2002.htm.

8 Ibid.

9 Alper, *Exploring Atlantis*, p. 16.

10 Gerber, *Vibrational Medicine*, p. 343.

11 Carrie Blakley.

12 Ibid.

13 Cayce, *Readings* 2285–1.

14 Alper, *Exploring Atlantis*.

15 Cayce, *Readings* 440–5.

16 Caldwell, *The Romance of Atlantis*, p. 18.

17 King, *Pyramid Energy Handbook*, p. 27.

18 Bethards, *Atlantis*, p. 22.

19 Van Auken and Little, *Lost Hall of Records*, p. 171.

20 Hope, *Practical Atlantean Magic*, p. 115.

21 Brodie, *The Healing Tones of Crystal Bowls*, p. 18.

22 Ibid., p. 46.

23 Ibid., p. 99.

24 Kasten, Len, *Atlantis Rising*, Number 15, pp. 68–70.

25 Two talented artists who channel Atlantean energy healing devices and heal-ing art are manifesting a spiritual healing center, the Center of Radiant Light. Their website, www.trlamb-art.com, offers interesting information.

26 Firman, *Atlantis, A Definitive Study*, p. 38.

27 Cosentino, *The Light Messenger*, Vol. IV, No. 9, p. 7.

28 Ibid.

13

ENERGY

IN BOTH LEMURIA AND AT-
lantis, a communal society with shared
storehouses and warehouses assured that
everyone worked at what best suited them.
Therefore, scientists and artists were relieved of the necessity to earn money, and
freely focused their efforts on contributing
to knowledge and aesthetic development.
The accomplishments of Lemurian and
Atlantean priest-scientists, with unlimited
facilities and thousands of years to develop
their technology, exceeded those of our relatively short civilization. The ability of
these skillful inventors to develop and use
their minds in a way that most scientists
today cannot comprehend contributed to
their amazing achievements.

At least twenty years of extremely de-
manding study and meditation were required to bring the intuitions and intellects
of potential priest-scientists into harmony.

During this time, the candidates not only studied the physical sciences, but also expanded their awareness and improved their psychic abilities. They learned to trust their intuition, in addition to the suggestions of their logical brain.[1] Focusing on understanding the natural laws, the Lemurians constructed a sophisticated type of windmill as a source of energy.

They also discovered that their mineral-rich land contained magnetic and radioactive rocks, which, when properly used, offered energy.[2] Ancient writings and carvings tell us that in volcanic regions the Lemurians found strange, powerful stones from the center of the Earth. When they placed one of them in water, it pushed the water away from it. They attached one of the stones on the bottom of a raft and, as the water moved away from the powerful object, the raft moved forward. Another stone, which seemed to have magnetic properties, was capable of turning wheels if there was some sort of metal on the outside of the wheel. A different stone or mineral, similar to the magnetic one, provided a continuous light.[3] Since we have not discovered duplicates of these unusual stones, references to them are difficult to interpret.

Using their highly developed skills, the Lemurians and the Atlanteans succeeded in obtaining energy from a wide variety of other sources, including the sun, the mind, the Earth's magnetic field, and sound. Conscious of the necessity of preserving the environment, their beloved sun proved to be the most beneficial. Throughout their long history, both civilizations worshiped the large body in the sky as a source of light, heat, and life. It was their symbol for the Creator, the one all-powerful mass of energy with feelings and love, which they believed formed the universe and everything in it. Before long, perhaps with the help of visiting extraterrestrials,[4] the Atlanteans perfected a magnificent crystal that enabled them to acquire efficient energy from the sun.

Edgar Cayce refers to the first important crystal in Atlantis as the Tuaoi stone. Initially, Atlanteans amplified the light its six sides received from the sun to enhance their meditation and contemplation, and communicate with the spiritual realm. After thousands of years, as the people became more materially oriented, priest-scientists perfected the Great Crystal that, when properly controlled, magnified and directed the energy it collected. With this source of infinite power, the Atlanteans acquired the ability to travel in the air and on and under the water.[5]

> *I remember the extensive use of crystals for power. I remember the building of the Great Crystal, which was pyramidal in shape. I remember the use of the Great Crystal for communication and warfare as well as for energy production. I remember the point-to-point transmission of electricity without wires through the land, from one pyramid to another.*
>
> —ANONYMOUS

Innumerable people recall the Great Crystal, even though they have never heard of Edgar Cayce, who describes it in detail. To build the huge, multifaceted "firestone," Atlantean scientists placed a large piece of precisely cut quartz crystal in the peak of a building that served as a solar type converter. In this exposed location, close to the heavens, the facets of the crystal focused energy from the rays of the sun, just as parabolic mirrors do today. A movable dome over the top of the complex quartz stone allowed skillful engineers to control the amount of exposure to the light from above. Atlanteans lined the crystal's building with a nonconducting material similar to asbestos.[6] Cayce describes a central power station on the ground which provided the energy from the Great Crystal that enabled Atlanteans to overcome gravity.

The Cayce readings have been interpreted to suggest that rays or beams of energy from the Great Crystal sent the power to receptor crystals, which rekindled it. From there the force could be used to run an electrical or thermal engine in a vehicle or other mechanical device.[7] It offers one of several examples of the Atlanteans' ability to transmit power without lines.[8] Cayce also refers to the Great Crystal obtaining energy from the stars, something that astronomers have recently explained. From various sources in the heavens, quasars and pulsars transmit strong electromagnetic radiation in the form of light, heat, and radio waves.

> *As a result of some regression sessions without the use of hypnosis, I could view the past. Not that I really saw full-colored pictures, but merely knew certain details and remember them. Here is what I saw—it certainly isn't the absolute truth, because this type of memory is very "colored." Still, I think it adds something.*
>
> *One of the things I was aware of was those energy towers in Atlantis. On the ground they had the shape of a pyramid, but from the top emerged a thin, very tall antenna. High above the ground there was another pyramid-like object built inside this antenna, much smaller though, and above that the antenna emerged again. The height of such an antenna exceeded 100 meters. All around there was a glow of some kind, a purple light that made it a living thing.*
>
> *The towers were used to exchange and intensify energy in its widest sense, making it possible to even amplify thought, so everybody throughout Atlantis could "tune in" and "hear."*
>
> —WIM ROSKAM, THE NETHERLANDS

Information about how to construct the crystal disappeared during disastrous catastrophes that agitated our planet's surface and totally destroyed the country. Only a select few in Atlantis were allowed access to the full picture of information, for the authorities hid technical secrets from the people so as to maintain power over them. Few of these scientifically oriented people heeded the dire warnings of the coming disaster, and those who did leave were among the last to go. They departed hurriedly and usually separately, traveling to different places. Even if they had some technical knowledge, without the necessary tools it was impossible for them to reconstruct any one scientific process, especially another Great Crystal. As centuries passed, all knowledge of it slowly vanished.

The Atlanteans had solar-charged crystal flashlights that projected a blue-white light to combat the darkness after sunset. The bulbs never grew hot. To turn them off, one moved a lightweight cover, which sealed in the power.[9] Since the Great Crystal produced more energy than the Atlanteans could ever consume, they may have developed solar cells that will last forever, similar to those we recently perfected. A copper material (copper indium gallium diselenide) in the batteries contains atoms that are diffused to light-damaged areas of the cells and effectively heal them, continuously extending a battery's life.[10]

The Bermuda Triangle, which includes the site of Poseidia in the Bahama Islands, is a large area that stretches from Puerto Rico to Bermuda to Miami, Florida, and then back to Puerto Rico. Many ships and low-flying planes have permanently disappeared without any explanation in the Bermuda Triangle. If their radios are operating, pilots sometimes report that their engines are losing power, that their compasses spin counterclockwise, and that other navigational equipment is behaving erratically or has ceased to function. Suddenly the travelers discover that they and their ships or planes are in a dense fog.

Perhaps a powerful crystal from Atlantis, hiding beneath the water, occasionally catches the sun's rays and transmits energy at the moment when a motorized vehicle is passing above. Reports of disappearances in the Bermuda Triangle are not as prevalent as they were years ago, when instruments were less sophisticated, which may indicate that either today's modern equipment is strong enough to combat the unknown culprit, or whatever was causing the difficulties has lost some of its power.

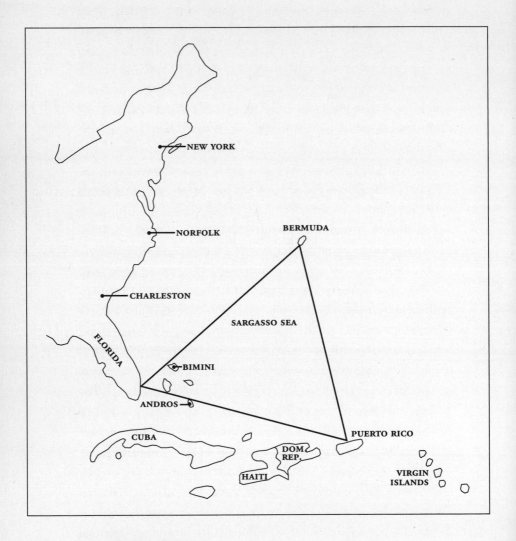

THE BERMUDA TRIANGLE

Straight through the Earth, almost directly opposite the Bermuda Triangle, is the Devil's Sea, an area with many of the characteristics of the Bermuda Triangle. The Devil's Sea, considerably larger than its counterpart, extends from the southeast coast of Japan to the northern tip of the Philippines and to Guam. Apparently a mysterious force also affects navigational equipment in the Devil's Sea, for ships and planes also vanished there, especially during World War II. Following the war, a Japanese research vessel that was sent to search for an explanation for the many losses permanently disappeared without a trace.[11] Perhaps energy from Lemuria is still present on the ocean floor in this strange region.

Many believe that, to more easily enter other dimensions, the Atlanteans attempted to create a powerful interdimensional portal in the area of the Bermuda Triangle. This offers another possible explanation for the communication problems and mysterious disappearances in that area. Portals are doorways to other dimensions. They enable a person to move through the curtain and sense what is happening in another period of time. Perhaps lack of comprehension of the deadly power of this enterprise contributed to the Atlanteans' doom, just as the Montauk Project was abandoned when our scientists were unable to control their unusual experiments.[12] Rumors abound that the United States has continued to secretly research the technology of interdimensional doorways. Rumors on the Internet report that scientists at Los Alamos, with the assistance of extremely high-powered holographic technology, have successfully created an entrance to other zones of time and place. Hopefully, knowledge that the Atlantean priest-scientists' experiments with their advanced technology were at least partially responsible for the destruction of their country will provide an incentive for our scientists to proceed cautiously until their spiritual development is comparable to their technical capabilities.

Quartz crystal was readily available in volcanic Atlantis, and many people, including Egerton Sykes, believe Atlanteans carved the life-size crystal skull, which Anna Mitchell-Hedges found in 1927 under the ruins of a temple in Belize. The age of the Mitchell-Hedges skull is undetermined because radiocarbon dating does not test quartz. After thoroughly studying it, scientists at Hewlett-Packard laboratories in Santa Clara, California, concluded that the people who made the skull were from a civilization which possessed a crystallographic ability equivalent to ours.

Before working with a chunk of crystal, modern sculptors always take into account the orientation of its molecular symmetry, since if they use lasers and other high-tech cutting methods and carve against the grain, the piece will shatter. The Mitchell-Hedges skull was carved against the natural axis of the original block of crystal. To compound the strangeness, Hewlett-Packard could find no microscopic scratches on the object to show it was formed with metal instruments. The scientists estimate that, if it was roughly hewn out with diamonds and then meticulously finished and polished with a mixture of silicon sand and water, the exhausting job would require man-hours adding up to about 300 years of effort. The skull was carved from clear crystal with piezoelectric properties, so it has a positive and negative polarity. It is capable of carrying an electric current from top to bottom or in the reverse direction.[13] Because the Mitchell-Hedges skull most closely resembles a female head, it is often referred to as "she." The object is strikingly beautiful, with a movable lower jaw and a network of prisms, lenses, and light-pipes that give life to her face and eyes. The realistic skull exhibits strange faculties. Sensitive people sometimes see an aura around her; others sense a sweet-sour odor. At times she seems to produce sounds like tinkling bells or a faint choir of human voices.

Initially, skilled persons probably used the head to stimulate and amplify their psychic abilities, but sensitive persons say her power also assists them in healing. If it is hung over a fire, when the firelight shines up through the passageways and focuses out from the lifelike skull's eye sockets, it produces a dramatic effect. The object would have provided a very effective way to control people, since its movable jaw offers unlimited opportunities to a person with the skills of a ventriloquist.

The Mitchell-Hedges skull is not the only crystal skull. An old Native American legend says there are thirteen ancient crystal skulls which contain important information about the origin, purpose, and destiny of the human race, as well as answers to questions about the universe. They believe that one day, when the human race is sufficiently morally and spiritually evolved, all the skulls will be brought together for their collective wisdom.[14] Many skulls have appeared which are said to have Central American origins, but a new type of test, performed in England in 1996 in preparation for a BBC documentary, determined that only two of the five skulls the scientists tested are ancient. Anna Mitchell-Hedges declined the invitation to include her skull in the program.

The results of the tests of their age were not made public, but "Max" was one of the skulls a BBC associate revealed was carved more than 5,000 years ago. Max was originally from Guatemala, and found his way to Texas via a Tibetan healer. Max has an exceptionally strong ability to transmit energy. Skilled people, utilizing crystals and sounds of toning, employ his power to energize small imitation crystal skulls that they use for healing.[15] Sha-Na-Ra, another skull which proved to be as old or older than Max, weighs over thirteen pounds. His previous home was in an ancient temple in the buried ruins of a city in Mexico. Sha-Na-Ra has an angular head with slanted eyes and prominent cheekbones.[16]

Skulls that were carved within the last five years are easy for experts to recognize, but there are other crystal heads which may have Atlantean origins, since their age has not been determined. Two clear quartz crystal skulls were found in Guatemala, as well as an amethyst skull, which was discovered in 1912.[17] A skull from Central America, which is smoky quartz, has a pointed cranium and is referred to as "ET" because it has the features of an extrater-restrial.[18] The Rose Quartz Crystal Skull, which is reported to reside near the border of Honduras and Guatemala, is the only skull that compares to the craftsmanship of the Mitchell-Hedges skull.[19]

Skilled craftspeople are making crystal skulls today from silicon quartz and they are available from a variety of sources. An artist in Brazil carves crystal skulls today that are available at the Gaila Goddess Specialty Shop at the Shambala Meditation and Training Center in Manchester, New Hampshire.[20] Some of the more recently produced skills have proved to be very useful to their owners, especially for healing. A few of the more recently carved skulls are especially powerful because they were crafted from crystal that was programmed in some way long ago. The following communication from the Netherlands offers an example:

> *Ohr Gesher is a newly carved skull, but the crystal from which he was carved has Atlantean memories. His name means "light." From what he told me, he was made to serve as some kind of library and also as a generator of some kind. When I first meditated with him I saw complete corridor-like structures with light in them. The light was a golden color. He's a bit of a mental little fellow and will not accept any thoughts that are below Christ-consciousness.*
>
> *Ohr Gesher told me that his mission is to connect the old and the new, and the young and the old, on as many levels as possible. He just came to me, so we still have a lot to learn from each other.*
>
> —GALIMAI, THE NETHERLANDS

Highly developed people who practice scrying believe they successfully obtain information from ancient crystal skulls or skulls made from age-old crystal. To follow this procedure, scryers intensely focus and concentrate in a dark, quiet place with only the light of a candle. Placing their hands on either side of the head, they look into its depths, projecting their minds into it with their gaze. The skull slowly becomes cloudy and the scryer perceives pictures deep within it. One problem is that they do not know if the information from the crystal head concerns the past, present, or future.

Crystal skulls have the power of light and dark within them. We have to be careful or we may absorb the negative as well as the positive. They are libraries of knowledge, for as they absorb all, they can return all if we have the keys to access it. Tone was used in Atlantis to gain admittance to the skull's libraries, and it can be used now if we know how to do it. However, our energy frequencies have changed over time, and few people today are capable of the necessary focus and are as in tune with the elemental forces of creation as those who once worked with the crystal skulls.

——HEATHER ROBB

Scientists at the U.S. National Bureau of Standards first discovered quasi-crystal in 1984. They reported that the strange stone possessed the same type of order usually associated with a crystal, except its atoms were arranged in a pattern that is physically impossible for any crystalline substance. Crystals can have only twofold, threefold, fourfold, and sixfold symmetry. Quasi-crystals have fivefold symmetry, which cannot be assembled to completely fill space.[21]

Atlanteans programmed quasi-crystals telepathically, using the energy of their minds. The result is something like a computer. With the assistance of the powerful stones they had access to mental time travel to explore the nature of the universe.[22] If they had a mental image of a desired destination, such as a geographical landmark, it was possible for their minds to go to any location in their present day, and also to journey in the past and the future.[23]

Some years ago in Norway, I met a man working with crystals, and he told me that some crystals have small triangles engraved on the faces. He said these are very precious because this is encoded information (he talked about a link with Atlantis). He said the triangles "come and go, you see them if you are ready to." He showed me some crystals with very tiny triangles on their faces. He said you should always look very carefully when buying crystals and choose these.

When I went home, I was curious and looked at my crystals. In fact, most of them had triangles. A couple didn't, and one or two (especially one) was literally covered with all sorts of triangles (from very small to bigger, overlapping each other.)

—ANONYMOUS

Holographically encoded quasi-crystals which receive psycho-electric programming are referred to as recorder crystals. When properly encoded with intense concentration and meditation, recorder crystals assume their own personality and are very powerful, especially for healing. See appendix I for one intuitive person's experience with a powerful crystal she believes priest-scientists worked with in Atlantis.

I was an Atlantean priest who taught in the temples. The classrooms were similar to mini-amphitheaters and I stood on a platform, facing the students who were reclining on pillows on the floor. When class began, each student took out their most precious possession—a Knowledge Crystal. Intensely concentrating, with the crystal in their hands, they absorbed and recorded the complex information I sent to them. Teaching and learning were such a joy.

—MICHAEL FESS

Dolores Cannon is a hypnotist who helps others explore experiences in previous incarnations with the goal of improving their present lives. In *Jesus and the Essenes,* Cannon offers a fascinating recollection of a very large recorder crystal which may have come from Atlantis. From the past life reflections of a girl from an isolated rural area who only had a minimum education, she received information about an amazing crystal in the library of the Essenes. The Essenes were a secret society of spiritual scholars who flourished in the Near East during the first century B.C. and perhaps for long before that time. They are most widely known as the probable authors of the Dead Sea Scrolls.

Dolores Cannon's patient described being a student in the school of the Essenes, and working in the library, where a huge crystal that was about two feet in diameter rested on a pedestal. The stone was shaped like a pyramid and seemed to change color. A waist-high wall surrounded the crystal, for it expelled so much more energy than was sent to it that it burned anyone who touched it.

In the library the students were taught to focus on an elderly professor, who was the only person who had the ability to come close to the powerful stone. He used the force he received from them to obtain knowledge from the crystal, telling the students they were not evolved enough to be exposed to this information; that once great damage was done by unenlightened people who gained access to it. The girl reported that she was told the powerful crystal had been with the Essenes for as long as anyone could remember and its origins were unknown. They thought it came to their land in a boat. Atlantis is a logical possibility.

The girl had never heard of the Essenes and knew nothing about the ancient Near East but, after carefully checking historical records with the minute details she received from her patient about the Essenes' daily life and surroundings, Dolores Cannon is convinced that the girl's report of the pyramid-shaped crystal is authentic.

The Great Pyramid of Giza in Egypt offers another example of the skills the Atlanteans exhibited as they attempted to record knowledge for us. Edgar Cayce states many times that when they anticipated the destruction of their land, Atlanteans traveled to Egypt and built the pyramid to preserve information. The building displays its builders' superior knowledge of mathematics, geometry, astronomy, and technology at a level we are just achieving. Its 2,500,000 granite and limestone blocks, some weighing seventy tons, occupy thirteen acres, or the equivalent of seven square blocks of Manhattan.

Those who planned this huge building had the ability to express their exceptional mathematical and astronomical data in structural form. The geometric design, which is all on the basis of the mathematical ratio of pi, accurately incorporates the sun's distance from the Earth, the weight of the Earth, its circumference at the equator, and other knowledge of our planet which our scientists rediscovered relatively recently. It is as if the builders, realizing that written records, tools, and machinery do not survive, used this building to display the level of their skills. Incorporation of their amazing understanding of the Earth's dimensions suggests that those who designed the Great Pyramid wished to let us know that their advanced race once inhabited our planet.[24]

Like a trick birthday candle that is difficult to blow out, so unanswered questions about the elaborate pyramid at Giza continue to disturb investigators. Contemporary archaeologists are unwilling to accept Cayce's construction date of approximately 10,000 B.C., but evidence that the unique building is older than they believe continues to appear. The recent discovery of the inaccuracy of radiocarbon dating, as described previously, also adds numerous years to the antiquity of this and other prehistoric sites.

In addition to its age, there is the problem of how the immense building was constructed. Cayce makes it plain that Atlantean mechanics went to Egypt to offer advice for creating the mechanical tools for cutting the stones.[25] Contemporary attempts to demonstrate that thousands of laborers spent innumerable years cutting boulders into precisely accurate blocks and piling them up to make the pyramid prove to many that this is *not* the way it was constructed.

After carefully studying Egyptian technology, engineer and laser technician Christopher Dunn believes that when they built Egypt's Great Pyramid, craftsmen successfully used ultrasonics to penetrated granite. The quartz embedded in granite vibrates sympathetically with the high-frequency ultrasonic waves and does not resist the cutting action.[26] Perhaps Aarth-Elth, a young Atlantean whom Cayce says moved to Egypt and worked to develop mechanical appliances to cut stone,[27] was involved in perfecting ultrasonic tools.

Cayce mentions that the pyramid builders, as they traveled upon the river in Egypt, learned the correct chants to overcome the force of gravity and lift heavy stones. Stories from all over the world tell of waves of sound lifting and raising heavy objects. Priests in Chaldea are said to have lifted the great stones at Baalbek with repeated and harmonious chants. At Tiahuanaco in Bolivia, narratives portray builders employing the sound of trumpets, and the walls of the Greek city of Thebes were supposedly constructed to the tones of Amphion's lyre. Legends report the builders of Stonehenge overcame gravity with drums, songs, and the clash of cymbals.[28] German travelers in Tibet depict monks using drums, trumpets, and chants to defy gravity and move heavy blocks up a hill, and accounts of visitors to India describe monks who rose in the air with the assistance of sound plus the power of their minds. Babylonian tablets reiterate that sonic energy can lift weighty objects.

More recently, sonic levitation was employed in a space shuttle. Sound waves securely held glass in suspension while it was experimentally melted and shaped into a delicate lens. This remarkable act is possible because in the space vehicle, due to the absence of gravity, less intense sound is required for levitation. Once this process is perfected, optical engineers will successfully create thinner, more complicated lenses with fewer layers of material.[29]

Scientists have learned the effect of the energy of sound on plants. When they played recordings of high pitched tones to crops of wheat, the vibrations significantly stimulated the plants to greater growth. Pulsations from people stamping and dancing on the land improved the growth of a variety of other plants. Varied species of flowering plants that were continuously subjected to different types of music reacted differently. Some grew toward rock music, others died.[30]

Ultrasonic vibrations above our hearing range enable skilled technicians to map ocean bottoms, increase molecular motion in liquids, generate heat, crack solids, and sterilize surgical instruments. Ultrasound is a well-known diagnostic technique that provides physicians with images of internal organs, and often offers successful therapeutic treatment. As we relearn and employ the power of sound waves, it is possible to believe the Atlanteans may have had the ability to harness it to move large rocks.

One situation for which the Atlanteans used the energy of sound has not been fully explored. A member of a former Nobel Prize-winning team told author and scientist Murry Hope that he recalls his days as a priest-scientist in "the Old Country" where he was engaged in advanced work on sonics. He said he did not pursue that line of scientific inquiry in this lifetime because it was too dangerous and he believes the world is not ready for it.[31] We know that very strong vibrations of ultrasonic waves are capable of killing animals and people. Equally powerful infrasonic vibrations below man's hearing have similar powers.[32]

Cayce also reports that in Mexico the Lemurians combined with others from Peru, Egypt, and Atlantis to build pyramids and temples, and that the lifting power of gases enabled them to construct the large structures of heavy stone.[33] Megalithic pyramids on numerous Pacific Islands, similar to the one on Tahiti on which stone altars once stood,[34] continue to remind us that the Lemurians and their descendants also found ways to overcome the force of gravity.

Scientist and inventor Nikola Tesla offers an example of how the highly developed minds of the Atlanteans enabled them to surpass us in their technology. Tesla (1856–1943), who invented alternating current, also explored the possibilities of electromagnetism, including its use to access other dimensions. It is thought that his knowledge was one of the sources of top-secret U.S. research with time and space, including the Philadelphia Experiment and the experiments at Montauk. Descriptions of Tesla's lethal Scalar Wave technology have a striking resemblance to Edgar Cayce's Atlantean death rays, which will be depicted in chapter 14.

To devise a new invention, Tesla first pictured in his mind what he wished to construct. In this solely visual state he corrected the device, turned it on to see if it worked well, and completed it in every detail. Only then did he make the drawings and diagrams. The final step was to actually build his invention, if there was money. Tesla's creations never failed because they were already designed and tested in his head. Einstein is reputed to have worked in a similar manner.

Although he was a genius, the establishment discredits most of Tesla's work and many of his inventions remain secret. His concepts of antigravity, time travel, flying discs, thought machines, ozone generators, and electric submarines were too much for the conservative scientific community of the early twentieth century. When he died, most of his papers mysteriously disappeared.

Edgar Cayce tells us that an abundance of Atlanteans returned to this planet in the twentieth century. Thanks to the wisdom and effort of many of them, our technology improved tremendously. However, he often cautions them to beware of developing radioactive forces as they had done in the past. He offered his observations on the dangers of breaking up the atom in 1935 before that was officially accomplished and became public knowledge.[35] As we follow in the footsteps of the Atlanteans, our physicists are expanding their minds and acquiring the ability to efficiently utilize solar energy, the Earth's magnetism, and the power of sound. Hopefully, we will simultaneously develop the ability to live in harmony and use this plentiful energy to benefit all humanity without destroying ourselves and our beloved Earth.

NOTES

1   Andrews, *Atlantis: Insights from a Lost Civilization.*

2   Cerve, *Lemuria.*

3   Ibid.

4   Montgomery, *The World Before*, p. 79.

5   Cayce, *Readings* 2072–10.

6   Cayce, *Readings* 440–5.

7   Donato, "Cayce's Masers," *Atlantis Rising*, Number 32, p. 61.

8   Cayce, *Readings* 262–39.

9   Hope, *The Ancient Wisdom of Atlantis*, p. 110.

10 *Boston Globe*, August 30, 1999.

11 Winer, *The Devil's Triangle*, p. 210.

12 For more information see *The Montauk Project* by Preston B. Nichols. For four decades, from 1943 to 1983, secret research at the abandoned U.S. Air Force base at Montauk, Long Island, focused on attempts to manipulate space and time. Initially they used a computer and technology that ITT developed that could pick up the electromagnetic functions or thoughts of human beings. As they experimented with moving and materializing objects, they often manipulated time without understanding why or how. The scientists came to realize that their work was doing irreparable damage to the people involved and the project was discontinued.

13 Morton and Thomas, *The Mystery of the Crystal Skulls*, p. 47.

14 Ibid., p.2.

15 Isabelle, *Crystal Skull Handbook*, p. 32.

16 Morton and Thomas, Ibid., p. 92.

17 Ibid., p. 93.

18 Ibid., p. 210.

19 Ibid., p. 93.

20 The Shambala Meditation Center at 865 Second Street in Manchester, New Hampshire, contains a large temple, a healing center, and a specialty shop. It offers a wide variety of lectures and classes. Many years ago, a Maya priest gave Susan Isabelle, the founder and director of the center, an ancient crystal skull, telling her he knew she would understand how to use it. He said its name was El Aleator (Lord of the Tones). Susan believes the skull is one of the ancient thirteen crystal skulls programmed so long ago. With tones and energy Susan uses El Aleator to activate the newer crystal heads from Brazil until some of them actually pulse in her hand. Some of the crystals take on a color frequency for specific uses in healing. These activated skulls are very

effective in healing as they gradually change the new owner's energy field, making the person more aware and energetic.

Lemurian seed crystals are also available at the specialty shop, and classes and groups have formed around the Lemurian crystals and crystal skulls. Students of Lemuria and those interested in the skulls have discovered the group consciousness enhances the experience for all. Using the Lemurian crystals in circlular formation, the groups have discovered an automatic link-age occurs in which each participant is "locked in at the heart center" one to another, forming a strong electromagnetic, energetic field and consciousness within the group. Gateways are formed and participants have experienced blue globes of light within the room and Lemurian consciousness contacts have occured. Their messages, psychically received, have spoken of their concern for the earth. The desire of the Lemurian consciousness as expressed within the group is to help us care for the earth. Actual photographs of the globes of light are available at the Shambhala Temple for all to see the light manifestations.

21   Hope, *The Ancient Wisdom of Atlantis*, p. 105.

22   Ibid., p. 106.

23   Carrie Blakley.

24   *Atlantis: Insights from a Lost Civilization* offers more information about the Great Pyramid.

25   Cayce, *Readings* 1177–1.

26   Dunn, *The Giza Power Plant*, p. 87.

27   Cayce, *Readings* 1177–1.

28   Michell, *The New View Over Atlantis*, p. 204.

29   Raloff, *Science News*, November 28, 1987.

30   Tompkins and Bird, *The Secret Life of Plants*.

31   Hope, *The Ancient Wisdom of Atlantis*, p. 111.

32   Donato, *A Re-examination of the Atlantis Theory*, p. 153.

33   Robinson, *Edgar Cayce's Story of the Origin and Destiny of Man*, p. 124.

34   Sykes, *Atlantis*, Vol. 21, No.1.

35   See *Atlantis: Insights from a Lost Civilization* for further information about nuclear energy in prehistory.

14

TECHNOLOGY

FREELY COMBINING THE IN-
tuitive abilities of their highly developed
minds with their advanced mathematical
and technical skills, the priest-scientists of
Lemuria and Atlantis learned to use the
forces of nature for the comfort, conve-
nience, and pleasure of all. They developed
a technology that, although different from
ours, was superior in many respects. Fields
of wildflowers and lush green forests in
those beautiful lands were not defaced by
strips of metal and concrete to facilitate
rapid trips in fast trains and automobiles,
but people managed to live happily and
well without polluting the environment
and depleting their natural resources.

Edgar Cayce's readings describe the Atlanteans' acquisition of power from the
Great Crystal, from sound, and from splitting the atom. He says that with currents
of energy from the crystal, the people who

lived so long ago enjoyed travel in the air, on water and under the sea, the transmission of voices over a long distance, and the benefits of lasers.[1] Airplanes, ships, long-distance communication, and lasers seem fantastic, but legends, recollections, and artifacts of prehistory do report instances of most of these amazing accomplishments.

References to boats that flew in the sky without sails or oars and vehicles like flying birds that carried people are common among the stories of the past on this planet. Written records are also available that depict the flying vehicles of long ago. The age-old vedic epics of India offer detailed descriptions of *vimanas*, the airplanes of the Rama, who were descendants of the Lemurians. They also cite *valix*, the flying ships of the Atlanteans, whom they called the "Asvins."[2]

The valix (*valixi* in the plural) is described in detail in *A Dweller on Two Planets,* which eighteen-year-old Frederick S. Oliver wrote in 1884. Oliver says that Phylos the Tibetan, who lived in Atlantis in 11,650 B.C., visited him at night and carefully described his Atlantean life. Phylos dictated *A Dweller on Two Planets* backwards, which is the way Oliver wrote it—from the end to the beginning. Although his manuscript was published long before our aircraft were invented, Oliver's descriptions of large cylindrical passenger vehicles, with windows along the sides in rows like portholes, are strikingly similar to contemporary jet-powered airplanes. The Atlantean valixi resembled hollow needles with sharp points at each end, 25 to over 300 feet in length, and were constructed from sheets of a bright lightweight metal that shone in the dark. With crystal windows in the floors and skylights in the ceiling, they were in some ways more advanced than contemporary aircraft. It is very unlikely that a boy from rural California in the nineteenth century would have had access to ancient Indian texts, but the name of the Atlantean's aircraft is the same and Oliver's report of Atlantean valixi is very similar to the vimanas in this remote Sanskrit literature. The Rama's vimanas will be described in chapter 16.

With the guidance of Phylos, Oliver depicts other amazing technological accomplishments in Atlantis such as air purifiers, electric guns, crystal lights that burned indefinitely, and an instrument for condensing water from the atmosphere. He portrays these astonishing achievements with convincing details, but they were unknown to our civilization when he wrote *A Dweller on Two Planets* in 1884.

Atlanteans carried messages through space, served as navigators and engineers on aircraft, moved goods above the surface, journeyed throughout their country, and traveled to distant lands.[3] They devised a flying machine that resembled a low, flat sled, which was capable of carrying heavy loads thirty feet above the ground for long distances in a straight line. Power from the Great Crystal motivated the conveyance, which a person on the surface directed.[4] We have recently developed the unmanned RQ-1 Predator spy plane, which a person on the ground directs with a remote-control console.

In Atlantis, rays from the crystal similarly energized small planes, which carried one or two passengers and flew two to three feet above the surface.[5] Edgar Cayce refers to Atlantean flying vehicles similar to those Ezekiel portrays in the Bible.[6] Ezekiel describes bright, shiny metal crafts that resembled living creatures. Fire, like lightning, continuously flashed from the creatures as they traveled in any of the four directions. The vehicles varied, but each had wheels and wings that didn't turn as they moved in the air. When the strange creatures stood still they let down their wings and the beasts were quiet, but they made a loud noise like thunder as they traveled.[7] In the final days of Atlantis, a few fortunate people escaped in these airplanes from their sinking country and flew to the Pyrenees and Egypt.[8] Atlanteans also had vehicles that not only flew in the air but also moved under the surface of the ocean like submarines.[9]

Taking advantage of the water that surrounded them and the power of the crystal, the Atlanteans became a great seafaring nation with outposts throughout the world. Each district of the country was required to provide at least four sailors for their navy of 1,200 ships to assist in their vigorous struggles for more land. At the height of their power, Atlantean kings ruled over all the islands in the Atlantic Ocean, parts of the American continent, and as far into the Mediterranean as the present countries of Egypt and northern Italy.[10]

It was important for the Atlanteans to regularly find new space for their bulging population, for the greedy ocean steadily devoured portions of their land, and their high standard of living and pleasant climate continuously attracted immigrants from Africa and Europe. As the need to acquire additional land grew more urgent, the Atlantean army became more assertive in their attempts. Finally, just before the final destruction in 10,000 B.C., when the aggressive Atlantean soldiers attempted to move more deeply into the Mediterranean, the stronger Greek army defeated them.[11]

Living in a land of many waterways that was surrounded by the Pacific Ocean, the Lemurians came to rely on the highways of the rivers and the sea for communication with others. Although nothing suggests the Atlanteans used sails to take advange of the power of the wind, evidence shows that large ships using sails were present in the Pacific Ocean in prehistory. Most of the Lemurian's seven sacred cities of religion and sciences were at the mouths of important rivers and, as a result of their ships and navigational skills, Lemuria became a worldwide center of learning, trade, and commerce.[12]

Sailors' charts from ancient times provide a source of information that portrays the skills of the sailors of long ago. Accurate maps that were preserved in northern Africa and in the dry Middle East surfaced in the thirteenth and fourteenth centuries A.D. when it became permissible again to believe the world extended beyond the Straits of Gibraltar. At that time, cartographers in western Europe who copied the maps were amazed to discover that they portrayed northern Europe with its lakes and ice as it was before the glaciers melted in 10,000 B.C. The very old charts also depicted unknown islands in the Atlantic Ocean. The accuracy of these ancient maps indicates the use of extremely precise clocks to measure longitude as well, something our civilization was unable to accomplish until the eighteenth century.

> *The crystal room in Atlantis was a room filled with crystals. The crystals were used for many things, such as clocks, healing and communication.*
> —CARRIE BLAKLEY

Edgar Cayce mentions the Sons of Belial meeting in a crystal room to communicate with those who descended from on high to bring messages.[13] Apparently shrewd Atlanteans were taking advantage of the numerous crystals in the room to increase their psychic ability to more easily communicate with their spirit guides, with extraterrestrials, or with those who had passed on.

Over fifty mysterious stone chambers near the Hudson River in Putnam County, New York, may resemble the Atlantean crystal rooms. One of them, the "Crystal Chamber," has a quartz vein in its ceiling that produces such strong energy that people sense it when they stand in the room beneath it. Visitors also experience strange visions and weird hallucinations in the vicinity of these unusual chambers.[14]

Science, magic, and religion were one in both Lemuria and Atlantis, and all things were related. As the priest-scientists expanded their minds to facilitate their acquisition of knowledge, they learned to enter the subtle worlds of spirits from which they believed they originated. Once there, they navigated by means of intuition tempered by reason. To ensure their ability to explore fruitfully, it was important that they first ground themselves with basic symbols such as one of the many variations of the equidistant cross. The ankh, caduceus, sacred eye, chalice, and winged disc were important in their ceremonial journeys, for they helped to project their consciousness beyond the realms of matter into a hidden universe.[15]

> *In the later days of Atlantis I was a man with very unusual dark eyes. Much of my time was spent working as a magician with colleagues and students in a laboratory in a large subterranean cave. Here, using meditation enhanced by crystals, I acquired esoteric knowledge and the ability to shift in and out of the etheric plane and to communicate with other masters. Under the influence of an older associate I was led to misuse these powers and control others, particularly women.*
>
> —ANONYMOUS

Of course the Lemurians and Atlanteans spoke aloud, but they also used their minds to communicate with each other. To successfully transmit information telepathically, one must never tell a lie and have nothing to hide. It is essential that a person's mind be completely open to giving and receiving information. The Hopi describe this as keeping the hole in the top of their heads open.

The Atlanteans perfected a machine similar to our telephone that transmitted voices over a distance,[16] and a type of telepathic telephone was also available at one time in Atlantis. If they pushed the correct buttons on the machine, like our dialing the number, it sent a signal that amplified the vibrations of the person with whom they wished to communicate.[17]

> *About six years ago, I had a very unusual dream unlike any kind of dream I had ever experienced. I only remember bits and pieces. I first remember being in a desert and witnessing the*

construction of a large pyramid. I saw many men working on it yet they were not using ordinary tools. The blocks were being cut by what appeared to be a laser-like beam. They cut through the blocks as if they were soft butter. The blocks were being put in place by one man alone using a small hand-held device which acted as a forklift, yet it used levitation to manipulate the block into place.

I saw aircraft being loaded with metals which appeared to be gold. As I was witnessing this, I heard a voice speak to me and say, "This is the way they have been built in the past when the fathers had arrived and as they always shall be constructed." I presume that the voice was talking about Atlantis. After the voice spoke, I realized that I was wearing the typical dress for an Egyptian male of the time period.

In another dream I remember seeing a woman moving a wand in a back and forth motion across a garden. The beam of the device was about six feet wide, instead of the typical laser focusing. It seemed to me this device might have multiple uses that rejuvenated or destroyed. If it helped agriculture, it could benefit the people. And if it could cut through stone, it could cut through flesh.

—CLARENCE OLINGER

Edgar Cayce first mentions Atlantean lasers in 1933 and predicted our scientists would produce them in twenty-five years. Twenty-five years later, in 1958, Bell Telephone Laboratory produced masers (Microwave Amplification by Stimulated Emission of Radiation). At that time, Cayce advised a patient that in order to avoid the mistakes he made with the powerful tool in Atlantis, he must meditate and listen to the advice of his soul.[18]

The Atlanteans utilized lasers as bloodless knives in surgery.[19] They also had a stronger, similar version that Cayce calls the death ray, or super-cosmic ray.[20] Death rays, which were so powerful that they were capable of killing with their intense light, were helpful to Atlanteans in their battles against aggressive animals during the country's earliest civilization. Like the Atlantean's lasers, our masers utilize quartz crystals to accumulate energy in a small insulating crystal with special magnetic properties. Upon signal, the crystal releases stored energy in excess of what it receives.

> *After years of practice I am able to travel through time or space, no matter where I am. All I have to do is close my eyes and focus on my destination, and I'm there in a near instant. I believe it is a skill I had in Atlantis which has made it possible to learn it again.*
>
> —CARRIE BLAKLEY

We use only a small part of our mind, but we are slowly learning to expand our senses and accomplish the feats of the Lemurians and Atlanteans. As they attempted to facilitate their ability to move beyond physical reality, they acquired the capacity to comprehend levels of awareness and dimensions that only a few individuals are beginning to reach today. They had access to the future and the past, in a manner similar to Edgar Cayce, and they came to realize that time is an illusion that keeps us in the third dimension.

NOTES

1 Cayce, *Readings* 1719–1, 17335–2, 262–39.

2 Childress, *Lost Cities of China, Central Asia & India.*

3 Cayce, *Readings* 2494–1, 2124–3, 2437–1.

4 Winston, Shirley Rabb, Lecture re: Edgar Cayce Readings at Association for Research and Enlightenment, Inc., September 22, 1988.

5 Ibid.

6 Cayce, *Readings* 1859.

7 Ezekiel 1:4–5, 15–28, *The New Oxford Annotated Bible.*

8 Cayce, *Readings* 2677–1.

9 Cayce, *Readings* 2157–1.

10 Plato, *Timaeus.*

11 Ibid.

12 Churchward, *The Lost Continent of Mu,* p. 49.

13 Cayce, *Readings* 830–1.

14 Brennan, Janet, *Fate Magazine* May 2001, "The Chambers of Putnam County," pp. 20–21.

15 Hope, *The Ancient Wisdom of Atlantis,* pp. 137–138.

16 Cayce, *Readings* 813–1.

17 Bethards, *Atlantis,* p. 13.

18 Cayce, *Readings* 440–1.

19 Cayce, *Readings* 470–33.

20 Cayce, *Readings* 262–39.

15

DESTRUCTION

I am a little girl. I live in Atlantis. I'm playing with some children in a grassy space like a park with houses close around it. The sky is getting dark, but I know it isn't nighttime. I'm running around having fun, and then I notice that the ground is rolling and shaking. Two big, sharp noises frighten me and I start to cry, but my father comes racing out of the house, grabs my hand and says, "Come with me." Ashes and dust are falling down like rain and the smoky air is hard to breathe. I realize some volcanoes exploded.

We run out to the street and it's full of screaming people all racing with us to the water. My father has a small boat, which is still there. After I get in, he rows us away from the heaving ground. Lots of people are swimming in the water and some manage to climb into our little boat and others desperately hang on to the sides. Hot coals from the volcano keep falling on us and burn our skin, so we go farther out to where we can hardly hear the terrified shouting people on the land. Suddenly a huge wave is coming, taller than a building. It tips over our boat. I hit my head on something as I fall into the water and I sink deeper, deeper . . .

This is my story. It helps me to understand why I have always been so apprehensive and uncomfortable swimming in deep water that's over my head or riding in a boat on a lake or the ocean. Perhaps it also offers an explanation for my unpleasant tendency toward sea sickness.

In those days of Atlantis, we knew about reincarnation. We knew the physical body is only used for a brief moment before it is replaced with another. I could have gone with others to Egypt before Atlantis sank. I was given that choice. But I decided to stay to the end, to experience the last moment of Atlantis with those who could not leave. I knew I would be reincarnated into Egypt for my next lifetime, and yes, this happened, and I lived many lives there.

I especially remember the very last day in Atlantis, the very last moments when the land turned to yellow mush like quicksand as it sank beneath me. Those terrifying last moments are as clear to me today as they were thousands of years ago. The sinking happened so quickly, there was hardly time to think, to feel. Yet, my last thought was that of horror when the land went down under my feet.

When I was a small child in this lifetime, I remember being asleep in my crib when an earthquake struck and my parents picked me up and quickly carried me out of the room. At that moment, as the house trembled, the feeling was the same as when the earth sank beneath me in Atlantis. I don't think any-

one ever forgets this. I am very glad I don't live today in an earthquake-prone area. I would have to leave. I could not repeat over and over the feelings of my last moments in Atlantis.
—BARBARA WOLF

In 50,722 B.C., as the Atlanteans searched for a means of destroying the dangerous large animals that were eating their crops and their children, they began to experiment with obtaining energy from natural sources. Desperately, the priest-scientists combined numerous chemicals and created powerful explosives, but these dangerous weapons were difficult to control.[1] One day, when they aimed them at the animals' homes on the ground, the tremendous blasts triggered terrible earthquakes that led to Atlantis cracking and splitting into five smaller islands.[2]

In 28,000 B.C., when Atlantean scientists tuned the crystal too high, it suddenly turned into a deadly, destructive force. The tumult from earthquakes, volcanic eruptions, and floods that followed devastated Atlantis once again until only three islands remained, one of which was Poseidia in the Caribbean. Plato adds that a string of lesser islands connected the Atlantic Ridge to the American continent.

When I read about Atlantis I sense this strange pain, of a land in distress, of people running for their lives, and I feel a terrible sadness for this place that was so loved by its citizens.
—ANONYMOUS

About 10,000 B.C., something happened that dramatically changed the climate on our planet. The warm northern lands of Siberia became intensely cold, and the glaciers on the European and North American continents rapidly melted. As a result of the cataclysmic weather and geological upheavals at that time, forty million animals, including woolly mammoths, saber-toothed cats, mastodons, dire wolves, great ground sloths, giant cave bears, and antique bison died on the North and South American continents, and many more in Europe failed to escape nature's wrath. The *Chilam Balaam*, one of the three remaining books of the Maya, describes the face of the heavens tilting, and the great tempest that arose and darkened the face of the sun and blew everything to the ground.[3] What a horrible time for the human beings who lived on our planet.

Just as a furious fire destroys a forest of tall, stately trees, so this savage natural event completely eliminated advanced civilizations as well as the animals. Lemuria and Atlantis suffered terribly. Beautiful homes and pyramid temples cracked and collapsed, and the waters of the ocean swept over both lands. Plato tells us "the island of Atlantis was swallowed up by the sea and vanished."[4] In the Motherland of Mu, the catastrophe happened so suddenly that 64 million people died as the doomed island went "down, down, down."[5] Memories of this frightful time lie deep in the unconscious of many individuals today.

> *Twice Mu jumped from her foundations: it was then sacrificed by fire. It burst while earthquakes violently shook it up and down. By kicking it, the wizard that makes all things move like a mass of worms sacrificed it that very night.*
> —CODEX CORTESIANUS (SEE CHAPTER 4)

Churchward proposes that the granite under the continent of Mu was interlaced with pockets of volcanic gases. Initially, the chambers which supported Mu were very near the surface of the land and isolated from those below, but violent earthquakes and volcanic action in the depths of the Earth opened passages from the lower caverns to those above. The tremendous pressure on the higher chambers as gases rose from below obliterated the cavern's roofs and completely broke up the land. At the same time, the gases burst into flames and engulfed the Motherland.[6]

Wishai S. Cerve adds that as tectonic plates moved, a remnant of submerged Lemurian land was pushed up against the western portion of the American continent. He points out that as one nears the Pacific coast in western California, the soil changes. As a result, redwoods, certain wildflowers, and ferns that are difficult to grow in the eastern portion of the state flourish there in the wild without cultivation.[7] Edgar Cayce also refers to remains of Lemurian land in lower California.[8]

Some researchers suggest that the combination of violent earthquakes, overpowering tidal waves, and rapidly rising ocean levels that killed most of the people on our planet in 10,000 B.C. were indirectly responsible for the cannibalism and infanticide people once practiced in the South Pacific Islands. When disaster struck, lucky survivors scrambled to higher ground but, as the land continued to shake and the ocean waters rose, those who survived were forced to crowd together on the remaining fertile land. The expanse of sea between them and other islands continued to increase and they were trapped, often without inadequate food. To survive they resorted to eating humans.[9]

It is impossible to reflect on the changed state of the American continent without the deepest astonishment. Formerly it must have swarmed with great monsters: now we find mere pigmies, compared with the antecedent, allied races. If Buffon had known of the gigantic sloth and armadillo-like animals, and of the lost Pachydermata, he might have said with a greater semblance of truth that the creative force in America had lost its power, rather than that it had never possessed great vigour. The greater number, if not all, of these extinct quadrupeds lived at a late period, and were the contemporaries of most of the existing sea-shells. Since they lived, no very great change in the form of the land can have taken place.

What then has exterminated so many species and whole genera in 10,000 B.C.? The mind at first is irresistibly hurried into

the belief of some great catastrophe: but thus to destroy animals
both large and small, in South Patagonia, in Brazil, on the
Cordillera of Peru, in North America up to the Bering's straits,
we must shake the entire framework of the globe.
—CHARLES DARWIN[10]

Scientists have several theories as to what was responsible for the disastrous event of 10,000 B.C. The most probable is that a terrific shock provoked the planet's axis to shift, and this disturbed the stability of the hot, thick liquid that lies beneath its surface. Inevitably, in vulnerable places, the fragile crust crumpled.

The ancient belief that comets, or huge stars in the sky with tails, were predecessors of a disturbance in the heavens (the gods were angry) is once again attaining credibility. Scientists are becoming increasingly aware that the Earth's surface is extremely exposed to a comet, or "dirty snowball," like the one that broke into twenty-one pieces and smashed into the face of Jupiter in July 1994. Each of the chunks of that comet had the force of several nuclear bombs. If pieces of a comet or remains of an exploded star landed in one of our oceans, in addition to the damage of the impact, the heat would evaporate immense amounts of water. This water, plus the liquid from the rapidly melting outer layer of the foreign body as it sped into our atmosphere, would produce heavy rains for several days. As debris from the pieces of the comet that crashed on the land sent immense clouds of dust into the sky, the sun's light would fade, and darkness would prevail.

Only those human beings who sought refuge in underground caves or lived high in the mountains escaped the massive tidal waves, and many of them died of starvation before plants were able to grow again. Ships at sea may have provided a temporary safe refuge and a means of finding areas where needed food was available, but even these lucky people were soon reduced to living in extremely primitive conditions. The story of Noah and his ark is repeated in legends throughout the world.

German physicist Dr. Otto Muck believes that at the time of the final sinking of Atlantis, an asteroid several miles in diameter plunged into the Atlantic Ocean off the eastern coast of the United States. The huge holes where pieces of the hot, destructive demon penetrated the Earth's crust near the Carolinas are quite visible today on the ocean floor, and photographs taken from the air show that hundreds of elliptical craters, called "Carolina Rings," pockmark Georgia, Florida, Virginia, Maryland, and North and South Carolina. Muck estimates that when it smashed into us, the rapidly moving asteroid was as strong as 30,000 hydrogen bombs.[11]

The Earth is a small, frail sphere compared to the larger planets. Its crust is only five to thirty miles thick. The oceans of hot magma inside it are constantly in motion and, if the activity of this liquid is disturbed, it swings around and contributes to the planet's instability. Muck believes the shock of the asteroid's impact was so strong that our globe, which is like a giant top, wobbled on its axis, instigating the shattering earthquakes, gigantic waves, and long-lasting, damaging volcanic action.

A plausible theory explaining the demise of Atlantis suggests that, as a result of the tremendous jolt when this fast-moving body from space hit our planet, cracks developed on either side of the Atlantic Ridge. Red-hot magma from inside the Earth shot up at terrific speed through those spaces and melted the bottom of the land and, as the island crumbled, the beautiful country sadly sank into the sea. Lemuria may have suffered a similar fate.

Agitation of the Earth's axis, earthquakes, volcanic eruptions, and floods offer the outward, physical explanations for the sinking of Atlantis, but another source of the catastrophic devastation lay in the thoughts and inclinations of the people. Their lack of affection for our lovely world, their selfish aspirations, and their immorality were contributing factors.

I have the memory of being the wife of one of the priests of science, a specialist in what we call electronics nowadays, who understood the workings of the Great Crystal. He was one of a group of twelve miscreants who fiddled with the settings, being a portion of the cause of the downfall of Atlantis.

—KATHLEEN KEITH

Interest in scientific achievement gradually supplanted compassionate relationships, the sharing of resources, and the harmony with nature that had characterized life in Lemuria and Atlantis for thousands of years. A class society evolved in both countries, in which the priest-scientists were extremely powerful, not always to the benefit of humanity.

From what I have seen of Mu, and from a channeled drawing that I was privileged to research, Mu was a battle of light versus dark. One part of the civilization was a farming community that was spiritual/religious, and dark energies dominated the rest of the society. Their collapse was destined if they never resolved their differences, which they did not. They had very little contact with each other.

—ANONYMOUS

The priest-scientists initially used their minds to access hidden spheres with the goal of benefiting others. The result was a remarkable technology blended with a spiritual base. The magician in the following experience is typical of those in the later days of Atlantis and Lemuria, who used their advanced information to obtain wealth and power at the expense of others. Although the Lemurians did not descend to the same level of corruption and evil as the Atlanteans, Llasa records portray a wealthy class in Mu who adorned themselves with fine clothes and jewels and lived in magnificent palaces.[12]

What I recall about my time in Atlantis is that I was a very powerful magician who was totally removed from humanity. I see a huge white tower with windows all around that look out on a land surrounded by sea. In this tower I experimented on life and abused my power horribly.

—ANONYMOUS

The actions of the priest-scientists were a factor in the unpleasant situation before the catastrophe of 10,000 B.C., but the behavior of the people in Atlantis also contributed. During most of their long history, Atlanteans and Lemurians practiced the Law of One. They were compassionate in their relationships with others and lovingly cared for the Earth with respect and consideration. Gradually, as the emphasis on technology increased and focused on scientific achievement, they lost respect for nature and tried to assume control over it. Natural resources became something to be used for their own benefit.

When technology assumed a leading role in their lives, it had a dehumanizing effect. People became obsessed with acquiring additional things and moved to the cities, where tangible objects were more readily available. Toward the end many people spent more and more time focusing on facts and possessions. They substituted machinery for mental tools in a manner similar to our dependence on calculators and computers. As they further fragmented their awareness into the physical, they lost respect for what they could not perceive with their five senses and all that lies beyond the third dimensional environment. The spiritual quality of life became unimportant to them. As they separated from their Creator and searched elsewhere for love, moral standards declined; anger, greed, hate, and envy increased; and crime was prevalent. Sexual orgies, robbery, and murder were common events. The Sons of Belial treated the "things" as slaves.

Intense, vivid dreams helped me to learn and understand some of my past lives. One of the most interesting of these recollections involved my being a "thing" in Atlantis.

My first wife, Hanna, remembered being my mother in Atlantis (although that wasn't what she said the first time we discussed the matter). She remembered that in Atlantis she was married to a rich and powerful man, but she had an affair with one of the "things" who worked as houseboys. When she got pregnant, she wasn't sure whether the father was her husband or the houseboy, but unfortunately it turned out that the houseboy was the father, a fact which was revealed when I was born and I was obviously part simian (not fully human, part ape).

Her husband had the houseboy executed, and she (my mother) was supposed to be put to death, too, but it was finally decided that we should be exiled to the wilderness, where it was presumed the two of us would not survive for long. I remember living in the forest in Atlantis with that human mother and having an intuitive knowledge which enabled me to look after her for many years, but one day she got sick and died.

After she was gone, I continued to live in the wilderness, but I was lonely and soon ventured into an Atlantean city. A number of people there seemed to know more about me than I knew about myself. I even met a judge who had spoken out against executing my mother. I was much more intelligent than people expected me to be, and that judge helped me to seek training as a mathematician. I spent the balance of my life doing theoretical work that was highly regarded. I clearly remember the dominant pure-human Atlanteans using their mental powers to manipulate many of the "things."

What was weird about this particular dream and past life was that, in addition to my first wife Hanna, I have met five or six people who remembered their roles in that Atlantean story without my having to prompt them. A good friend in Denver

recalled that he was the executed houseboy, and another friend in New York remembered being the judge.
—ANONYMOUS

A correspondent suggests that dissension between the virtuous Children of the Law of One and the immoral followers of Belial contributed to the problems in another way.

I remember classes in the temple in Atlantis. We were taught spirituality and Cosmic Law which were the principles of the Children of the Law of One, but they were watered down and we weren't encouraged to remember them. We also learned the tenets of the Sons of Belial. The students who adopted the principles of the Sons of Belial got the easiest tests. If those who wished to follow the Law of One didn't change their minds, they were harassed both physically and mentally until many of them died or went insane. The final result was that the good people who should have been involved in the management of the Great Crystal never had the opportunity.
—ANONYMOUS

Invariably, the portrayal of the last days of Atlantis focuses on the corrupt, immoral state to which many of the people had fallen and asserts that it was at least partially responsible for the fate of the land. Plato describes the change in the people: "The portion of divinity in them became weak . . . they lost their comeliness, through being unable to bear the burden of their possessions, and grew ugly to look upon, in the eyes of him who has the gift of sight." He writes that "Zeus, the God of gods . . . marked how this righteous race was in evil plight, and desired to inflict punishment upon them." Cayce agrees that many of the inhabitants of Atlantis were so sinful that the elements combined to bring a conclusion to their dreadful actions.[13]

It is difficult for modern science to explain how the energy of emotions and thoughts have any effect on the forces of nature, but indigenous people knew and understood this concept. When rain was needed, shamans supervised specific melodious dances, chants, and prayers, and their strength drew energy from clouds. As the clouds dissolved, moisture fell to the thirsty land and people below. Societies maintained elaborate planting ceremonies during which they danced on the earth and even kissed it. As they danced they chanted, for they knew the combination of love, vibration, and sound was beneficial to the newly planted, living seeds, and to their beloved planet.

> *I am a carpenter and my father and grandfather were carpenters. My grandfather told me that long ago carpenters used their minds, he said "hypnotism," to move heavy objects.*
> —ANONYMOUS

This carpenter's statement emphasizes how little we understand about the powers of the mind. Some people are capable of moving small objects without touching them, and others know how to produce enough energy to bend forks and spoons. We realize that a focused mind, utilizing meditation and visualization, can sometimes relieve health problems as well as the unpleasant symptoms of stress.

Edgar Cayce tells us that thoughts are things or deeds, and they may become miracles. When many individuals concentrate on an identical desire or aspiration, the thought acquires additional power, and their intention gradually becomes reality. It is said that if you focus on a thought or feeling for at least seventeen seconds, without introducing a contrary image or emotion, your intention will be manifest in the physical world.

How is this possible? The process of creation starts with a thought or a conception. Thoughts are energy that travels through the atmosphere. As the currents of energy from our minds move around us, they give off signals. We know that thoughts are contagious between people and can produce mass hysteria. If a group of furious individuals assemble, their animosity creates a field of energy that affects others and soon the situation turns into an angry mob. In this same way unfavorable energy travels from this planet throughout the cosmos and disturbs the universe. In the final period of Atlantis, the unfavorable vibrations resulting from crime, immorality, and conflicts between groups of people over treatment of the "things" was extremely strong. As Plato and Cayce tell us, overpowering negative thoughts and actions disturbed the natural forces. A catastrophe sent the fertile land and the people who dwelt on it into the greedy ocean. If we are not careful, there is always the danger that our universe will choose to do with us as it did with Atlantis and Lemuria, wrinkle the Earth's skin like a dog with fleas, and destroy our civilization.

NOTES

1   Cayce, *Readings* 621–1 and 419–1.

2   Cayce, *Readings* 877–26.

3   Hatt, *The Maya*, p. 14.

4   Plato, *Timaeus*.

5   Troano Codex.

6   Churchward, *The Lost Continent of Mu.*

7   Cerve, *Lemuria*, p. 214.

8   Cayce, *Readings* 1473–1.

9   Brown, *The Riddle of the Pacific*, p. 54.

10 Darwin quote from chapter 8 of *The Voyage of the Beagle*; http://www.literature.org/authors/darwin-charles/the-voyage-of-the-beagle/chapter-08.html.

11 Muck, *The Secret of Atlantis*, p. viii.

12 Churchward, *The Lost Continent of Mu.*

13 Cayce, *Readings* 5750–1.

16

OTHER
CIVILIZATIONS

IN ABOUT 570 B.C., WHEN
Athenian lawyer Solon, "the wisest of the
Seven Sages," went to Egypt to study history, the priests he consulted told Solon
that natural disasters had obliterated almost all tangible information of the civilizations of the past. The learned Egyptians
said that there have been, and there will be,
many destructions of human beings, the
greatest by fire and water. The priests told
Solon about Atlantis and the sacred knowledge, which was eventually passed down to
Plato who, toward the end of his life, revealed it for us.

Plato's fame as a scholar and his admirable writing skills ensured that knowledge of the Atlantean people would survive
for us, and Colonel Churchward's discovery of recorded information about the
Motherland of Mu has helped to preserve
the memory of that superior civilization.

Data about the countries that preceded, coexisted with, or closely followed Lemuria and Atlantis is not as readily available, and most pieces of the puzzle are still missing. However, researchers are slowly collecting enough details to confirm that those two civilizations were not alone. Prior to 10,000 B.C., spiritually and technically evolved people, who were very similar to ourselves, thrived throughout the world.

Edgar Cayce tells us that at an international conference in 50,722 B.C., representatives from five countries assembled in Atlantis to discuss a permanent solution to the problem of the omnipresent dangerous wild animals that were overrunning the Earth. The Atlanteans provided transportation to their country in what may have been the first flying vehicles, airships that contained gas and resembled balloons.[1] People from Lemuria, the Uighur Empire in the Gobi, west and north Africa, and the Carpathian Mountains of central Europe came to the first conference. Delegates from Peru and India were included in later meetings.

SOUTH AMERICA

Edgar Cayce offers information about some of the first Lemurians to flee to Peru, which he also referred to as Oz, Og, or On. They came after the earth changes of 50,000 B.C., and soon built new homes and temples. Religion was the main focus of their lives. As priests, priestesses, ministers, and teachers, they excelled in music, art, and the braiding of beads and designing of jewelry from abundant precious stones and metals. After many, many years the Ohlms, as Cayce calls them, designed an excellent system of democratic self-government, which was to influence governments throughout the world.[2]

Hundreds of years later, when Atlanteans arrived in Peru, the leader of the Ohlms was a weak person given to sexual excesses.

After a brief war, the Atlanteans took over and taught the Law of One, mined gold and silver, and built walls across mountains.[3]

Dramatic changes in the land have altered the topography of South America, but megalithic constructions remain to demonstrate the skills of the advanced human beings of long ago who lived in an extensive chain of cities which stretched as far north as Columbia. The buildings in these cities, with their many-sided enormous stones tightly arranged in earthquake-resistant patterns, were similar to those of the massive city of Tiahuanaco, which thrived on the banks of Lake Titicaca during the time of Mu and Atlantis.[4] The Incas did not construct as many buildings as the previous mysterious civilization. They used small rectangular stones and often placed their temples on top of the ancient, larger structures of their predecessors.

A "Garden of the Gods" on the Marcahuasi Plateau high in the Andes provides additional evidence of the prehistoric occupants of South America. Here, burial tombs and stupendous sculptures carved from granite cover an area of several square miles. The statues represent a variety of birds, animals, and human races. Some are so large that it is believed they were made by giants at least twelve feet tall. The descendants of the native Huanaca in this area describe the strange place as the home of the wizards and Giant Gods.[5]

Lake Titicaca, the highest navigable lake in the world, lies partly in Peru and partly in Bolivia. Today it is 13,500 feet above the Pacific Ocean, but once it was at sea level, 460 miles long and 30 to 100 miles wide. A canal from the lake gave access to the Pacific Ocean. A variety of oceanic plants still live in its brackish water. Nearby Lake Poopo and Lake Coipassa are also salty and were once included in gigantic Lake Titicaca.

In an ancient monastery in western Tibet, Col. Churchward found a map of South America on a large tablet. The person who made the map drew a group of constellations on it to indicate its

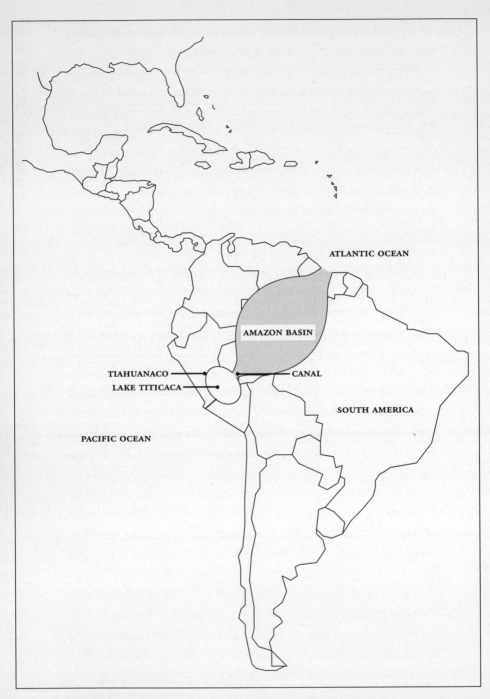

ROUTE FROM PACIFIC OCEAN TO ATLANTIC OCEAN AS DESCRIBED
BY COL. CHURCHWARD IN "THE CHILDREN OF MU"

date, and astronomers said those stars were in that position 25,000 years ago. The age-old map shows the present Amazon Basin as a huge inland sea, comparable to the Mediterranean today, with a narrow opening to the Atlantic Ocean, and a short canal from the basin to Tiahuanaco. Churchward believes the crumpled remains of the canal that connected Tiahuanaco with the Amazon Basin may be seen on the tops of the mountains which now stand between the city and the Amazon.[6] Traces of another canal which formed a boundary of the city and continued on to the Pacific Ocean are visible today,[7] as are docks for ships, cut from solid rocks,[8] with rings on them, which served as attachments for cables for fastening oceangoing vessels.[9]

Before movements of the Earth's crust pushed Tiahuanaco far above the level of the sea, people traveled in boats from one ocean to the other across the South American continent. Edgar Cayce makes several references to those who went back and forth between Mu and Atlantis, often to discuss principles of human behavior. The city of Tiahuanaco was a favorite destination. When Spanish friars discovered the ruins of the city in the sixteenth century, signs and symbols from the Far East indicated people from all over the world visited and inhabited the magnificent metropolis.

On the top of a truncated pyramid, the citizens of Tiahuanaco built the largest Sun Temple in the world, complete with an astronomical observatory. When German-Bolivian Professor Arthur Posnansky of the University of La Paz carefully studied its stone calendar, he determined that at the time the observatory was abandoned in 9550 B.C., the astronomers were studying the North Star.[10]

The Spanish were amazed to see that artisans had embellished buildings throughout the ancient city with gold and silver, including silver bolts weighing over three tons that served as rivets in huge monoliths.[11] Remains of lifelike sculptures of citizens holding upraised drinking glasses lined the pleasant lake shore.[12]

The Gateway of the Sun, one of the largest carved monolithic structures in the world, displays some of the skills of Tiahunaco's prehistoric citizens. The expert craftsmen cut the gate, which is over thirteen feet wide and nine feet high, from a solid block of thick andesite. Andesite, the material of most of the stonework at Tiahuanaco, is an extremely hard rock which blunts all but the strongest steel tools. In addition to our inability to understand how they accurately cut blocks of andesite weighing over eighty tons, no one really understands how the builders of Tiahuanaco moved the huge stones into position from quarries that were many miles away.

Space shuttle imaging indicates that we have excavated only a small fraction of the magnificent city of Tiahuanaco, and that 90 percent of it is below ground. As we penetrate the remains of its five layers of civilizations, we will gradually learn more about those who lived in this beautiful city so long ago.

UIGHUR EMPIRE

The wild and barren Gobi Desert in northeast Asia was once a fertile and beautiful land, where the Uighur Empire prospered during the time of Lemuria and Atlantis. The magnificent cities of the Gobi, including the capital of Kara Khota, are well remembered in Far Eastern stories and legends. From the Chinese we know that the successful Uighur Empire was at its height around 17,000 B.C., and it spread from the Pacific westward through Asia and northern Europe.[13]

After struggling to dig down through fifty feet of gravel, boulders, and sand, Russian explorers finally uncovered ruins of Kara Khota south of Lake Baikal. From remnants in the city, archaeologists determined that the Uighurs knew astrology, mathematics, writing, reading, and medicine. They mined extensively, made textiles, and engaged in agriculture. Long before the history of Egypt began, the Uighurs made statues of gold, silver, bronze, and clay and were experts in decorating silk, metals, and wood.[14]

Atlantean priestesses frequently traveled to the distant land of the Uighurs to minister to the people and teach them the power of right and wrong.[15] They worked together with the Lemurians, who joined them to teach the tenets of the Law of One. The two cultures are memorialized in an ancient painting of a Uighur queen and her consort. Poseidon's trident, a symbol of Atlantis, appears with the queen, and lotus buds, symbolic of the land of Mu, are arranged at her feet.[16] Cayce's references to a City of Gold, a Temple of Gold, and a Temple of the Sun in Mongoloid land[17] lend support to the Chinese legends that describe the prosperity of the Uighur Empire in the Gobi in the distant past.

When the biblical flood destroyed the eastern half of the Uighur land, the few people who remained were reduced to living in extremely primitive conditions.[18] Today the desert's shifting sands cover the bones of these talented people and their long-forsaken cities, but some day space satellites will detect additional enlightening evidence of them beneath the desert floor.

Many believe that Shambala, the home of highly evolved mystics and scholars who exist in another dimension, is positioned over the Gobi Desert.[19] Esoteric tradition adds that when their land disappeared, Lemurian priests migrated to Shambala, where the highest known vibrations on our planet make it possible for them to more easily contact spiritual realms.

RAMA EMPIRE

Ancient Greek, Egyptian, Mexican, Hindu, and mystical writings all portray the Rama Empire, which once prospered in the Indus Valley of Pakistan and northern India.[20] The Vedas, as described in the preface, offer the most extensive information about the Ramas' advanced civilization. The seven greatest cities of the Rama are often referred to as "Rishi cities." In Sanskrit, *Rishi* means "Master or Great Teacher,"which relates to the highly developed mental and psychic skills of the Rama leaders.[21] Dravidian, the Rama's undeciphered writing, is almost identical to the script of Easter Island, thousands of miles to the southeast,[22] which suggests a connection with the Motherland of Mu.

The intelligent Rama developed flying vehicles called vimanas.[23] In about the fourth century B.C., Bharadwaja the Wise compiled information about the vimanas from at least eighty earlier texts and Vedic epics for his book *Vaimanika Shasta*. Scholars, who found the *Vaimanika Shasta* in 1918 in the Barbuda Royal Sanskrit Library north of Bombay, have verified the authenticity of Bharadwaja's work as well as the manuscripts he consulted when he assembled it.[24]

The *Vaimanika Shasta* includes elaborate descriptions of two- and three-decker planes, cargo-carrying aircraft similar to helicopters, and passenger planes capable of transporting 400 to 500 people. It even furnishes detailed directions for building the flying vehicles, including accurate dimensions and descriptions of what type of metal would be most suitable for various parts. Bharadwaja's monumental work includes elaborate instructions for training pilots to fly the vimanas, functions the vehicles could fulfill and more.[25] The well-known *Mahabharata* and the *Ramayana*, compiled from ancient temple records, contain further extensive information about the vimanas of the Rama Empire.

Chants and dances which the Pueblo, the Yaqui, and other Native Americans have passed down describe a long-lasting conflict between the Atlanteans and the people of a lost empire in the Indian Ocean. The war took place when the glaciers were still large,[26] about 20,000 years ago.

Esoteric tradition describes one encounter in this conflict between the Ramas and the Atlanteans and a strange way in which the wisdom of the Ramas overcame their foes from the Atlantic Ocean. In their search for more land, the Atlanteans, who are referred to as the "Asvins," once attempted to take over the capitol city of the Rama. The Indian ruler declared that, although the Rama only believed in peace, they would never succumb to the aggressive army of Atlantis. The Atlantean soldiers completely ignored him and, despite the Rama's sincere and numerous attempts to avoid a battle, they proceeded to advance toward the city. At that point, the Rama priest-king raised his arms and, using a powerful mental technique which certain yogis in the Himalayas understand today, caused the leaders of the invading Atlanteans to drop dead one by one. It was as if huge rocks were falling on their heads from a great height and, as a result of the blow, their hearts just stopped beating. The remaining, terrified Atlanteans quickly retreated to their waiting valix (aircraft) and flew away.[27]

Archaeologists in India have recently begun to excavate Kot Diji and Harappa and the nine or more layers of civilization at Mohenjo Daro. They've discovered that residents of two of these ancient cities enjoyed running water, indoor toilets, and covered sewers.[28] The level archaeologists are working at currently dates to about 3,000 B.C., but scientists have recently discovered an underwater city off the northwestern coast of India with a similar grid-style layout which thrived 9,500 years ago. This city, which is in about 120 feet of water, is five miles long and contains the oldest known group of manmade structures in the world.[29] As research continues, modern equipment will undoubtedly produce evidence of life in the Pacific during the time of the Motherland of Mu.

ANTARCTICA

The continent of Antarctica, which was not rediscovered until 1818, was once a land without snow and ice. Copies of ancient maps portray its lakes, rivers, and mountains as they are today beneath the glaciers. Some day we may find and explore the homes and buildings of seafaring Lemurians and Atlanteans who happily lived in Antarctica before unending snow suddenly covered the land.

A recent book that describes Antarctica as Plato's Atlantis is filled with ifs and maybes. Its authors' proposal that the plates of the Earth shifted from time to time is probable, but that an island which Plato describes as lying "within the mouth of the Pillars of Heracles" (the Straits of Gibraltar) moved to the present location of Antarctica is difficult to comprehend. Plato says the sea swallowed the island of Atlantis, but Antarctica is still above the surface, it did not sink.

OSIRIAN CIVILIZATION

Long ago, the area the Mediterranean Sea now covers was dry, fertile land. The Nile River was known as the River Stix, and it flowed through Africa as it does today, but continued on to a lake in the Mediterranean valley. From the lake, the river moved foreward and flowed into the Atlantic Ocean at the Pillars of Heracles.[30] Legends say that during the time of Atlantis the Osirian people lived around the large lake in this attractive Mediterranean valley. Over 200 of the Osirian's megalithic buildings are visible today on the floor of the Mediterranean.

Little is known about this civilization, although it is assumed that the Osirian religion of Egypt, which focused around Osiris, originated with them.[31] Osiris, the Egyptian god of the dead, is portrayed as a mummy with his hands out of the wrappings and holding the symbols of a ruler. Myths about Osiris often connect him with water, either drowning in the Nile or submerged in water and then coming forth with life-giving moisture and fertilizing power. Perhaps this symbolizes the fate of the Osirians. When ocean levels rose about 10,000 B.C. and earthquakes changed the land at the Straits of Gibraltar, water from the Atlantic Ocean poured in and flooded the peoples' cities. Those who could, quickly moved to the higher ground of Egypt and other surrounding lands.

On the island of Malta, ancient ruins offer evidence of the advanced people who once lived there. Numerous large monuments and structures, built with huge blocks of stone, are sometimes arranged in patterns. Ancient tracks on Malta are carved into the rocks on flat areas, and even on hillsides. The tracks form a network over the whole island, and some of them descend directly into the sea to the remnants of Osirian cities. Like railroad tracks, the mysterious ruts are parallel and equidistant, always curving and straightening together. Undeciphered writing on stone tablets in Malta will probably offer information about the strange tracks and those who formed them.

EGYPT

When the first Atlanteans arrived in Egypt they failed to perceive the spiritual qualities of the native people. They thought the Egyptians were ignorant and inferior because they were not technologically advanced.[32] This is similar to the way the Europeans assessed the inhabitants of Central and South America in the sixteenth century, whose civilizations were superior to theirs in many ways.

The land of Egypt was attractive, however, and Atlantean families continued to flee there from the unstable Atlantic Ridge. In their new homeland, they joined existing communities, worked in the schools and hospitals,[33] and struggled to gain political power.[34] The Atlanteans in Egypt even engaged in archaeological activities as they searched for evidence of prior inhabitants.[35] They built a Temple of Sacrifice and a Temple Beautiful, whose activities offered a focus for those who wanted to devote themselves to helping the less fortunate and improving the lives of others. Preservation of Atlantean records, which will be discussed in chapter 18, was a full-time occupation for many of the newcomers.

Cayce tells us that Lemurians also moved to Egypt.[36] As a result of extensive research, Churchward believes that the original Egyptians were Lemurians and Nagas who established a colony in the fertile delta of the Upper Nile, whereas the first Atlanteans lived in the Lower Nile Valley.[37] (The word "Naga" comes from Cambodia, where at Ankor Wat the carved forms of the Great Seven-Headed Serpents are referred to as Naga. Churchward believes the design, which symbolizes the Great Creator of all worlds, came from the Motherland of Lemuria when people moved to the Asian continent thousands of years ago. *Nagas* refers to descendants of those Lemurians who settled on the mainland, and in this case moved to the Upper Nile.) After some conflicts, the two cultures combined and the country became a spiritual, scientific, and cultural center.

NOTES

1   Cayce, *Readings* 953–24.

2   Robinson, *Edgar Cayce's Story of the Origin and Destiny of Man.*

3   Ibid.

4   Sykes, *Atlantis*, Volume 4, No. 4, 1951.

5   Brother Philip, *Secret of the Andes*, pp. 58–60.

6   Churchward, *The Children of Mu*, pp. 80–82.

7   Sykes, *Atlantis*, Volume 4, No. 4, 1951.

8   Steiger, *Atlantis Rising*, p. 17.

9   Tomas, *The Home of the Gods*, p. 1.

10 Hansen, *The Ancient Atlantic*, p. 422.

11 Wilkins, *Mysteries of Ancient South America*, p. 189.

12 Ibid., p. 188.

13 Churchward, *The Lost Continent of Mu.*

14 Ibid.

15 Cayce, *Readings* 1273–1, 1648–1, 3420–1.

16 Churchward, Ibid., p. 162.

17 Cayce, *Readings* 1648–1.

18 Churchward, Ibid., p. 291.

19 Milanovitch, *Sacred Journey to Atlantis*, p. 145.

20 Childress, *Lost Cities of China, Central Asia, and India*, p. 218.

21 Ibid.

22 Berlitz, *Mysteries from Forgotten Worlds*, pp. 128–129.

23 Childress, Ibid.

24 Childress, *Vimana Aircraft of Ancient India & Atlantis*, pp. 34–36.

25 Ibid., p. i of Foreword.

26 Hansen, *The Ancient Atlantic*, p. 307.

27 The information in this paragraph is from Childress, *Lost Cities of China, Central Asia & India*, p. 243.

28 Childress, *Lost Cities of Atlantis, Ancient Europe & the Mediterranean*, p. 15.

29 Little, *Ancient Mysteries*, April 2002.

30 Childress, Ibid., p. 27.

31 De Camp, *Lost Continents*, p. 98.

32 Cayce, Edgar Evans, *Mysteries of Atlantis Revisited*, p. 125.

33 Cayce, *Readings* 516–2, 500–1.

34 Robinson, *Edgar Cayce's Story of the Origin and Destiny of Man*, p. 77.

35 Cayce, *Readings* 2799–1.

36 Cayce, *Readings* 1472–10.

37 Churchward, *The Children of Mu.*

17

SEARCHING FOR LEMURIA AND ATLANTIS

OVER THIRTY OF THE ISLANDS in the Pacific, which once provided shelter- to Lemurians and their descendants, continue to turn the clock back as they display evidence of the people of ancient advanced civilizations who lived on them. Remains of megalithic buildings of the past lie on the Maldives, Vinapu, the Marquesas, the Carolines, the New Hebrides, the Mariana group, Yap, Truk, Rarotonga, Lele, Kiribti, New Caledonia, and many other islands. In Hawaii petroglyphs enhance stones in Kauai, Oahu, and Kaunolu Lanai. Giant platforms in Molokai, Tahiti, Huahine Island, Tonga, and Easter Island stir one's curiosity about the lives of the ancient people who constructed them so long ago. The pyramids of Rapa Iti Island, the Marquesas, Huahine Island and Guam, Rota, and Saipan in the Marianas remind us of their builders' impressive knowledge. In a manner similar to the coast of the Yucatan, mysterious roads on Pacific Islands lead down into the sea. Archaeologists will eventually reconsider the myths of native people who claim their distant ancestors lived in the Motherland of Mu.

The innumerable megalithic ruins in the Pacific present concrete evidence of the skilled people who once lived there, but Plato's description of the great capitol city of Atlantis is what inspires many explorers today. The search for tangible evidence of Atlantis occupies the time and thoughts of numerous people, just as it has since 350 B.C. when Plato wrote about the extraordinary civilization on land outside the Straits of Gibraltar. Although Plato describes buildings of stone whose chances of survival are much greater than our concrete structures with their metal framework, it is extremely difficult to find ruins on the Atlantic Ridge where layers of lava that has erupted in the last 12,000 years often cover the ocean floor.

In many places the seabed is over a mile below the surface, so submarines, such as deepdiving *Alvin* from Woods Hole, have been the only means of careful investigation. *Alvin* is a small vehicle which holds three or four people who sit in a cramped position and look through a circular window only three and a half inches in diameter. The view opens outward, but it is very limited. During their short time inside the small submarine, the occupants are restricted to a camera, notebook, tape recorder, lunch, musical tapes, and warm clothes. In the Mediterranean, where it was considerably easier to search than on the Atlantic Ridge, *Alvin* was helpful in locating a lost hydrogen bomb but, although it has two external robot arms to grasp and break off rock samples for later analysis, it has made little progress on the Atlantic Ridge.

In spite of the difficulties, like persistent dandelions whose bright yellow flowers appear overnight, detailed glowing accounts of remains near the Atlantic Ridge continue to circulate on the Internet. A site 250 miles southwest of the Azores in 2,800 feet of water is said to contain structures, circular canals, and bridges. Nearby mountains rise within 300 feet of the surface. Reports describe military ships flying a United States flag which seem to be guarding the area, so inspection of these intriguing formations is not possible.[1]

I grew up in Poland and we learned about Atlantis in school there.
—ANONYMOUS

In eastern Europe scholars and scientists who focus on Atlantis research are highly respected by their colleagues, and for many years the Russians have actively searched for the lost country. In 1974 Russian investigators photographed some ruins in the Atlantic Ocean which they claim are on the Amphere Seamount near Madeira. These include five steps and a platform with blocks that are about five feet square. In the photos the ruins are quite visible, but dense masses of seaweed and sea fans are growing on them. In 1978 the pictures finally appeared in a Russian magazine which is similar to our *Life* magazine. The photographers, who were on a Soviet research ship, the S.S. *Petrovsky,* included a scientist from the Russian Institute of Oceanography and another who was a specialist in underwater photography. The ship was equipped with elaborate lighting equipment and a special camera.

Egerton Sykes was intrigued by the photographs and carefully analyzed them. In his opinion, the S.S. *Petrovsky* was a Russian spy ship and the pictures were taken near the Azores between Santa Maria and Sao Jorge, where the Russians should not have been. Sykes believed the Russians released only a small number of their photographs, and there are 100 or more additional steps which lead downwards from those in the pictures. He concluded that the platform and steps were part of a structure similar to a Mayan pyramid.[2] Russian geologist Viatcheslav Koudriavtsev believes remains of Atlantis lie in relatively shallow regions on the Celtic Shelf west of the southwestern tip of Great Britain. He points out that the ley line which runs for hundreds of miles in southern England, through Avebury to Land's End in Cornwall, leads directly to this area.[3] Legends say the land of Lyonnaise, with its beautiful cities, fertile lands, and a noble race of people, was once located in this submerged area. In 1998 a Russian expedition spent time on the Celtic Shelf searching for Atlantis without spectacular results.

Plato's circular city, with its canals and tremendous palaces and temples, may never be found, but Edgar Cayce says records of the Atlantean civilization and information about the construction of the crystal are in three locations. One is in a temple beneath the sea near Bimini, another is in Central America under a temple, and the third is in a Hall of Records near the Sphinx in Egypt.[4] Deep memories of ancient times, and hopes of recapturing them, have led numerous searchers to the three locations.

Lava does not cover the ocean floor in the Caribbean as it does the Atlantic Ridge, but ever-shifting sands produce a substantial problem. Portions of objects tantalizingly appear and almost immediately disappear when blankets of sand cover them during the next storm. In spite of this, stone buildings and walls Atlanteans constructed in Poseidia when the thousands of square miles of the Bahama Bank were dry land are slowly revealing themselves. If the water level around Bimini were to drop, many secrets would be uncovered.

In 1933 Edgar Cayce foresaw that in 1968 or 1969 a portion of an Atlantean temple would rise in the vicinity of Bimini. When that time came, airplane pilot Bob Brush reported sighting what appeared to be cut stone blocks and columns under the surface north of Andros Island, about fifty miles to the west of Nassau in the Bahamas and 150 miles east of Bimini.

It has been said that the tongue of the ocean lies at Andros, the largest island in the Bahamas. As a former citizen of the Bahamas who once lived in Andros, I know for a fact that there are several "black holes," inexplicable ponds or "spring puddles," and caves on that island, and that the ocean surrounding Andros is very deep with mysterious occurrences that the locals simply dismiss as pure folklore. As a child growing up in the islands, I am personally aware of what has become known as UFO sightings, but back then they were dismissed by American military personnel and media as something to do with meteorites.
—ANONYMOUS

Andros Island is the site of the Atlantic Undersea Test and Evaluation Center (AUTEC), and although this top-secret base occupies only one square mile of land on the island, it also includes over 1,000 square miles of the surrounding Caribbean. AUTEC tests underwater weapons systems, but many believe that in this area the United States government is conducting secret research on UFOs. This would help to account for the numerous sightings of unidentified flying objects around Andros Island.

The ocean waters near Andros are known for their strange "blue holes." Blue holes are small openings of fresh water, apparently formed from within. The unusual energy they exhibit leads to the belief that they are related to microwormholes. It is suggested that blue holes are "star gates" and offer the opportunity to access another dimension, although star gates usually do not move and blue holes tend to fluctuate in and out of existence. Perhaps they are a remnant of the powerful energy Atlantean scientists once manipulated in this area.

Dr. J. Manson Valentine, one of the first archaeologists to search for prior civilizations in the Bahamas, was often accompanied by his friend Bob Brush, who was an amateur photographer. The pictures Bob Brush took have proven very valuable to those who are exploring anamolies off the coasts of Andros Island today.

Valentine also reported the flooded caves with stalactites that he found on an underwater plateau southwest of Andros Island. More recently, Jacques Cousteau partially explored these caverns, as described in chapter 4. Hopefully, scuba divers will investigate the concealed caverns near Andros Island, for Egerton Sykes believed the crystal skull was not the only Atlantean treasure in the Bimini area and that other precious objects are hidden in nearby caves, some of which are now under the sea.

In April of 2003 husband-wife research team Drs. Greg and Lora Little announced they had discovered a gigantic stone platform off the north coast of Andros Island in twelve feet of water.[5] The three-tiered structure is composed of large, thick, rectangular blocks placed on top of other blocks, side by side in rows. The Littles' extensive research did not reveal any similarities to beach rock or any type of reef, and they assume that the structure is man-made. At Andros the Littles also inspected what appear to be ancient remains of a stone temple on a high overlook. Continued investigations in the vicinity of Andros will verify that thousands of years ago, during the Ice Age, an advanced civilization lived on the Bahama Bank.

Edgar Cayce's suggestion that if geologists and archaeologists explore under the sea water near Bimini they will discover Atlantean ruins[6] has inspired interested investigators to focus in that area. In 1968, a group of divers led by Dr. Valentine discovered an unusual formation of massive stone rocks near the west coast of Bimini. The site, at a depth of fifteen to twenty feet, is easily accessible to scuba divers. Large stones, some of them eight feet square or rectangular or irregular in shape, lie in adjoining rows on the ocean floor in the shape of an immense reversed J.

Many of the sizable rocks with square corners appear to have been shaped by man. Some of the blocks lie on top of others. There is a Bimini story that these were once layers of rocks, but a man from Miami carried them off and they were used to build jetties on the southeast coast. The blocks of stone, which are often referred to as the "Bimini Road," resemble the remains of a prehistoric passageway or wall which does not run parallel to the sea coast.

Recent satellite mapping of the shallow waters of the Bahama Bank to the east of Bimini reveals large (over 200 feet wide) geometric patterns of turtle grass in the shapes of pentagons and rectangles with perfectly square corners. It is believed that whatever is causing these turtle grass configurations is twelve to fifteen feet beneath the sand-covered ocean floor. Excavations of the sand to that depth would be difficult and have not yet been attempted. Further analysis of them is costly and difficult because these apparent ruins are only visible from the air, but researchers are using submersibles and global positioning devices to locate a variety of sites, including some Manson Valentine identified many years ago. Side-scan sonar would be helpful in some situations, but it costs many thousands of dollars to lease for one day, and in many instances the water is too shallow to tow the sonar device.

Edgar Cayce also advised those who were searching for remains of Atlantis in the Bahamas to look in the vicinity of the nearby Gulf Stream.[7] Investigators from the GAEA Project who are working in that area hired professional technical divers, and they photographed what appear to be streets, pillars, and terraces. The objects are covered with sea fans and almost impenetrable coral, and are in 180 to 300 feet of water. If the pictures are verified, they will lend support to the proposition that intelligent persons once lived here.[8] GAEA stands for Global Approach to Earth Antiquities and is the ancient Greek name for the Earth Mother Goddess. "Gaia" is the Roman spelling for the same goddess.

Vestiges of a former civilization in the mangrove swamps of East Bimini include the apparent remains of a rectangular temple, a large mound in the shape of a cat or perhaps a sperm whale or a lemon shark. The shallow water in the vicinity of these ruins

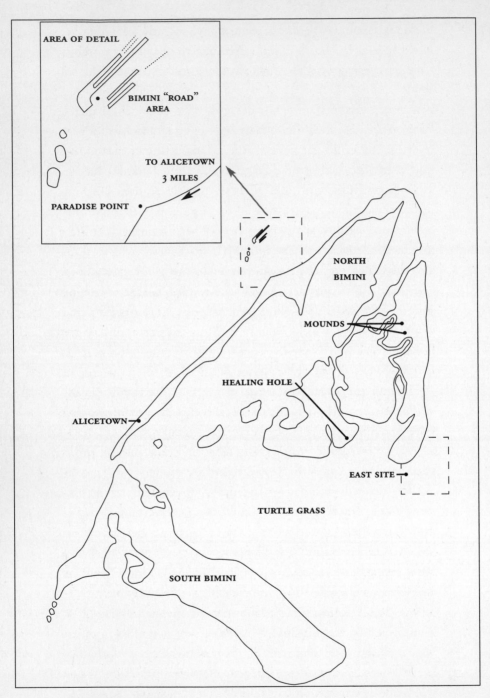

AREA OF DETAIL

BIMINI "ROAD" AREA

TO ALICETOWN
3 MILES

PARADISE POINT

NORTH BIMINI

MOUNDS

HEALING HOLE

ALICETOWN

EAST SITE

TURTLE GRASS

SOUTH BIMINI

THE BIMINI ISLANDS

makes it necessary to travel in a small boat, so entrance and exit to the area must be timed with the tides. Swarms of hungry mosquitoes make one's presence extremely unpleasant. To add to the difficulties, ground-penetrating radar, which costs $2,000 to $3,000 a day, is relatively ineffective because of the high water table. In spite of the problems, members of the GAEA Project consider Bimini to be the most promising archaeological undertaking of this century and that they will find, as Edgar Cayce said, evidence that Atlanteans and their descendants lived and thrived here for thousands of years.

Archaeologists from Brigham Young University have spent time uncovering ruins in a remote area in northern Guatemala, where they hope to find indications of Jewish families from remnants of the Lost Tribes, whom they believe reached Central America around 3,000 B.C. A variety of clues led these fearless searchers to fight their way through dangerous rapids and travel up the Usamacinta River to where the deserted ruins of the Mayan city of Piedras Negras lie amidst deadly snakes, ticks, scorpions, and dense jungle growth. An interpretation of Edgar Cayce's readings suggests the possibility that Piedras Negras may be one of the sites where Atlanteans carefully concealed their records.[9]

Atlanteans undoubtedly hid records and treasures in the numerous dark caves that honeycomb Central America, but entering many of them is difficult because pyramids and temples are constructed over their secret entrances. Robbing caves has proved to be a lucrative business, for illegal sales of ancient artifacts contribute much-needed financial support to local people. However, some caverns with unusual energy, such as Actun Tunichil Muknal in Belize, have not been touched for many, many centuries. The Maya, sensing their spiritual nature and considering them to be sacred, respect them and do not disturb them. Predecessors of the Maya also left them alone, for they regarded caves as foul, gloomy places that were sacred entrances to the underworld. Only secret rituals were permitted inside the hidden underground rooms.

Intrepid investigators from Earthwatch Institute are attempting to explore the vast cave network of Central America, but searching is not pleasant. Assassin beetles, botflies, and spiders of all sorts, including tarantulas and barking spiders, consider the caverns to be their homes and do not welcome intruders. Che Chem or poison-wood, which is worse than poison ivy, often guards entrances to the enticing underground world, hoping to assault the unwary intruder. Inside the caves, tortuous passages, very steep stepwork, and sudden dropoffs in darkness that were meant to cause confusion add to the difficulties of exploration.

When North American glaciers rapidly melted and sent torrents of water racing down the Mississippi River, the level of the Gulf of Mexico quickly rose. Before long, seawater covered thousands of square miles of dry land. When the dreadful waters threatened, in a futile effort to keep out the floods that endangered their precious homes, desperate descendants of Atlanteans employed their engineering skills to build Cyclopean walls. Extensive fortifications, some with huge blocks of stone, are visible underwater near Mexico, northern Cuba, and Florida. Adjacent to Venezuela, another substantial wall, thirty feet high, reaches for miles into the sea.

For fifty years, airplane pilots and scuba divers have reported artifacts and stonework in the shallow waters near the coasts of Cuba, but until recently no one has had access to the modern technology of underwater archaeology that is capable of providing the means to examine and verify the ruins. Off the western end of Cuba, scientists from Canada's Advanced Digital Communications Company, known as ADC, have the assistance of a satellite-integrated ocean bottom positioning system, two-person submersibles, remote operated video recorders, and side-scan sonar. Side-scan sonar, which is called a "fish," looks like a torpedo. As the "fish" is dragged behind a boat, highpitched sounds from either side of it hit rocks and sand below and reflect them back as an image. A video imaging camera is necessary to distinguish metal from stone, and since it is very dark one-half mile under the surface, strong lighting equipment must accompany cameras.

Paulina Zelitsky of ADC reports seeing from above what appears to be a submerged megalithic city not far from Cuba with "shapes that resemble pyramids, roads, and buildings."[10] At a depth of 2,100 feet, the area covers about 7.7 square miles. Many thousands of years ago, when the land was above the surface, the underwater structures in this area were erected with huge stones as large as six feet square and sixteen feet high. Using sonar and underwater robots, U. S. and Cuban scientists have obtained additional information. An anthropologist with the Cuban Academy of Sciences, whom the ADC consulted, pointed out that some of the images contain signs and inscriptions.[11] Those who have seen photographs of the inscriptions report that they are hieroglyphic signs, similar to some found on Central and South American structures and in caves in the Canary Islands and the Loltun Caverns, which no one has successfully deciphered.

Cayce often describes the work of the Atlanteans who heeded the warnings of the prophets, anticipated the destruction of their country, and went to Egypt to preserve information about their sciences, the arts, their ceremonies, the construction of the fire-stone, and all other aspects of their civilization. His specific description of the location of this secret storage place of Atlantean information on the Giza Plateau in Egypt has encouraged scientists from all over the world to focus on the area.

My father's cousin is a leading Egyptologist and I believe they now know of the "Hall of Records" existence and are refusing to allow any access to actually doing the archaeological dig on it. I have tried to contact him through my father and he takes the attitude that all Egyptologists seem to have, that my beliefs of Egyptian-Atlantean connections are ridiculous! Well, I guess Troy, the crystal skull, the ancient computer remnants discovered in the Aegean Sea, and space travel are all figments of my imagination! I think he is ridiculous for not even taking the time to talk about the possibilities of this "Hall." Fox did a cheesy TV show on Egypt's pyramids, etc., and they actually showed access tunnels under the Sphinx and suggested they led to the Hall of Records, yet the leading Egyptologist doing the show discounted its importance despite the overwhelming evidence that points to even a shred of possibility.

—ANONYMOUS

Cayce said the Atlanteans' information is in a Hall of Records that can be accessed through an entrance under the right forepaw of the Sphinx. The Egyptians have been reluctant to allow an extensive investigation because they believe the advanced civilization of ancient Egypt was not the product of a superior race who came there from elsewhere: it originated and grew in their country. However, the international search continues. Until now, ground-penetrating radar, pneumatic cameras, and sonic devices have disclosed only coffins and debris in the numerous tunnels that interlace the Giza Plateau, but hope of discovering the well-hidden information never dies.

NOTES

1 www.ancientamerican.com/issue41.html.

2 Hope, *Atlantis: Myth or Reality?*, pp. 84–89.

3 www.geocities.com

4 Cayce, *Readings* 2012–1.

5 The Littles are associated with the Association for Research & Enlighten-ment, the international headquarters for the work of Edgar Cayce.

6 Cayce, *Readings* 587–4 and 440–5.

7 Cayce, *Readings* 364–3.

8 www.gaeaproject.com.

9 For more information on the explorations in Piedras Negras, see *The Lost Hall of Records* by John Van Auken and Lora Little.

10 Paulina Zelitsky, interview with Reuters of London, May 14, 2001.

11 *El Nuevo Herald*, "Sunken City Resurrects Atlantis Myth," December 16, 2001.

18

RESTORING THE
GOLDEN AGE

DURING MOST OF THEIR LONG
histories, the citizens of Lemuria and Atlantis were enlightened and connected
with their source. They remembered their
previous lives and understood who they
were, why they were on the Earth, and
how to serve others. Although this is not
the prevailing situation today, it is possible
to return to this Golden Age of the distant
past. Many people are working hard to
make it a reality and each of us may contribute to the effort.

Cayce describes an elaborate ceremony
that took place in 10,500 B.C. when a
group assembled to seal information in the
Hall of Records in Egypt. With the assistance of incense from the temple altars,
the priests carefully worked to cleanse the
minds and alleviate the bodily desires of
the participants.[1] This suggests that those

who enclosed knowledge in sacred places were being prepared to move into another state of consciousness.

Edgar Cayce cautions that we will not be capable of comprehending the information in the Atlantean record chambers until we have the necessary understanding,[2] which may be interpreted to mean until we are more spiritually developed—until we return to the higher frequencies of the early Lemurians and Atlanteans. To interpret the concept of our reaching a higher vibrational tone, it is necessary to believe that we are spiritual beings, not simply a material body, and that it is possible to sense and experience more than the three-dimensional world that we see, feel, and touch.

Ancient cultures were well aware of other worlds, and their healers often contacted this spiritual realm from whence they obtained assistance. Most well-known is the Brazilian who, when asked the source of his amazingly successful plant remedies, replied that it came from the Other World, where he went when in a trance or hypnotic state. Edgar Cayce easily put himself into a trance-like state and traveled through the screen to read information from the Akashic Records.

It would be extremely difficult to attain Edgar Cayce's skills but, to access and comprehend the wisdom the Atlanteans so carefully preserved for us, it is essential to cultivate the ability to see through the veil that separates us from the Other World. Our minds must open and learn to take us where computers cannot.

In the past, ceremonies of initiation helped individuals to awaken their awareness and increase the subtle energy frequencies of their minds. Depending on the culture, the object of initiations varied, although the primary focus was to expand the person's consciousness. In secret societies, after the initiates were fully prepared, their superiors offered them hidden knowledge, such as histories of past civilizations, instructions for unfolding one's mind and increasing spiritually, and information about the other worlds and the various forms of life in the universe. Often these truths were concealed in symbolic stories or preserved in mysterious rituals and ceremonies, so only the initiated would understand them.

In some initiations, such as those in ancient Egypt, priests assisted the subjects through a rehearsal of the death experience so that the feeling of transition would be familiar when death actually occurred. As their physical senses witnessed the passage from this world to another, their tangible encounter with immortality increased the initiates' understanding and taught them to believe in and trust the Other World. In a similar way, people today who survive a near-death experience no longer fear passing on and have a strong belief in some type of immortality. They find that, after viewing the Other Side, their focus has changed and they are apt to spend their time caring for the Earth's environment and serving others.

On the once-spiritualized American continent, descendants of Atlanteans among the Maya and the Inca called themselves Children of the Sun or Children of Light. They believed their ancestors built their temples on high energy sites that acted as portals or doorways to other worlds. The Maya and Inca erected pyramids in these powerful locations and placed their temples high on the top, where they were closer to the heavens. The heights also provided secrecy in sacred initiation ceremonies. Indigenous healers used similar high energy sites, hallucinogenic drugs, frantic dancing, meditation, fasting, sleep deprivation, and concentration on symbols to help them gain a different perception of reality in another level of consciousness.[3]

All humans have the natural ability to perceive dimensions other than the three we know, and it is possible for us to follow the examples of our predecessors and learn to do this without enduring the physical hardships which shamans and initiates of the past inflicted upon themselves. The Lemurians believed the unseen spiritual part of the world was the most important and, with their highly developed sixth sense, they instantly perceived what was invisible to their physical experiences.[4] They understood that Heaven and Earth were all one place, and that the loving God or Creator, or Cosmic Consciousness, was everywhere in everything.

Einstein expressed his comprehension of the rewards of expanding our minds when he said: "Imagination is more important than knowledge." There is a story that one day a student offered Einstein a unique interpretation of a problem. When the distinguished scientist asked how the young person had arrived at that solution, the student replied that it had just come to him. Einstein replied, "Good, if you had told me anything else I wouldn't have believed you."

Edgar Cayce portrays the Atlanteans as a "thought people, those of an intuitive influence." How did they get this way? They focused on developing their children's natural skills, such as their intuitive instincts, and respected their insights and dreams. The life-style of the early Lemurians and Atlanteans gave them the opportunity to retain and develop their natural psychic skills, for they did not have the numerous distractions of a materialistic society and were always in close touch with their natural environment. As adults, some of them developed tremendous discipline of the mind and dedicated their lives to applying the knowledge they acquired.

Cayce describes Children of the Law of One in Atlantis who, with the increased power of group meditation, left their bodies and entered into fourth-dimensional consciousness[5] to acquire increased knowledge and understanding. Incense, crystals, symbols, and particular sounds facilitated meditation and enabled our ancestors to penetrate the darkness and more easily access the energy and wisdom of the universe. The initial function of the Tuaoi stone in early Atlantis was to help bridge the gap between outer and inner reality.[6]

In our more modern world, Cayce's statement that we have to increase our understanding before we retrieve Atlantean records also refers to the necessity to fully understand ourselves, to grow spiritually, and to make a transition to a higher state of consciousness. Since meditation requires one to be still and quiet and centered, it helps us to perceive the spiritual aspect of the universe. If one becomes completely absorbed in music, it sometimes gives rise to a brief sensation of tuning into higher consciousness. Group meditation is beneficial, for the energy inner reflection generates is enhanced when people gather together. With contemplation, in addition to learning about ourselves and the universe, we will realize that it is important to readily monitor our thoughts and actions so as to increase our compassion for others, always choosing the path which has truth and light.

The parallels between the last days of Atlantis and the development of our civilization are obvious and disturbing. In addition to lack of respect for the Earth's gifts, the crime, adultery, and immorality that characterized the final days of Atlantis are widespread. Attaining personal wealth and power are of primary importance to most of those who live in technologically advanced nations. Scientific materialism has once again gained an upper hand, with the result that many people believe they do not need a relationship with their Creator or a strict moral code. There is danger that we cannot control our deadly weapons and will extinguish life on this planet.

Prevailing selfish thoughts create a general disharmony, just as they did in late Atlantis. The destructive energy of these thoughts extends beyond this planet into the cosmos. Perhaps the unusual current weather reflects the disturbances that are flowing through the group consciousness of the human race. Frequent dire prophecies of pole shifts, devastating earthquakes, and drastic changes in the Earth's surface are also damaging.

Edgar Cayce asserted that the future is not fixed, and that we have control of our own destinies. We must believe this is correct, that it is possible for us to avoid the terrible fate of the Atlanteans and create a world in which we benefit from our amazing achievements. Ideally computers and our other mechanical accomplishments will eventually enhance our lives, rather than dominate and dehumanize us.

The Hopi have a story of a gentle fawn who, as she started up a trail, came to a terrible monster who was guarding it and preventing people from reaching the top. With eyes full of compassion and love, the fawn looked at the ugly monster and pleaded that he let her pass. The demon was amazed that no matter what he said or did, she was not afraid of him. He felt her love penetrating his whole being, and he could not resist it. As he calmed down, the monster's heart melted and his body shrank to the size of a chipmunk. As a result of the deer's unconditional love, others were now able to climb the path to the top of the mountain without fear.

Gandhi said: "You must be the change we seek in the world." And Einstein's belief that "Today's problems will never be solved by the same level of thinking which caused them" is similar. If each of us attempts to raise our consciousness and pattern our lives after the lives of the first Lemurians and Atlanteans whose civilization existed in peace and harmony for thousands of years, the effect will expand, gradually reaching more and more people. Numerous individuals and groups on the Earth are working toward this goal.

Edgar Cayce reports that former Atlantean souls who have incarnated again on Earth are here for a variety of reasons. Some realize that in the past they failed to direct their energies toward the survival of the land and simply continued in their daily lives without confronting what was happening. Others who are here today were instrumental in the development of deadly, destructive devices. Since the condition of our world is very similar to that ultimate time of Atlantis, these souls have returned to take advantage of the opportunity to help, as a way of making amends for their previous sins. Hundreds of people are devoting themselves to working for the good of all human beings, hoping that their efforts will contribute to preventing our civilization from following in the footsteps of Atlantis. I believe the work of these good persons will, and has, made a difference in changing the direction of the world.

In the later stages of the Atlantean civilization, the Children of the Law of One, who focused on love and prayer to promote knowledge, secluded themselves to ensure ideal conditions where they were free to meditate and concentrate on combating the sinful, unprincipled Sons of Belial. However, separateness was not the total solution, and it didn't work. Without the moral guidance of the Children of the Law of One, the nation became more and more corrupt. Robbery, rape, and murder increased rapidly, and scientists proceeded with their destructive experiments without regard to the possible outcome.

The numerous people who are attempting to restore harmony on our planet today are using quite a different approach from the Children of the Law of One. Rather than isolating themselves, they work together to combine their positive energies for the benefit of the planet and humanity. Participants in this new approach of cooperation realize that planetary illnesses may be changed by sending positive energies to the problems, just as many prayers can speed the recovery of a patient.

During World War II, Winston Churchill used the approach of huge numbers of people focusing on a positive outcome when he initiated a Minute of Silence project. He encouraged everyone to pause and pray for peace each day when London's Big Ben struck the hour of twelve noon. In 1999, when Kosovo was being torn apart, Internet organizations revived Churchill's Minute of Silence concept, and within a week, busy individuals in every corner of the world were stopping to pray for peace in Kosovo.

The theory behind mass participation as a means of changing a destructive situation to a more positive one is similar to what happens when one candle is lit, and then many candles are lit. One candle produces light and positive energy, and this is substantially increased by adding more and more candles. An area of negative energy, such as a conflict area, if subjected to intense light and positive energy, has the possibility of becoming a place where the energies of hatred and anger no longer predominate.

The Global Meditations Network, which quickly reaches approximately 200,000 individuals, is an example of an Internet organization taking advantage of the Computer Age to help the planet and its people. After the September 11, 2001, bombing of the World Trade Organization, the increase of fear was countered by the network globally sending peace, love, and light. When Afghani representatives met in Germany in an attempt to form an interim government, participants in the Global Meditations Network directed positive thoughts to them. When the first global positive energy event after September 11 occurred in Salt Lake City at the 2002 Olympics, the Global Meditations Network sent continuous positive thoughts to help deflect any negativity.

The theory is simple. What we create with our thoughts is what we can expect. If we focus on disaster, this increases that possibility. If, on the other hand, we focus on positive matters, we have a chance to build a better world.

In addition to thinking positively and not expecting disasters, it is important to realize that many of our ancestors survived because they resolutely persevered as natural catastrophes destroyed their families, their friends, their homes, and their land. These survivors were intelligent, innovative, and supportive of others but, in their constant struggles against floods, volcanic eruptions, and sinking land, it was sometimes necessary for them to be brutal, cunning, and opportunistic. Similar personal characteristics were essential for those who moved to new homelands, where they combated human foes as well as natural problems. Brutal behavior to achieve goals in our society is partially a reversion to the conduct of our ancestors, who were forced to fight with all their strength to endure, and their survival traits continue to characterize the human race. The realization that some descendants of those survivors live on the Earth today will empower us to cope with our fellow humans' ingrained aggressive tendencies with increased skill, understanding, and compassion.

Basically all on this planet and in the universe are spirits from the same source, not just material beings. There is only one supreme Creator. We are one family. It is said that if you arrange the doctrines of all the religions of the world around an imaginary mountain, they culminate with one very similar god at the top. As we emphasize the similarities rather than the differences among people, unity will prevail and we will come together on the higher plane of consciousness that characterized the Golden Age of early Lemuria and Atlantis.

> The children of the New Age are involved with light, love, spaceships, and peace.
> —SENECA FRED KENNEDY[7]

Careful examination of those born within the last twenty years indicates that the consciousness of the human race is rapidly expanding and our evolution is progressing in a variety of ways. The enlightenment of this next generation is reflected in IQ tests where, because of improved results, a rating of genius now requires a much higher score than in the past. In addition to increased intelligence, many of the newcomers possess unique skills, which Native Americans describe as the "wisdom of the Elders."

Scientists in the United States, China, and Mexico are studying a new type of children who are appearing in ever-increasing numbers throughout the world. They are commonly referred to as Indigo Children or Starseed Children. The "indigo" description results from intuitive observers who see a greater concentration of that color in the young person's auras. "Starseed" comes from those who believe these children are from other worlds and have come to assist us in these difficult times.

Like shamans or those who underwent an initiation process in the past, or people who have had a near-death experience, these youngsters display an unusual amount of psychic talents. These include telepathy, precognition, telekinesis, intuition, remote viewing, teleportation, levitation, and interdimensional awareness. Of course, every Indigo or Starseed child does not possess all of these skills, but they each seem to sense when others are in trouble and have an ability to console and heal, which they freely utilize.

The Indigo and Starseed children are a bewilderment to many of today's parents and teachers who have only a third-dimensional understanding of life. The youngsters already "know" who they are, and many of them understand the purpose of their present stay on Earth. They are apt to focus on the etheric rather than the linear, making it difficult for them to adapt to conventional classroom discipline and fit into mainstream society. Frequently these children are diagnosed with attention deficit disorder or some form of hyperactivity, which alarms those who attempt to help all young people avoid frustration and achieve balance and harmony in their lives.

Many believe these leaders of the future are ancient souls from Mu and Atlantis who have returned to help humanity find its way out of the world difficulties. We've had spiritual impoverishment and would benefit from listening to these children with the wise old eyes. As we encounter the current problems of social upheavals, crime, and our inhumanity to one another, the wisdom of the Indigo and Starseed Children will offer us a bridge from the third dimension to higher levels.

Indigenous people who are close to nature realize that the Earth is out of balance, and they attribute the disharmony to our polluting and plundering of our world, as well as the extensive worldwide discord. They believe our once-beautiful planet is a living being who is so sick she is unable to heal herself. In their efforts to care for her, they are reviving old prayers, offerings, customs, and ceremonies. The practice of drum circles to reinstate the planet's basic rhythms and heartbeat is becoming increasingly common in Canada and North America. The Kogi, who inhabit a remote jungle area of Bolivia, believe they have the spiritual responsibility of maintaining the heartbeat of Mother Earth. Praying twenty-four hours a day, they continually dissolve the out-of-balance thought-forms that are being projected into the atmosphere.[8]

The Hopi, who live in the southwestern United States, regularly perform rituals and offer special prayers to hold the world in balance, just as their ancestors did thousands of years ago. They believe they are responsible for maintaining the proper rotation of our planet by keeping the twin spirits Poqanghoya and Palongawhoya in position—one at the north pole of this planet's axis and one at the south pole. Hopi elders spoke at the United Nations in New York City, warning that we must join together in spiritual peace with love in our hearts for one another and for Mother Earth.

As we strive to counteract the omnipresent problems and help the Earth regain its balance as an intelligent, living superorganism, the thoughts and quality of life of each of us will extend into the whole world and on to the universe, for all is interconnected. Placing more emphasis on balance and simplicity in our lives and feeling enhanced compassion for others will increase the amount of positive energy. To diminish fear and reduce our own apprehension about the future, it helps to appreciate what we have today, for we are where we are right now. It is important to try to live in the moment and find and enjoy something beautiful in whatever we are doing. There is a well-known, very appropriate phrase of the Buddhists: "Live in the present moment." Nothing is a reality until it becomes a reality.

The world situation will not change immediately but, from observing the mistakes of the past, we have the knowledge to create a society free of greed, oppression, hatred, and violence, where differences in religion are unimportant, and technology and wisdom are in balance. It is possible to restore the Golden Age of the past.

NOTES

1   Cayce, *Readings* 378–16.

2   Cayce, *Readings* 5748–6.

3   See *Atlantis: Insights from a Lost Civilization* for descriptions of a typical initiation ceremony in Atlantis.

4   Cerve, *Lemuria*, pp. 132–4.

5   Cayce, *Readings* 2464–2

6   Cayce, *Readings* 2072–10.

7   Red Star, *Star Ancestors*, p. 48.

8   Ibid.

AFTERWORD

THE HOPE AND CHALLENGE
of finding knowledge or material remains
from the ancient civilizations of Lemuria
and Atlantis continue to inspire explorers.
In the Pacific, where ocean waters rose
hundreds of feet during the conclusion of
the last Ice Age, recent discoveries of underwater ruins that must have been built
before that time confirm that intelligent
people lived and worked there more than
10,000 years ago. A wall-like structure in
the ocean near the northeast side of
Tungchi Island, Taiwan, and large, sophisticated buildings in 120 feet of water
twenty-five miles off the coast of Gujurat,
India, offer two examples. Another interesting location is in the sea near the tiny
island of Yonaguni off southern Japan.
Here, scuba divers' photographs reveal
what appear to be underwater structures
with carved steps, flat terraces, platforms,

and engravings similar to etchings on the nearby island. Obviously, knowledgeable people spent time here thousands of years ago when the area was above the surface.

As we move into the twenty-first century numerous well-meaning individuals make dire predictions that the Earth's surface will experience catastrophic changes. Prophecies from psychics combined with the end of Mayan calendars in 2012 reinforce these negative thoughts. It is important to realize that "Earth changes" does not necessarily mean a disastrous physical commotion. "Changes" in life on our planet are present now due to crime, social upheavals, and our inhumanity to one another. Mayan elders believe that we are in a time of transition and chaos as we approach the World of the Fifth Sun, which begins on December 21, 2012. They explain that at sunrise on that day, as the sun rises it conjuncts the intersection of the Milky Way and the plane of the ecliptic. The ancient Maya were aware of this astronomical event, and it offered a convenient time for them to end their timetables. Maya elders believe the world will not end in December 2012, it will be transformed, as a channel from far above opens and cleansing cosmic energy flows toward the Earth, raising all to a higher level of vibration.

Edgar Cayce correlates "Earth changes" with the time of our finally gaining access to the Atlantean Hall of Records, and researchers are focusing on the areas he recommends. Of the three places Cayce describes, the Giza Plateau in Egypt is the most accessible. Modern techniques such as satellite imagery and ground-penetrating radar for viewing what's beneath the surface reveal a complex network of tunnels under the area. Exploration discloses that some of the tunnels are natural and others are manmade. Edgar Cayce refers to three buried pyramids here.

Efforts to access the underground maze have received little publicity, although many assume that a strange round building the Egyptians erected in 2001 may have covered a possible entrance while workers undertook to hide a newly constructed doorway. Placed behind the Great Pyramid and aligned with the rear end of the Sphinx, this would be a logical location to access the passages below. The secrecy surrounding the affair, such as the government diverting all local people from the area just before the edifice appeared, encourages speculation.

Another unusual structure is emerging on the Giza Plateau. A huge barricade is being built that will eventually surround approximately eight square miles of land that includes the pyramids and a large unexcavated area with underground structures yet to be uncovered. The concrete construction, which is 6½ feet wide and rises 22 feet into the air, extends more than six feet below ground. It is reinforced with massive rebars. Posts for security guards at intervals along the wall are equipped with video cameras and lighting for surveillance. The extensive fortification seems to be designed for something more than simple "crowd control." An explanation of the source of the estimated $300–$500 million to finance this tremendous project is not available.

Investigations in the Great Pyramid continue to suggest that an advanced scientific civilization existed in prehistory. In September 2002, scientists who used a robot to open a door in the Queen's Chamber's southern shaft were surprised when the robot's camera detected another smaller door in the shaft. Two days later they discovered an identical door with intact brass handles in the Chamber's north shaft. This find leads some researchers to believe there is another room in or below the complicated building that sophisticated persons designed and constructed so long ago.

Engineer Christopher Dunn has carefully studied the Great Pyramid for twenty years. In *The Giza Power Plant: Technologies of Ancient Egypt* he explains that powered saws and drills were used to cut precise corners and perfectly flat surfaces of the sarcophagus in the King's Chamber and other granite artifacts within the pyramids. Dunn offers convincing, detailed evidence to demonstrate that the immense structure with its highly crystalline granite was once a power generator comparable to modern electric plants. In the future, if his proposition is accepted the techniques the ancients utilized here may help us to obtain energy without further polluting our planet.

Two respected Greek historians, Diodorus Siculus (first century B.C.) and Herodotus (fifth century B.C.), describe another site where prehistoric inhabitants of Egypt left knowledge of all history and astronomy. They depict in detail an elaborate labyrinth, more impressive than the pyramids of the Giza Plateau, with networks of intersecting passages, courtyards, and thousands of chambers. No one is certain of the location of the enormous building now buried beneath the desert sands, but some believe it is at Hawara, south of the Giza Plateau. Perhaps, when investigators have access to this extensive network of underground tunnels they will find a branch that leads to this unusual source of information from prehistory.

Just as children playing hide and seek will not remain hidden forever, so remnants from long ago continue to reveal themselves. Egerton Sykes' description of the Temple of Murias and Edgar Cayce's predictions of rising temples offer inspiration to searchers in the Caribbean. Near Bimini and Andros, where the water is relatively shallow, investigators from the A.R.E. (Edgar Cayce's Association for Research and Enlightenment) are locating convincing evidence to indicate that intelligent people lived here before the ocean rose and covered their homes and temples.

When vegetation, either above the surface of the water or below, occurs in regular geometric patterns it strongly suggests human activity in the area in the past. Since the late 1960s when Dr. J. Manson Valentine observed regular formations in the ocean near Bimini scuba divers have attempted to examine them. Modern technology assists in the search but it is still extremely difficult, as the following episode demonstrates.

By correlating older Landsat satellite imaging with the recently surveyed high resolution IKONOS satellite imaging of the Bimini Archipelago, common points were found on each image that allowed Jonathan Eagle to compute the GPS coordinates for a large dark pentagonal-shaped area, seen on the Landsat imaging but outside the scope of the IKONOS imaging. The general accuracy of the computations and the existence of the feature were confirmed by Bill Donato, with the assistance of pilot Thomas Coleman, as they flew over it. Later, the computed coordinates proved to be highly accurate when Bill Donato and Jonathan Eagle took the thirty-seven-foot research vessel *Sea Spirit*, chartered from Don and Sally Tondro, across five miles of shallow shoals directly to the center of the "pentagon" using nothing but the computed GPS coordinates. Although they probed with rods several feet into the turtle grass that defines the shape, they were unable to detect any underlying structure to account for it. It will be necessary for A.P.E.X. Institute, their nonprofit corporation, to find additional funds to determine what the underlying structure is through the use of sub-bottom profiling.

Doctors Greg and Lora Little have returned twice to Andros Island as they continue the A.R.E.'s search for Atlantis. In June 2003 the husband-wife team continued to explore the gigantic three-tiered submerged platform described in chapter 17. Since the top layer of the structure lies in approximately ten feet of water and the bottom tier is only about fifteen feet below the surface, it is possible for a scuba diver to study it carefully. Rectangular and square blocks 25 by 30 feet plus many smaller ones are arranged to form a platform with three layers that is about 1,500 feet long, 150 feet wide, and 50 feet high. In *The A.R.E.'s Search for Atlantis* the Littles describe their unusual find and their further explorations in and around the islands of Bimini and Andros in hopes of proving that the Bahama Bank was inhabited at the time of Atlantis.

Scientists are continuing to verify Edgar Cayce's amazing knowledge of the Earth's history, lending credibility to his information about Atlantis, Lemuria, and the Hall of Records. However, the underlying principle of Cayce's work was to instill tolerance, compassion, and understanding plus a comprehension of the oneness of all life. As Heather Robb said to me: "To open the Halls of Records around the Earth we need the same purity of interaction as those who enclosed the knowledge so successfully." That is the key to our acquiring higher knowledge and surviving.

APPENDIX I

DIADENON

AN E-MAIL FRIEND FROM Australia, Heather Robb, contributed the following story of her experience with a powerful crystal:

I have an old friend and teacher who came to me many years ago. She is not human or spirit but a recorder crystal, one of the Atlantean master crystal energies. My connection to her goes back to the time in Atlantis when my father worked in the caverns with crystals, and I tried to warn him of the coming destruction because of the work he and others did.

The Atlantean magicians had the power to manifest thought into crystals for experiments against man and nature. Back then I saw it as a kind of rape of the crystals and the Earth of which they were an important part. I knew that such manipulation could only lead to destruction. As I got to know her energies, I realized that the crystal was feminine, like a reflection of Gaia. She asked me to call her Diadenon.

Diadenon is a cluster of what looks like a mixture of cloudy quartz, pale amethyst, and tourmaline, and fits comfortably into my hand. When I first saw the crystal, I was very drawn to her, even though the owner was obviously relieved to get rid of her. I soon found out why—she used to stab me in the heart chakra and give others nightmares and headaches. One day I took her to my yoga class and her energies distressed everyone so much I had to take her away.

When Diadenon first came to me, she had a silver figure of a man attached to her. At that time it was popular to buy crystals with figurines. I found this demeaning but, whatever I did, I couldn't get the man off.

Diadenon sat on the window ledge above my kitchen sink so that I had a lot of contact with her. I would tune in and send her love. It seemed important to me to make her a part of my world, and I formed a close connection with her energies. One day as I stood at the sink, I heard someone calling from inside her. "Help—please help me."

The plea puzzled and, I think, frightened me. I picked her up and looked deeply into the clusters and saw what appeared to be a crystal city, with a woman with long hair pacing up and down, as if trapped in a room. Something seemed to trigger inside me and, without thinking, I picked up the crystal and held it above my head and stepped into the energies. I immediately felt I was in a huge maelstrom with enormous power swirling around me. As the calling became even louder, I sensed the female energy trapped inside, and I prayed for her release with an authority I did not know I possessed. At that moment, it seemed as if she and I recognized each other across space and time. The memory was like some echo from my past and, as I tried to identify it, I was suddenly jolted out of the vision to find that the silver man had fallen off Diadenon. The female energy in the crystal was stronger, but less frightening. I heard her name, "Diadenon," and I realized she was the energy of the crystal itself and that I saw her elemental form in the vision I just had of the woman inside her.

The crystal continued to attack my chakras. Eventually I put her in a glass container with sea salt crystals around her and and placed the jar in a shallow stream on our farm. It seemed like a safe place as summer had been very dry and still. I hoped the clear water and the Earth energies would heal her.

That night we had a massive storm, the stream became a raging torrent, and Diadenon disappeared. I was relieved she was gone, as I was sick of her attacks on my heart chakra and on my friends, but even so, I felt protective and loving, and over the following months I would visualize Diadenon next to my heart and give her all the love I had without fully understanding why.

And then one day I felt her presence again. It was like a calling. Sure enough, after a few days our farm hand brought the container to me. He had found it far away, half buried in the stream, glistening in the sun like a beacon, and he somehow knew he had to give it to me. Despite myself, I held the crystal to me again and gave her a great love, as I would to a beloved friend returning. I could never understand the connection, but I had to honor it. Her energies did seem calmer somehow, more in balance, and I was happy to be reunited with her.

Over many years, I gave love and respect to Diadenon, and we both grew in wisdom. As I learned, it seemed she did as well—we seemed to share our spiritual path together, like osmosis. Was she awakening in this bright world as I opened more to spiritual understanding? Perhaps I created a safe healing space here and thus it allowed her the freedom to be herself again. I felt she had been asleep, and now, as I acknowledged her presence, she came alive.

One evening I had an amazing experience. I was ill and lying in bed, frustrated because everyone had gone to a party and I had to stay at home. Our home is full of crystals. Many are never used or cleansed, but simply enjoyed for their presence. Feeling sorry for myself, I called on the crystal circle in our bedroom to heal me. They started to hum or tone, and gradually all the other crystals in the house joined in. It was a beautiful, harmonious song, like a celestial choir.

I lay there awed, and then in my mind sought out Diadenon. Nothing. I said to her, "Well, I've helped you—what about helping me?" Almost immediately her etheric form came floating into the room on a parallel plane and hovered in front of me. I said, "Okay, I'm going to trust you, I'm going to allow you to enter my third eye and help with the healing." I was a bit afraid as I was allowing her into my head and intuition, but I knew that she needed trust. She sent a beam of blue light into my forehead. It was gentle and cool, like calming waters, and then her form returned to my study. All became still. The crystals stopped singing, and I slept. When I awoke later I was completely well.

Recently I did a healing on a young mother who has Behchet's syndrome. This is a particularly nasty autoimmune disease, and the woman was panicking when she phoned. Her distress was so strong that I felt myself shaking all over, and I knew I had to really work hard to help her.

Before she arrived to see me, I did my usual room cleansing and preparations. I filled my small burner with water, and added the aromatherapy oils. As I was about to light the candle to warm it, Diadenon said as clearly as a bell ringing, "Pass the water over me and I will add to its harmonies." I did as I was told, and I watched in awe as blue rays radiated again from inside her and entered the water.

Diandenon was there throughout the healing, as if she had fully come awake. Her presence was as tangible as another person, and she showed me how to do the healing. It was a very powerful experience, and when it was over the woman shone so brightly she looked like a pure crystal. By pushing out all the darkness, Diadenon's energy and light had made a space for my patient to really heal herself. Afterward I held Diadenon in my hand and felt a great love between us. At last I knew our union was complete. Our working relationship and the opening of us was just truly begining.

Diadenon is unlike any crystal I have ever encountered because she thinks for herself and manifests her independence, which I would never have thought possible. The first time I encountered it was when I tried to photograph her. She kept folding in on herself and her energy remained hidden. She also did this when I showed her to others and only twice did she reveal herself. Both times I was awed to watch her wrap what looked like tenacles of light around my friends. It felt like a love song—like a deep contented sigh—and each time they were swept away by the experience.

One day as I held Diadenon close to me, she gifted me this vision of myself in an Atlantean past life. I saw myself as a young adolescent girl entering the Great Crystal caverns of Atlantis, and running to my father. "Father, you must stop manipulating the crystals with your mind, for that will destroy us!" And I remembered my father's laconic, intelligent gaze as he looked at me but did not listen. Later, when part of Atlantis was breaking apart, I rushed to get him, but he would not come. He stayed because he believed he could stop the carnage from happening. When the caverns started to crumble around us, I held on to my father and I gave my love to him and the crystals there and vowed that in my next life I would work with them, not against them. The last thing I remember was the energy of Diadenon reaching out to me with love—a pact had been made.

This memory helps me understand my commitment to Diadenon and why the bond between us is so strong. Our relationship also helps me recognize other crystal energies and the nature of their communication. It gives me a deeper perception of the elemental kingdom—that all on Earth are truly alive. Diadenon's memories were of the priest-magicians' mental power blocking her natural light energy as they harnessed and focused the crystals for other uses. As Atlantean priest-scientists like my father programmed the stones to distort energy, they were manipulating the inanimate but intelligent crystal kingdom. Diadenon's experiences were of darkness and abuse in the final destructions—not of love and nurturing. Years later, I understand that the compassion I give to her enables her true light to shine once more.

NOTE

Heather Robb is a talented healer and teacher who lives in Australia. Information she channels from the spirit world greatly enhances her understanding and knowledge. She is a Reiki master who works and studies within many areas in addition to crystals. To contact her, write to Robb@virtual.net.au.

APPENDIX II

BIOGRAPHIES

EDGAR CAYCE (1877–1945), who grew up in the southern United States as a poor farm boy with very little education, is a fruitful source of information about Atlantis. As a young adult, Cayce discovered that when he was in a state of self-hypnosis he was able to diagnose and prescribe sophisticated beneficial guidance for physical and mental problems of troubled individuals who were often far away. His treatments were so successful that he is sometimes referred to as the father of holistic medicine.

Cayce's responses to questions were called "readings." For forty-three years he gave over 14,000 of these sessions, and in many of them, as he attempted to point out a person's strengths and weaknesses, he referred to one or more of their past lives. Over 700 of these previous incarnations were in Atlantis. Cayce's readings offer interesting details about the surface of the

Earth in prehistory and life on this planet so long ago. Although hundreds of different persons were involved, Cayce was perfectly consistent in his data, and no one has found any contradictory statements of dates or events in his information on any subject. His data is always consistent with more conventional reports with which he could not have been familiar. In addition, scientists and scholars are slowly confirming Cayce's descriptions of geography and incidents in prehistory. His sons are certain that he never read Plato's material on Atlantis or other books about that country. With his talent for accessing information about civilizations as far back in history as Lemuria and Atlantis, Edgar Cayce could easily have used his skills to further his own interests, but he devoted his life to offering healing advice to those who sought his help. He was truly an admirable person. For more information about Edgar Cayce see *Atlantis: Insights from a Lost Civilization*.

WILSHAR S. CERVE was a pen name of Harvey Spencer Lewis. Using this name, he wrote *Lemuria: The Lost Continent of the Pacific*, which the Rosicrucian order (AMORC) of San Jose, California published in 1931. He also compiled *Unto Thee I Grant . . .*, also known as *The Economy of Life*, a collection of secret spiritual and ethical teachings of the Tibetans. Cerve obtained the material in these books from a portfolio of very rare manuscripts a representative of the Rosicrucian brotherhood in China brought to the Rosicrucian office in San Francisco. The information had been preserved for thousands of years in ancient archives of China and Tibet.

The Rosicrucian Order is an extensive, ancient worldwide organization which explores natural laws that govern all aspects of life—physical, mental, emotional, psychic, and spiritual. It is reasonable to assume that the brotherhood in China, anticipating the coming suppression of information in that country and Tibet, decided to make the sacred knowledge available to others. A priest carried the valuable manuscripts to the Rosicrucian headquarters in California for safekeeping and publication. Cerve was selected to write these books because of his interest in archaeology, geology, and meteorology. His intent was solely to present information from the manuscripts, not to prove it.

COLONEL JAMES M. CHURCHWARD (1851–1936) was born in Devon, England, where he received an Oxford education. A true Renaissance person, he was a soldier, scholar, inventor, painter, engineer, explorer, expert angler, metallurgist and a Mason. As a young man, Churchward lived in India where he spent time with a Hindu priest who taught him to decipher Naacal, an ancient symbolic writing.

As their friendship increased, the priest shared with Churchward sacred Naacal tablets, which had been carefully hidden for thousands of years in secret archives of his temple. From the Naacal records Churchward learned that the extensive civilization of Mu once thrived on land in the Pacific Ocean. The Naacals, priests in India and Burma who long ago taught science and religion to others, wrote 10,000 clay tablets to preserve information that had come to their countries from Mu. The priests used symbols, rather than writing, which described explicit facts, to keep their historical knowledge secret. Only initiates and those of the highest standing were taught to interpret the images which relate to the sacred mysteries. To preserve the valuable documents, they also carried tablets to Egypt and the Gobi where they were carefully hidden.

Col. Churchward invented NCV steel, an almost impenetrable alloy, which the Americans used for helmets in World War I. The income it produced provided Churchward with time and money to travel and learn more about the lost continent of Mu. He spent twenty years searching in Tibet, Burma, and other temples in India for additional Naacal tablets and investigating hundreds of sources. As he compiled his data, he carefully studied traditions, customs, languages, legends and statuary of indigenous people. Churchward's 168 sources include the Troano Manuscript, Codex Cortesianus, and other books from Central America, the Lhasa Records from Tibet, inscriptions in Central America and the Pacific, and documents from Greece, India, Egypt, and the Maya. His close relationships with Augustus Le Plongeon and William Niven provided him with additional information. The extent of Churchward's facts and his cross-referencing at a time when there were no computers is truly amazing. He is primarily remembered as the author of *The Lost Continent of Mu, the Children of Mu, The Sacred Symbols of Mu,* and *Cosmic Forces as They Were Taught in Mu.*

In his books, Churchward's convincing interpretations and explanations of numerous Naacal symbols lend additional credibility to the mysterious tablets, even though there is no concrete evidence of the sacred books. His numerous cross-references to inscriptions on ruins, legends, and many other sources also provide reliable proof that he really did spend a tremendous amount of time translating and recording information from the Naacal tablets.

As one reads Churchward's five books, a clear picture emerges of how often his numerous sources cross-prove each other. Several farflung temple inscriptions match the information in an ancient scroll and duplicate some tribal lore. Similarities in architecture and protolanguages of extremely ancient and extinct civilization provide unusual examples of the spread of culture to distant places.

Although Churchward does not receive the respect he deserves, the scientific community is slowly considering his works more seriously. The large body of knowledge he assembled, combined with the sophisticated technologies available today, will certainly provide a basis for further investigation and exploration of megalithic ruins in the Pacific.

An excellent 62,000-word biography of Col. Churchward by Joan Griffith is available from Dick Lowdermilk (phone: 864-224-7945).

LUCILLE TAYLOR HANSEN. Archaeologist and anthropologist Lucille Taylor Hansen spent twenty-five years studying Native American cultures and slowly gaining the confidence of leaders such as Apache Chief Aso Delugio and Chief Sedillo, the great war chief of the Yaqui who studied with the Egyptian priesthood and also acquired degrees from European universities. Gradually the leaders revealed closely guarded ancient wisdom that had been repeated only in secret oral and family traditions since the the white people arrived in the sixteenth century. In *The Ancient Atlantic*, Hansen combines this Native American knowledge with information from museums and libraries to present a convincing mass of evidence to indicate that Atlanteans from an island in the sunrise sea and from the Caribbean area settled in central and northeastern North America.

MURRY HOPE, a British author and scientist, is one of the foremost authors on esoteric wisdom, ancient magical religions, and parapsychology. In 1977 Dr. Carl Sargent of Cambridge University tested her psychic abilities under the auspices of the BBC and she achieved an extraordinarily high percentage of accuracy. In 1988 she established the Institute for the Study and Development of Transpersonal Sensitivity in America. Recently she has concentrated on effecting a bridge between ancient and metaphysical beliefs and the new approach to physics and allied disciplines, which is being espoused by many respected scientists.

Hope is the author of *Time, The Ultimate Energy, Atlantis— Myth or Reality?, The Ancient Wisdom of Atlantis, Ancient Egypt: The Sirius Connection, The Psychology of Healing, The Greek Tradition, The Nine Lives of Tyo, The Psychology of Ritual, The Way of Cartouche*, and several other books.

ZECHARIA SITCHIN. (1920–) Biblical scholar and archaeologist Zecharia Sitchin is an expert in the Sumerian, Assyrian, Babylonian and Hittite languages, as well as the history and archaeology of the ancient Near East. After thirty years of study and travel, he published numerous scholarly works that provide little-known information about our extraterrestrial forefathers and some of their actions on the planet Earth in the past hundreds of thousands of years. His books include: *The Twelfth Planet, Stairway to Heaven, The Wars of Gods and Men, When Time Began, The Cosmic Code, The Lost Realms, Genesis Revisited, The Cosmic Code,* and *Divine Encounters.*

JAMES LEWIS THOMAS CHALMERS SPENCE (1874–1955) was a highly respected Scottish mythologist and ancient historian who was vice-president of the Scottish Anthropological and Folklore Society and was awarded a Royal Pension "for his service to culture." Membership in an age-old, reputable occult organization offered him access to manuscripts of the Arcane Tradition (records of occult fraternities) written over 1,000 years ago. The age-old books are in English, French, Spanish, German, Greek, and Arabic, all languages Spence mastered. Since there were few available copies of these aged documents, they were read aloud to potential new members of the occult group during sacred initiation ceremonies. Spence's expertise at memorizing folk tales and legends helped him to accurately retain the interesting information he received orally during his initiation. The numerous references to Atlantis in the ancient Arcane Tradition intrigued Spence and he began to earnestly pursue the subject.

As is true of many scholars who tackle the enormous job of researching Atlantis, Spence developed a passionate interest in the unique prehistoric country and its people. In his studies he assessed Herodotus' *History, The Historical Library* by Diodorus Siculus, Plato's *Critias* and *Timaeus,* and other classical authors who wrote hundreds of centuries ago. For additional material Spence studied Jewish rabbinical works, Arabic writings, the oldest documents from the Far East, the early chapters of the Bible, and reports and stories from early explorers and treasure seekers.

Spence was convinced that the occult arts, because they are unusually similar wherever they occur in the lands around the Atlantic Ocean, must have originated in one place. He found no region in western Europe with a culture sufficiently ancient to have served as the focal point from which the adjacent countries could have received their similar earliest ideas of religion, myth, and magic.

To reveal the results of his far-ranging research, Spence published *The Problem of Atlantis, The History of Atlantis, The Gods of Mexico, The Mysteries of Britain, Encyclopaedia of Occultism, Magic Arts of Celtic Britain, The Occult Sciences in Atlantis, Atlantis in America, The Myths of Mexico and Peru*, and *Atlantis Discovered.* Despite his enthusiasm for the topic, Spence decided his position as a trustworthy, accomplished scholar was in danger if he continued to talk openly about the quality of life at the time of Atlantis and the occult arts he believed were practiced there. He stopped all his work on the subject and, according to those who knew him, refused to ever discuss Atlantis again.[1]

EGERTON SYKES (1894–1983) was an erudite British student of antiquity who focused on Atlantis. In addition to serving in the British diplomatic service, he was an engineer, a soldier, a journalist, and a fellow of the Royal Geographical Society. Shortly after World War II Sykes founded the Atlantis Research Center in Brighton, England. Here, with the assistance of others devoted to the subject of prehistory, he assembled a large collection of classical references, ancient literature, and legends pertaining to Atlantis and other civilizations long ago. During his lifetime Sykes published four periodicals, *New World Antiquity, Atlantis, Uranus,* and

Pendulum. After his death in 1983, the Edgar Cayce Foundation in Virginia Beach acquired Sykes' valuable books and papers from the Atlantean Research Center. The Atlantis Research Center was founded in Italy in 1945 and found its final resting place in Brighton, England after WWII.

J. MANSON VALENTINE (1902–1994), a scientist with a doctorate from Yale, spent over twenty years locating ruins on the Great Bahama Bank. As a result of innumerable flights over the area, combined with information from onsite investigations, Valentine compiled a dossier of no fewer than sixty areas of potential archaeological interest located in the shallow waters on the Great Bahama Bank. As a result of his findings, Valentine was convinced he had found remnants of the lost civilization of Atlantis. He died at the age of 92 as the result of complications following a recluse spider bite that rotted away his flesh.

NOTES

1   Michel, *The New View Over Atlantis,* p. 200.

BIBLIOGRAPHY

Alper, Frank, Dr. *Exploring Atlantis.*
Irvine, CA: Quantum Productions,
1981.

Asher, Maxine. *Ancient Energy.* New York:
Harper & Row, 1979.

Bahn, Paul G., and Vertut, Jean. *Images of
the Ice Age.* London: Bellow Publication
Co., Ltd., 1988.

Berlitz, Charles. *Atlantis: The Eighth Continent.* New York: Fawcett Crest, 1984.

———. *Mysteries from Forgotten Worlds.*
New York: Doubleday & Co., Inc.,
1972.

———. *The Mystery of Atlantis.* New
York: Grosset & Dunlap, 1969.

Bethards, Betty. *Atlantis. What It Was
Then . . . Why It Is Important Now!*
Novato, CA: The Guidance Series,
Inner Light Foundation, 1974.

Braghine, Alexander Pavlovitch. *The Shadow of Atlantis*. Wellingborough, Northamptonshire: The Aquarian Press, Ltd., 1940.

Brennan, Janet, "The Chambers of Putnam County," *Fate Magazine*, May 2001.

Brodie, Renee. *The Healing Tones of Crystal Bowls*. Vancouver, Canada: Aroma Art Ltd., 1996.

Brother Philip. *Secret of the Andes*. CA: Leaves of Grass Press, 1976.

Brown, J. Macmillan. *The Riddle of the Pacific*. Kempton, IL: Adventures Unlimited Press, 1996.

Butler, G. I. *Giants*. Reprint from "A Collection of Valuable Historical Extracts," pp. 171–172, 1885, *Ancient American*, Volume 7, Number 43, p. 17.

Caldwell, Taylor. *The Romance of Atlantis*. New York: William Morrow & Co., Inc., 1975.

Cannon, Dolores. *Jesus and the Essenes*. Bath, UK: Gateway Books, 1992.

Cavalli-Sforza, Luigi Luca. "Genes, Peoples and Languages." *Scientific American*, November 1991.

Cayce, Edgar. *Atlantis* Readings. Volume 22. Virginia Beach, VA: Compiled by the Readings Research Department, Association for Research and Englighenment, Inc., 1987.

———. *Egypt at the Time of Rata* Readings. Volume 24, Part II. Virginia Beach, VA: Compiled by Ann Lee Clapp, Association for Research and Englighenment, Inc., 1989.

———. *Auras*. Virginia Beach, VA: A.R.E. Press, 1945.

Cayce, Edgar Evans. *Mysteries of Atlantis Revisited*. San Francisco, CA: Harper & Row, 1988.

————. *On Atlantis.* New York: Hawthorne Books, 1968.

Cerve, W. S. *Lemuria, the Lost Continent of the Pacific.* San Jose, CA: Rosicrucian Library Volume XII, Supreme Grand Lodge of AMORXC, 1931.

Childress, David Hatcher. "Subterranean Tunnels, Part 2," *World Explorer* Vol. 2, No. 3.

————. *Lost Cities of Atlantis, Ancient Europe & the Mediterranean.* Stelle, IL: Adventures Unlimited Press, 1996.

————. *Lost Cities of Ancient Lemuria and the Pacific.* Stelle, IL: Adventures Unlimited Press, 1988.

————. *Lost Cities of China, Central Asia & India.* Stelle, IL: Adventures Unlimited Press, 1985.

————. *Vimana Aircraft of Ancient India & Atlantis.* Stelle, IL: Adventures Unlimited Press, 1991.

Churchward, James. *The Lost Continent of Mu.* New York: William Edwin Rudge, 1926.

————. *The Lost Continent of Mu.* Albuquerque, NM: The C. W. Daniel Co. Ltd., Essex, England, and BE Books ⅝ The Brotherhood of Life, Inc., 1987.

————. *The Children of Mu.* Ives New York: Washburn, 1933.

Collins, Andrew. *Gateway to Atlantis.* New York: Carroll and Graf Publishers, Inc., 2000.

Cosentino, *The Light Messenger,* Vol. IV, No. 9, Sept. 2000.

Countryman, J. *Atlantis and the Seven Stars.* New York: St. Martin's Press, 1979.

Cummins, Geraldine. *The Fate of Colonel Fawcett.* London: The Aquarian Press, 1955.

De Camp, L. Sprague. *Lost Continents; The Atlantis Theme in History, Science and Literature.* New York: Dover, 1970.

Donato, William M. *A Re-Examination of the Atlantis Theory.* Fullerton, CA: Donato, 1979.

———. "Cayce's Masters," *Atlantis Rising,* No. 32.

Dunn, Christopher. *The Giza Power Plant.* Santa Fe, NM: Bear & Company, 1998.

Firman, George. *Atlantis, A Definitive Study.* Hallmark Litho, Inc., 1985.

Fix, William R. *Pyramid Odyssey.* New York: Mayflower Books, 1978.

Flemath, Rand and Rose. *When the Sky Fell: In Search of Atlantis.* New York: Martin's Paperbacks, 1997.

Gerber, Richard. *Vibrational Medicine.* Rochester, VT: Bear & Company, 2001.

Goodman, Jeffrey. *American Genesis.* New York: Summit Books, 1981.

Griffith, Joan T. "James Churchward and His Lost Continent." *World Explorer,* Volume 3, No. 1, 2002.

Hadingham, Evan. *Secrets of the Ice Age.* New York: Walker and Co., 1979.

Halifax, Joan. *Shamanic Voices.* New York: Penguin Books, 1979.

Hall, Manly P. *The Secret Teachings of All Ages.* Los Angeles: Philosophical Research Society, 1977.

Hancock, Graham. *Fingerprints of the Gods.* New York: Crown Publishers, Inc., 1995.

Hansen, L. Taylor. *The Ancient Atlantic.* Amherst, WI: Amherst Press, 1969.

————. *He Walked the Americas*. Amherst, WI: Legend Press, 1963.

Hatt, Carolyn. *The Maya*. Based on the Edgar Cayce Readings. Virginia Beach, VA: A.R.E. Press, 1971.

Heinberg, Richard W. *Memories and Visions of Paradise: Exploring the Golden Myth of a Lost Golden Age*. Quest Books, 1995.

Hesemann, Michael. *The Cosmic Connection*. Bath, UK: Gateway Books, 1996.

Homet, Marcel P. *Sons of the Sun*. London: Hapgood, 1963.

Hope, Murry. *The Ancient Wisdom of Atlantis*. London: Thorsons, 1991.

————. *Atlantis: Myth or Reality?*. London: Arkana, Penguin Books Ltd., 1991.

Hope, Murry. *Practical Atlantean Magic*. London: The Aquarian Press, 1991.

Hunt, Immanual. *Elephants and Chakras*. Las Vegas, NV: Spiritual Endeavors, 1996.

Isabelle, Susan. *Crystal Skull Handbook*. Manchester, NH: Shambala Gold Publications, 2000.

Kasten, Len. "Healing Technology from Atlantis," *Atlantis Rising* No. 15.

King, Serge V. *Pyramid Energy Handbook*. New York: Warner Books, 1977.

Kueshana, Eklal. *The Ultimate Frontier*. Quinlin, TX: Stella Group, 1963.

Le Plongeon, Augustus. *Sacred Mysteries*. New York: Macoy Publishing and Masonic Supply Co., 1909.

Le Plongeon, Alice, and Augustus Le Plongeon. *Queen Mu and the Eastern Sphinx*. New York: Steiner Publications, 1973.

The Light Messenger—A newsletter from Mount Shasta. ℅ Bev Dombrowski, 218 E. Hinckley St., Mt. Shasta, CA 96067. pegasusiam@snowcrest.net.

Little, Gregory L., and Lora H. Little. *The A.R.E.'s Search for Atlantis*. Memphis, TN: Eagle Wing Books Inc., 2003.

Little, Gregory L., John Van Auken, and Lora Little. *Ancient South America*. Memphis, TN: Eagle Wing Books, 2002.

Little, Laura. *Ancient Mysteries*. Virginia Beach, VA: Association for Research and Enlightenment, 2002.

Marciniak, Barbara. *Bringers of the Dawn*. Santa Fe, NM: Bear & Co., 1992.

May, Wayne. *The X-Factor DNA* Issue #42. Colfax, WI: Ancient American.

Mertz, Henriette. *Atlantis Dwelling Place of the Gods*. Chicago, IL: 1976.

Michell, John. *The New View Over Atlantis*. San Francisco, CA: Harper & Row, 1983.

Milanovitch, Norma J., and Meltesen, Jean. *Sacred Journey to Atlantis*. Albuquerque, NM: Athena Publishing, 1992.

———. *We, The Arcturians*. Alburquerque, NM: Athena Publishing, 1990.

Montgomery, Ruth. *The World Before*. New York: Ballantine Books, 1976.

Moore, William L., and Berlitz, Charles. *The Philadelphia Experiment*. New York: Fawcett Crest, 1979.

Morton, Chris, and Ceri Louise Thomas. *The Mystery of the Crystal Skulls*. Santa Fe, NM: Bear & Company, 1998.

Muck, Otto Heinrich. *The Secret of Atlantis.* New York: Times Books, 1978.

Nova. "The Gulf Stream." February 28, 1989.

Oliver, F. S. *A Dweller on Two Planets.* Los Angeles, CA: Phylos, Borden Publishing Co., 1952.

Paiva, Anton Ponce de Leon (I. A. Uma). *In Search of the Wise One.* Woodside, CA: Bluestar Communications, 1996.

Paulsen, Norman. *The Christ Consciousness.* Salt Lake City, UT: Builders Publishing Co., 1980.

Pinkham, Mark Amaru. *The Return of the Serpents of Wisdom.* Kimpton, IL: Adventures Unlimited, 1997.

Plato. *Timaeus and Critias.* Translation by R.G. Bury, Litt.D. Cambridge, MA: Harvard University Press, 1929.

Raloff. *Science News.* November 28, 1987.

Red Star, Nancy. *Star Ancestors.* Rochester, VT: Destiny Books, 2000.

Roberts, Anthony. *Atlantean Traditions in Ancient Britain.* London: Rider & Co., 1975.

Robinson, Lytle. *Edgar Cayce's Story of the Origin and Destiny of Man.* New York: Berkeley Publishing Corp., 1972.

Samsel, W. T. *The Atlantis Connection.* Sedona, AZ: Mission Possible Commercial Publishing, 1998.

Scott-Elliot, W. *The Story of Atlantis and the Lost Lemuria.* London: Theosophical Publishing House Ltd., 1930.

Sitchin, Zecharia. *The 12th Planet.* New York: Avon Books, 1976.

Solomon, Paul. *Excerpts from the Paul Solomon Tapes.* Fellowship of Inner Light, 1974.

Spence, Lewis. *Atlantis in America*. Santa Fe, NM: Sun Publishing Co., 1981.

———. *The Occult Sciences in Atlantis*. New York: Samuel Weiser, Inc., 1978.

Steiger, Brad. *Atlantis Rising*. New York: Dell Publishing Co., Inc., 1973.

———. *The Fellowship*. New York: Doubleday & Co., Inc., 1988.

Sykes, Bryan. *The Seven Daughters of Eve*. New York: W. W. Norton & Co., Inc., 2001.

Sykes, Egerton. *Atlantis*. Volume 4. Brighton, England: Markham House Press, 1951.

———. *Atlantis*. Volume 27, Nos. 3 & 4. Brighton, England: Markham House Press, 1952.

———. *Atlantis*. Volume 21, Jan./Feb. Brighton, England: Markham House Press, 1968.

———. *Atlantis*. Volume 27, No. 3, May-June. Brighton, England: Markham House Press, 1974.

———. *Atlantis*. Volume 27, No. 4, July-August. Brighton, England: Markham House Press, 1974.

Temple, Robert K. G. *The Sirius Mystery*. Rochester, VT: Destiny Books, 1998.

Tomas, Andrew. *Atlantis From Legend to Discovery*, London: Robert Hale & Co., 1972.

———. *The Home of the Gods*. New York: Berkeley Publications 1972.

"Science and Technology, the First Americans." *The Economist*. Feb. 21 (1998): 79-80.

Tompkins, Peter. *Mysteries of the Mexican Pyramids*. New York: Harper & Row, 1976.

———. *Secrets of the Great Pyramid*. New York: Harper & Row, 1971.

Tompkins, Peter, and Christopher Bird. *The Secret Life of Plants*. New York: Avon Books, 1973.

Van Auken, John, and Lora Little. *Lost Hall of Records*. Memphis, TN: Eagle Wing Books, 2000.

———. *The Lost Hall of Records*. Memphis, TN: Eagle Wing Books, 2000.

Vigers, Daphine. *Atlantis Rising*. London: Aquarian, 1952.

Walton, Bruce, ed . *Mount Shasta: Home of the Ancients*. Pomeroy, WA: Health Research, 1985.

Watkins, Alfred. *The Old Straight Track*. London: Methuen & Co., 1925. Reprinted London: Garnstone, 1970.

Watkins, Frank. *Ley Hunter's Manual*. Wellingborough, Northamptonshire: Turnstone Press Limited, 1983.

Weil, Andrew. *Spontaneous Healing*. Columbine, NY: Fawcett Press, 1995.

Wilkins, Harold T. *Mysteries of Ancient South America*. New York: The Citadel Press, 1956.

———. *Secret Cities of Old South America*. London: Rider & Co., 1950.

Williams, Mark. *In Search of Lemuria*. San Mateo, CA: Golden Era Books, 2001.

Winer, Richard. *The Devil's Triangle*. New York: Bantom Books, Inc., 1974.

Winston, Shirley Rabb. *Music as the Bridge*. Based on the Edgar Cayce Readings. Virginia Beach, VA: Association for Research and Enlightenment Inc.

Winters, Randolph. *The Pleiadian Mission*. Yorba Linda, CA: The Pleiades Project, 1994.

Ywahoo, Dhyani. *Voices of Our Ancestors*. Boston: Shambhala, 1987.

Zapp and Erikson. *Atlantis in America: Navigators of the Ancient World*. Stelle, IL: Adventures Unlimited Press, 1998.

Zhirov, Nicolai F. *Atlantis*. Moscow: Progress Publishers, 1970.

Zink, David D. *The Stones of Atlantis*. New York: Prentice-Hall, Inc., 1990.

INDEX

Free Magazine

Read unique articles by Llewellyn authors, recommendations by experts, and information on new releases. To receive a **free** copy of Llewellyn's consumer magazine, *New Worlds of Mind & Spirit,* simply call 1-877-NEW-WRLD or visit our website at www.llewellyn.com and click on *New Worlds.*

LLEWELLYN ORDERING INFORMATION

Order Online:
Visit our website at www.llewellyn.com, select your books, and order them on our secure server.

Order by Phone:
- Call toll-free within the U.S. at 1-877-NEW-WRLD (1-877-639-9753). Call toll-free within Canada at 1-866-NEW-WRLD (1-866-639-9753)
- We accept VISA, MasterCard, and American Express

Order by Mail:
Send the full price of your order (MN residents add 7% sales tax) in U.S. funds, plus postage & handling to:
Llewellyn Worldwide
2143 Wooddale Drive, Dept. 0-7387-0397-4
Woodbury, MN 55125-2989, U.S.A.

Postage & Handling:

Standard (U.S., Mexico, & Canada). If your order is:
$49.99 and under, add $3.00
$50.00 and over, FREE STANDARD SHIPPING

AK, HI, PR: $15.00 for one book plus $1.00 for each additional book.

International Orders (airmail only):
$16.00 for one book plus $3.00 for each additional book

Orders are processed within 2 business days.
Please allow for normal shipping time. Postage and handling rates subject to change.

ATLANTIS

Insights from a Lost Civilization

SHIRLEY ANDREWS

The legend of lost Atlantis turns to fact as Shirley Andrews uniquely correlates a wealth of information from more than 100 classical and Atlantean scholars, scientists, and psychics to describe the country and its inhabitants.

Review the scientific and geological evidence for an Atlantic continent, which refutes the popular notion that Atlantis was located in the Mediterranean. Follow the history of Atlantis from its beginnings to its destruction, and see a portrait of Atlantean society: its religion, architecture, art, medicine, and lifestyle. Explore shamanism, the power of crystals, ancient healing techniques, pyramid energy, ley lines, the influence of extraterrestrials, and the origin of the occult sciences. Learn what happened to the survivors of Atlantis, where they migrated, and how the survivors and their descendants made their mark on cultures the world over.

1-56718-023-X
288 pp., 6 x 9, illus. $12.95

PSYCHIC DEVELOPMENT FOR BEGINNERS

An Easy Guide to Releasing and Developing Your Psychic Abilities

WILLIAM HEWITT

Psychic Development for Beginners provides detailed instruction on developing your sixth sense, or psychic ability. Improve your sense of worth, your sense of responsibility, and therefore your ability to make a difference in the world. Innovative exercises like "The Skyscraper" allow beginning students of psychic development to quickly realize personal and material gain through their own natural talent.

Benefits range from the practical to spiritual. Find a parking space anywhere, handle a difficult salesperson, choose a compatible partner, and even access different time periods! Practice psychic healing on pets or humans—and be pleasantly surprised by your results. Use psychic commands to prevent dozing while driving. Preview out-of-body travel, cosmic consciousness, and other alternative realities. Instruction in *Psychic Development for Beginners* is supported by personal anecdotes, forty-four psychic development exercises, and twenty-eight related psychic case studies to help students gain a comprehensive understanding of the psychic realm.

1-56718-360-3
216 pp., 5¼ x 8 $9.95

To order, call 1-877-NEW-WRLD
Prices subject to change without notice

REIKI FOR BEGINNERS

Mastering Natural Healing Techniques

DAVID VENNELLS

Reiki is a simple yet profound system of hands-on healing developed in Japan during the 1800s. Millions of people worldwide have already benefited from its peaceful healing intelligence that transcends cultural and religious boundaries. It can have a profound effect on health and well-being by re-balancing, cleansing, and renewing your internal energy system.

Reiki for Beginners gives you the very basic and practical principles of using Reiki as a simple healing technique, as well as its more deeply spiritual aspects as a tool for personal growth and self-awareness. Unravel your inner mysteries, heal your wounds, and discover your potential for great happiness. Follow the history of Reiki, from founder Dr. Mikao Usui's search for a universal healing technique, to the current development of a global Reiki community. Also included are many new ideas, techniques, advice, philosophies, contemplations, and meditations that you can use to deepen and enhance your practice.

1-56718-767-6
264 pp., 5³⁄₁₆ x 8, illus. $12.95

Also available in Spanish!

To order, call 1-877-NEW-WRLD

Prices subject to change without notice

AURA READING
FOR BEGINNERS
Develop Your Psychic Awareness
for Health & Success

RICHARD WEBSTER

When you lose your temper, don't be surprised if a dirty red haze suddenly appears around you. If you do something magnanimous, your aura will expand. Now you can learn to see the energy that emanates off yourself and other people through the proven methods taught by Richard Webster in his psychic training classes.

Learn to feel the aura, see the colors in it, and interpret what those colors mean. Explore the chakra system, and how to restore balance to chakras that are over- or under-stimulated. Then you can begin to imprint your desires into your aura to attract what you want in your life.

1-56718-798-6
208 pp., 5³⁄₁₆ x 8, illus. $9.95

CHAKRAS FOR BEGINNERS
A Guide to Balancing Your Chakra Energies

DAVID POND

The chakras are spinning vortexes of energy located just in front of your spine and positioned from the tailbone to the crown of the head. They are a map of your inner world—your relationship to yourself and how you experience energy. They are also the batteries for the various levels of your life energy. The freedom with which energy can flow back and forth between you and the universe correlates directly to your total health and well-being.

Blocks or restrictions in this energy flow express themselves as diseases, discomforts, a lack of energy, fears, or emotional imbalances. By acquainting yourself with the chakra system, how they work and how they should operate optimally, you can perceive your own blocks and restrictions and develop guidelines for relieving entanglements. The chakras stand out as the most useful model for you to identify how your energy is expressing itself. With *Chakras for Beginners* you will discover what is causing any imbalances in your life, how to bring your energies back in to alignment, and how to achieve higher levels of consciousness.

1-56718-537-1
216 pp., 5³⁄₁₆ x 8 $9.95

Also available in Spanish!

To order, call 1-877-NEW-WRLD
Prices subject to change without notice

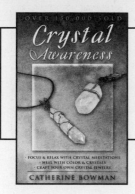

CRYSTAL AWARENESS
CATHERINE BOWMAN

For millions of years, crystals have been waiting for people to discover their wonderful powers. Today they are used in watches, computer chips, and communication devices. But there is also a spiritual, holistic aspect to crystals.

Crystal Awareness will teach you everything you need to know to begin working with crystals. It will also help those who have been working with them to complete their knowledge. Crystal topics include: forms, colors, single points, clusters and double terminated crystals, energy fields, etheric and spiritual bodies, energy generators, cleansing and programming, meditation, the value of polishing, personal spiritual growth, chakras, how to make crystal jewelry, the uses of crystals in the future, compatible metals, and several healing techniques, including The Star of David Healing.

Crystal Awareness is destined to be the guide of choice for people who are beginning their investigation of crystals.

0-87542-058-3
224 pp., mass market, illus.   **$3.95**

To order, call 1-877-NEW-WRLD
Prices subject to change without notice

CRYSTAL MEDICINE
MARGUERITE ELSBETH

Tribal peoples the world over have always revered and worked with stones for communicating, healing, or seeing the future. They as well as scientists mutually agree that the magnetism produced by an electric current is inherent in the atomic structure of certain stones. Now, *Crystal Medicine* offers a hands-on, down-to-earth view of how indigenous peoples have always recognized and worked with the power of stones. It uses ancient and contemporary anecdotes, myth, and folklore and combines shamanism, alchemy, astrology, sound and color, science and quantum physics to explore crystals, gems, and minerals with a mental edge geared toward the current Earth changes. You will learn to appreciate the sacredness in even the littlest pebble as you study a variety of practical, time-proven healing methods.

1-56718-258-5
264 pp., 6 x 9, illus., photos $17.95

To order, call 1-877-NEW-WRLD
Prices subject to change without notice

CRYSTAL HEALING
The Next Step

PHYLLIS GALDE

Discover the further secrets of quartz crystal! Now modern research and use have shown that crystals have even more healing and therapeutic properties than have been realized. Learn why polished, smoothed crystal is better to use to heighten your intuition, improve creativity, and healing.

Learn to use crystals for reprogramming your subconscious to eliminate problems and negative attitudes that prevent success. Here are techniques that people have successfully used, not just theories. This book reveals newly discovered abilities of crystal now accessible to all, and is a sensible approach to crystal use. *Crystal Healing* will be your guide to improve the quality of your life and expand your consciousness.

0-87542-246-2
224 pp., illus., mass market $4.99

CRYSTAL BALLS & CRYSTAL BOWLS

Tools for Ancient Scrying & Modern Seership

TED ANDREWS

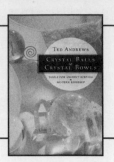

Despite the popular use around the world of the traditional quartz crystal ball and the modern crystal bowl as magical tools, there has been little practical information on their applications and use—until now. *Crystal Balls & Crystal Bowls* takes the ancient processes of divination and scrying out of the realm of the supernatural and places them in the domain of natural knowledge.

This book reveals why crystal balls and crystal bowls are dynamic instruments for transformation, and how they can be used to divine the future, astral project, connect with spirits, heal and balance the human energy system. This book explores their many functions, and reveals the secrets of vibrational energy, as well as its application for increasing intuition and activating creativity. Step-by-step, you will learn techniques for crystal gazing, scrying, attuning to spirit guides, developing clairvoyance, healing, and more.

1-56718-026-4
320 pp., 6 x 9, illus., photos $14.95

TO WRITE TO THE AUTHOR

If you wish to contact the author or would like more information about this book, please write to the author in care of Llewellyn Worldwide and we will forward your request. Both the author and publisher appreciate hearing from you and learning of your enjoyment of this book and how it has helped you. Llewellyn Worldwide cannot guarantee that every letter written to the author can be answered, but all will be forwarded. Please write to:

Shirley Andrews
℅ Llewellyn Worldwide
2143 Wooddale Drive, Dept. 0-7387-0397-4
Woodbury, MN 55125–2989, U.S.A.

Please enclose a self-addressed stamped envelope for reply,
or $1.00 to cover costs. If outside U.S.A.,
enclose international postal reply coupon.

Many of Llewellyn's authors have websites with additional
information and resources. For more information,
please visit our website:
http://www.llewellyn.com